Women united, women divided

Women United, Women Divided

Comparative Studies of
Ten Contemporary Cultures

Edited by PATRICIA CAPLAN
and JANET M. BUJRA

INDIANA UNIVERSITY PRESS
BLOOMINGTON

FIRST MIDLAND BOOK EDITION 1982

Manufactured in the United States of America

Library of Congress Cataloging in Publication Data

Main entry under title:

Women united, women divided.

Includes indexes.
1. Women—Addresses, essays, lectures.
2. Solidarity—Addresses, essays, lectures.
I. Caplan, Patricia. II. Bujra, Janet M.
HQ1154.W889   301.41′2   78–14085
ISBN 0-253-12215-5
ISBN 0-253-20297-3 PBK

2   3   4   5   85   84   83   82

Contents

Preface

Although this book has two editors, it is in fact very much a collective work. It has its origins in the London Women's Anthropology Group, which met regularly for two years between 1972 and 1974, during which time the possibility of compiling a book was mooted on several occasions. However, with the departure of several members of that group to the field, and others to jobs in different parts of the country, the group disbanded.

In the spring of 1977, a group of women anthropologists and sociologists, several of whom had been active in that group, began meeting to work out ideas for a collection of articles on various aspects of female solidarity. Our aim was to produce a book that would contribute to the growing academic debate on women, and yet at the same time be accessible and relevant to matters of concern to the Women's Movement.

We agreed to circulate our papers to one another, and to meet regularly to discuss our work. In spite of not being able to do this as often as we should have liked, we did manage to discuss our theme of solidarity at some length, and most of the authors in this collection benefited from the comments and views of their sister contributors. Although inevitably, individual perspectives and approaches differ, we have to acknowledge the mutual strength and support that we drew from each other.

Notes on contributors

JANET BUJRA is at present Lecturer in Sociology at the University College, Aberywstwyth, and has previously taught at the University of Dar es Salaam, and the American University in Cairo. She received her Ph.D. from the University of London in 1968, and has carried out research in Kenya and Tanzania. She is the author of articles on factional politics, on women in urban and rural Kenya, and on class formation in the context of underdevelopment.

PATRICIA CAPLAN did fieldwork on Mafia Island, Tanzania from 1965–7 and subsequently obtained her Ph.D. from London University in 1968. She then worked in a Hindu village in west Nepal and in 1974–5 carried out a study of women's organizations in Madras City, India. Her publications include *Priests and Cobblers* (1972) and *Choice and Constraint in a Swahili Com-*

munity (1975). She is Lecturer in Social Anthropology at Gold-smiths' College, University of London.

GAYNOR COHEN received her Ph.D. from the University of Surrey after carrying out fieldwork in West Africa and Britain. She was formerly a lecturer at Brunel University, and now teaches social policy at the Civil Service Staff College. Her publications include *Community and Leadership* (1973), a schools' text-book, as well as articles on a British middle-class housing estate, and equal opportunity policy. She is presently engaged in research on communications between central and local government on policy relating to ethnic minorities.

PAMELA CONSTANTINIDES did her Ph.D. at the London School of Economics in 1972. Her fieldwork has been carried out in the Northern Sudan, on women's spirit possession cults (1969–72), and also among Greek Cypriots in London and Cyprus (1972–5), and she has published articles on both peoples. She has been a Social Science Research Council-funded Research Officer and subsequently Lecturer in Anthropology at the London School of Economics.

ELISABETH CROLL was formerly a Fellow of the Contemporary China Institute, University of London, and is now consultant for the International Labour Organisation. She has carried out interviews in China and is the author of *Feminism and Socialism in China* (in press) and *The Women's Movement in China* (1974), as well as numerous articles. She recently obtained her Ph.D. from the University of London and is currently Visiting Fellow at the Institute of Development Studies, University of Sussex.

MELISSA LLEWELYN-DAVIES is a Ph.D. student at Harvard University. She did fieldwork among the Maasai in Kenya between 1970 and 1972. She subsequently worked for Granada TV's *Disappearing World* series of ethnographic films. In particular, she was associated with the films *Masai Women* and *Some Women of Marrakech*.

JULIA NAISH did fieldwork for her Ph.D. in anthropology in Désirade, French West Indies, focusing on race relations and rank. She now teaches and writes materials for English as a second language to adult immigrants.

NICI NELSON has carried out fieldwork in a slum settlement in Nairobi, Kenya and obtained her Ph.D. from London University. She is currently working at the Institute of Development Studies, University of Sussex on rural women in India.

URSULA SHARMA obtained her Ph.D. from London University in 1968. She carried out fieldwork in a village in Himachal Pradesh, India, in 1966 and is currently studying the role of women in agricultural production both in that state and the Punjab. She is the author of *Rampal and His Family* (1971) and numerous articles, and lectures in social anthropology at Keele University.

MAILA STIVENS is currently completing a Ph.D. at the London School of Economics. She has done research in Sydney, Australia on middle-class kinship (1968–70), and in Malaysia on women and underdevelopment (1975–6). She is temporary lecturer in anthropology, University College, London.

ONE

Introductory: Female solidarity and the sexual division of labour

JANET M. BUJRA

'Women are not so well united as to form an Insurrection. They are for the most part wise enough to love their chains, and discern how very becomingly they sit.' (Mary Astell, quoted in Mitchell and Oakely 1976:390)

'... a material foundation for "sisterhood" [could be found in] the social activity, the work which the female personality was shaped to submit to. That work was housework.' (Power of Women Collective, Dalla Costa and James 1975:3)

'housewives .. will not provide the decisive motive force of the women's struggle ... it will be primarily [women wage workers and students] who will inject radical women's consciousness back into the population of women who remain exclusively housewives.' (Secombe 1974:24)

This collection of papers had its origin in a discussion of the cross-cultural parameters of 'female solidarity'. Our interest in this theme arose out of a concern to explain the very striking differences that are apparent in the degree to which women support one another in different social contexts. However, it can also be seen as a contribution to the current debate in the women's movement over the notion of 'sisterhood'. In this introductory essay I will attempt to draw together some of our findings and present my own interpretation of the general theme.

Though we share a common interest in the theme of female solidarity we do not necessarily share a common interpretation of it. Our differing interpretations are coloured both by our varied theoretical positions and by the differing ways in which reality presented itself to us in the field. In the course of our collective discussions, however, we did forge a common set of concerns in relation to our theme. In attempting to understand the mainsprings of female solidarity, the kinds of questions we decided to consider were as follows: in what context does solidarity typically arise; in what situations is it inhibited; what forms does it take; and to what extent is it a phenomenon specifically of *feminist* consciousness?

As we began to work through our material it soon became clear that 'solidarity' expressed itself in many different ways: ranging from tacit moral support, through instrumental assistance, to organized activities specifically focused on women's concerns. More significantly, though, we became aware that the goals of solidarity were as varied as its form. 'Solidarity' in fact was no unitary concept, susceptible of simple definition and unproblematic application to cross-cultural material. It became fairly obvious that if female solidarity entailed a feminist consciousness – in other words an awareness of gender inequality *and* the desire to end it – then perhaps only one of our case studies, that of China (Chapter 2), would qualify for inclusion in the book. Gradually it emerged that, in considering women co-operating and supporting each other, we were facing a different analytical issue, which had more to do with the social and ideological manifestations of various forms of the sexual division of labour, than with feminist activity *per se*.

Few of the women we discuss in this book are consciously aware of being oppressed *as women*, even though their objective situation might be highly circumscribed. Furthermore they may

14

act together in ways that, far from challenging their oppression, actually reinforce it. We give examples of 'female solidarity' oriented towards the policing of women's domestic roles, or towards the assertion of *class* privilege rather than the rejection of gender subordination. Other forms of 'solidarity' merely entail the passive restatement of structures imposed on women by patriarchal social formations. We concluded, however, that these varied configurations of solidarity were not the less interesting for being apparently alienated forms.

We also discovered situations in which women exhibited no unity whatsoever, and where they were deeply divided among themselves. Sharma's study (Chapter 10) of peasant women in a village in Northern India reveals that where village exogamy and virilocal marriage is the norm, village women are initially strangers to each other. Within the extended household the older women have seniority over those more recently arrived. The power that older women have over younger women is derivatory – it stems from the relations of the older women with the senior males in the household. Women labour in the fields but the product of their labour is controlled by the males who own the land. Women thus lack independent access to productive resources, and are divided among themselves. Not surprisingly, in this situation, they fail to develop any solidarity.

The women of Désirade (a dependency of the French overseas department of Guadeloupe) described by Naish (Chapter 9), are not only lacking in solidarity, but are also mutually antagonistic. Naish shows how this is an outcome of their physical isolation within the domestic unit (the nuclear family is the norm here) and their almost total economic dependence on males. Women perceive themselves competing for husbands, because it is only through a satisfactory marriage that a woman may obtain the comfortable life to which all aspire. Women's lack of solidarity in Désirade parallels the individualism of their men-folk, for this, in general, is a fragmented and competitive society.

Our other seven studies exemplify various forms of female solidarity. In two cases women's solidarity is focused on their reproductive powers and/or their sexuality. Constantinides (Chapter 7) describes how Sudanese women in an urban context organize themselves into Islamic cult groups devoted to the treatment of women's illnesses. One latent function of such groups, she suggests, is as institutions of urban adaptation in a situation where women are usually secluded, and hence isolated from each other. Maasai women, described by Llewelyn-Davies (Chapter 8), organize their own rituals of reproduction, on which their identity as women rests. At the same time, however, they cover up for each other's adulterous affairs – women standing together in an attempt to control their own sexuality.

Three other contributions indicate that in class-divided societies, women's consciousness and forms of organization cannot be considered apart from their position within the class structure. Caplan (Chapter 4) and Cohen (Chapter 5) both analyse situations where women organize themselves to protect class privilege in activities that complement their husbands' objective positions in the class hierarchy. Caplan's study concerns upper- and upper-middle-class Indian women in Madras, who form themselves into clubs and associations devoted primarily to philanthropic activities. Cohen's contribution lays bare the underlying similarities between what might, at first sight, seem to be unrelated cases. There may appear to be little in common between English women on a housing estate coming together to share child-care chores and Creole women in Sierra Leone organizing Old Girls' Dances. However, as Cohen shows, both sets of women are organizing themselves to define, perpetuate, and improve their families' class position.

The 'female solidarity' described by Stivens (Chapter 6) takes a much more covert form. Analysing the situation of suburban women in Sydney, Stivens suggests that solidarity is mediated through kinship relations in which women play a focal and creative role. Kin relations in this context, she argues, are central to the processes both of class reproduction, and of the reproduction of the sexual division of labour within which these women play a subordinate role.

Two papers describe women pursuing a more active unity. Nelson (Chapter 3) analyses the situation of women beer brewers in Nairobi, whose economic success depends on their mutually supportive activities in a range of contexts. These are independent women, mostly divorced, widowed, or unmarried. Their way of earning a living (commercial beer brewing is illegal) isolates them from the wider society; their productive relations bring them into constant interaction with each other. These women are contemptuous of men, even while their solidarity is not consciously directed to changing the terms of the gender relationship – indeed they depend on the good will of male customers in order to survive.

Only in the Chinese case, described here by Croll (Chapter 2), are women working within a wider revolutionary context which structures their own consciousness of oppression, and which directs women's activity towards the goal of equality with men. Croll's paper is an account of the activity and development of women's associations among the Chinese peasantry.

Each of us has analysed the issue of female solidarity in relation to our own particular data. To what extent can these studies be pooled together to generate a more general analysis? I would argue that underlying our theme of female solidarity there lie other, more fundamental problems.

Women as a sociological category

Although all of the nine examples we have discussed in this book are contemporary, they deal with women operating in very different contexts, and, in particular, in societies at very different levels of economic development. Most of the women we describe are dependent on male income earners, but a few have asserted a degree of economic independence. They operate in the context of a range of family structures, from the isolated nuclear family set-up of the Désiradiens, to the extended and joint families of Maasai pastoralists and Indian peasants. The ideologies of femininity and of women's place which these women experience vary in many respects, though none is egalitarian.

To embark on a study of female solidarity in such diverse circumstances is to court the accusation that one is treating 'women' as a 'universal category' – as Mathieu has accused Ardener (Ardener 1975). At issue here is the validity of the comparative method. As Nadel remarked many years ago, use of this method is 'bound up with judgements on the identity and difference of social facts. The "same" social fact in different social contexts could be seen either as "the same thing varied", or as something "essentially" different' (Nadel 1951:224-25). To what extent, then, does it make analytical sense to set the wives of Maasai pastoralists alongside those of an Australian middle-class suburb, as comparable phenomena?

An answer to this problem is directly bound up with our main concern here – female solidarity. One product of the women's movement in recent years has been the celebration of 'sisterhood', with its implicit assumption that women, as *women*, have a necessary basis for solidarity. Mitchell and Oakley have voiced their scepticism of such assumptions:

> 'We do live in a hierarchical world; the women's movement does not just combat structures of dominance, it is also surrounded by them and embedded in them ... Sisterhood can undoubtedly be a relationship of solidarity and support ... [but] literature and mythology ... has some nasty things to say about sisters too ... ideology not only reflects but also influences social reality. [They conclude that 'sisterhood'] cannot be an instant and transcendent unification of women, [and that it] must to some extent repeat the terms of women's [existing] social relationships with one another.'
>
> (Mitchell and Oakley 1976:13)

The contemporary outburst of academic writing on women is a direct product of the women's movement, and not surprisingly incorporates some of its assumptions: in particular the assumption that women, as women, can be treated as a uniform analytical category. The paradox here is that while on the one hand the women's movement rejects the ideological claim that 'anatomy is destiny', on the other, academic writings assume that 'anatomy is a sociological category': that one can have an 'anthropology of women', or that there is a 'problem of women'.[1] Wallman has some salutary comments to make on such facile assumptions. Although her critique is of mainstream sociology and not of feminist writings, it is her conclusion that 'there is no analytic meaning in such concepts as "the position of women" or "the female role" in society, since the inevitable presence of the sex attribute tells us nothing at all about its general social relevance' (Wallman 1976:2–3). Such notions, she argues, must be tempered, since, 'the significance of being female ... varies with technology, setting, class, context, task, rank, race, age, profession, kinship, wealth and economics ... with any or all of the dimensions of a situation of which it can form only a part' (Wallman 1976:12).

There are in fact three senses in which the concept 'women' cannot adequately stand as an analytical category in sociological investigation. The first is that within any one society women are often divided against themselves in terms of their differential relation to class and status hierarchies, as well as factors such as age and kinship affiliation. To equate the mistress of a Victorian household with the maid does not make much sociological sense. Second, although gender may be a universal social category, its categorical imperatives differ widely, and may vary not only between societies, but even within the same society according to situation or social location. In one society women may be forbidden to make pots, in another it is prescribed that they do so. The third point is that in some contexts (granted they may be very few) women can more usefully be classed along with men in asexual categories, where the fact of sexual difference is irrelevant to the problem at issue.

So far, then, my line of reasoning would tend towards the position that any notion of 'female solidarity' must be critically evaluated, and cannot simply be taken for granted. As Wallman cautions: 'The plain presence of a number of female people together does not constitute a group of women playing a/the women's role' (Wallman 1976:12). Mitchell and Oakley also point out that the biological fact of sisterhood does not automatically engender 'sisterly' feelings – there can be no 'instant and transcendent' sisterhood.

Domestic labour and modes of production

It is clearly important that we resolve the analytical confusion that conflates women as an immutable biological category, with 'women' as a social category – historically, hierarchically, spatially, ideologically, and situationally varied. Leacock is apparently thinking along these lines when she rejects the mystification of such concepts as 'the status of women': 'The point I want to suggest here ... is that the notion of a somehow separate "women's role" hides the reality of the family as an economic unit ...' (Leacock 1975:601). Richards also, in an illuminating comment, points out that in cross-cultural comparisons of 'the "position" of women' one comes to the conclusion that: 'women cease to be a separate problem and become part of the system of child production, child-rearing and domestic economics' (Richards 1974:7). Unfortunately she does not build on this insight.

In my opinion what is required here is a mediating concept, to build a bridge between the biological fact of women's existence and the infinitely varied forms of her social existence. I would suggest that in domestic labour (socially reproductive labour expended in the context of the domestic unit) we have such a concept. Rather than analysing 'the position/role/status of women', attention should be diverted towards understanding the articulation of domestic labour with differing modes of production. It is also necessary to analyse the groupings (for example, family forms) that are built up on the basis of interlocking productive and reproductive processes.

Modes of production are the historically specific forms taken by the social and economic organization of production. In one sense the process of production is itself a process of *reproduction*. As Marx says in respect of capitalism:

> 'The capitalist process of production regarded as a connected whole, or as a process of reproduction, therefore produces not only commodities, not only surplus value, for it also produces and reproduces the capitalist relation itself; produces and reproduces, on the one side the capitalist, and on the other the wage worker.'   (Marx 1930:635)

Conversely, however, any mode of production entails, as its 'indispensable condition', the reproduction of labour power, that is, the renewal of the capacity or energy to labour expended in production. It is at this point that *domestic* labour enters into any understanding of modes of production. Following Secombe (1974) and others, one can, in fact, see domestic labour as entailing socially reproductive activity in three senses. First, it involves the day to day recreation of labour power, in activities such as cooking, servicing the domestic area, and the provision of sexual services. Second, it entails reproduction in an explicitly biological sense, the bearing of children and thereby the recreation of the next generation of labour power. Third, in the socialization of children, domestic labour is related to socio-ideological reproduction; in other words to the recreation of the relations of production and their corresponding ideological forms.[2]

It is women rather than men who are anchored in domestic labour simply because of their innate link with biological reproduction. The consequences of this for women's position in general social terms will depend on the character of the mode of production within which domestic labour is embedded. Not all women are rooted in domestic labour and they may individually bear a differential relation to this process of socio-biological reproduction. Some categories of women may be able to delegate the major responsibilities of domestic labour to a dominated class or to younger female relatives. Women past the menopause are generally less rigorously tied to the domestic domain: in some societies old women come to have a public status more or less equivalent to that of males (Murphy and Murphy 1974; Richards 1974). More significantly, women are (in cross-cultural terms) rarely domestic labourers and nothing else. They are often found combining their reproductive roles with more directly productive activities, but with their primary anchorage in domestic labour.

Analysis of the situation of women in terms of their relationship to domestic labour is of course common among writers on capitalist society (see for example, Benston 1969; Dalla Costa and James 1972; Rowbotham 1973; Secombe 1974). However, it has been applied less often in cross-cultural studies. An apparent exception is found in the work of Rosaldo (1974) where she differentiates between a 'domestic' and a 'public' domain in social life. It is women's universal association with the former which, she argues, underlies her generally lowly social position. Rosaldo's distinction, however, bears only a rough resemblance to the categories of domestic labour and mode of production specified above. She defines the 'domestic orientation' as referring to, 'those minimal institutions and modes of activity that are organized immediately around one or more mothers and their children; "public" refers to activities, institutions, and forms of association that link, rank, organize or subsume particular mother-child groups' (Rosaldo 1974:23). It will be noted that in this formulation the 'public' domain becomes little more than a residual category. In neither case are these domains seen as structured systems; rather they have the status of descriptive categories.

Nevertheless much of what Rosaldo has to say is illuminating. My main disagreement with her lies in the fact that her analysis is restricted to impressing a polarity on the data of sociological investigation (note she writes of an '*opposition* between domestic and public orientations' (Rosaldo 1974:24, my emphasis)). According to my position, to have any *explanatory* value what must be investigated is the *relationship*, the character of articulation, between domestic and non-domestic spheres of action. Domestic labour, in some form or other, is universal, but it takes on differing significance in contrasting modes of production. This is not the place to elaborate on such a scheme, but one may note a few basic points relevant to the cases discussed in this book.

The first is the great qualitative divide between the role of domestic labour in capitalist as opposed to precapitalist modes of production. Secombe notes the 'historical transition of the domestic unit from its feudal location', where it is 'coterminous with production', to its capitalist form where it is 'divorced from production' (Secombe 1974:6). In the former case domestic labour is on a par with, and to some degree indistinguishable from, subsistence production. In the latter case it has become 'invisible', its contribution to capital obscured by the separation effected between domestic and industrial units, between production and consumption, between wage labour and 'free' labour.[3]

Under capitalism domestic labour creates the *preconditions* for the production of surplus value (rejuvenated labour power and so forth). However, its relationship to capitalist production is obscured by its appearance as an individuated service relation of the domestic labourer to her spouse and family. Even when women enter the labour market they do not shake off their situational disabilities as domestic labourers. As Beechey (1977) has argued, female wage labourers cannot be considered as structurally equivalent to male workers. They can be paid wages that fall beneath the value (the cost of reproduction) of their labour power, since these costs of reproduction are already taken account of in their husbands' wages. Much of the labour of women may thereby be directed into the production of pure surplus value. In the capitalist mode of production, then, the role of domestic labourer, though highly specialized, is also a socially dependent one. While vital to capitalism, it appears in a trivialized form as non-work.

The second point concerns the qualitative break in precapitalist modes of production between those based on the appropriation of natural products and those organized around property relations. In hunting and gathering societies, some of which have survived to contemporary times although increasingly under pressure, a very low level of development of the

22

productive forces goes along with communal rights over the important life-giving resources, for example, territories within which to hunt and collect food, access to water supplies, and so on. Domestic labour is inextricable from other activities related to survival, and social reproduction is subordinated to simple physical reproduction. Within small bands of hunter-gatherers moreover, the tasks relating to child-care and socialization are less strictly the province of females. The latter are equally if not more active than males in directly productive activities, since the provision of staple foodstuffs is often their responsibility (Rohrlich-Leavitt 1975).[4] In performing these undifferentiated tasks, the domestic labourer relates to the survival of the whole group: her labour is communalized rather than privatized.[5]

In societies based on property ownership domestic labour is caught up in the web of property relations. Indeed Aaby argues that in order for property relations to emerge, the assertion of control over the reproductive powers of women becomes essential. He relates this development to the adoption of horticulture, and subsequently agriculture, systems that demand the long term planning of productive activity and hence, the reproduction of organized labour power: 'For the continued existence of these groups the reproduction of labour power becomes a critical element, and thence the need to control the reproductive potential of women' (Aaby 1977:38). Such an economic system allows for accumulation, the production of a surplus over immediate subsistence needs, and consequently the emergence of relations of control over this surplus or over the conditions of its production. In this situation the access of the domestic labourer to the means of production, and her control over the products of her labour come to depend on her relationship to the owner of those means. It is property relations that now determine the character of the local group, and hence the relationship of domestic labourers to each other. In this context domestic labour becomes, as Engels noted, 'a private service' (Engels 1972:81).

We do not have among our case studies any instance of hunting-gathering societies. Most of the cases we consider would fit into the model of capitalist society described above, with women primarily as domestic labourers, dependent on their husbands' incomes. This remains true even though some of the examples we discuss represent nations on the periphery of the world capitalist system – India, for example, or Sudan. In so far as we consider urban women in such countries, however, residing with and dependent on income-earning husbands, the pattern of articulation of domestic labour with the overriding mode of production is similar to that in the developed capitalist world.

In the case of the Maasai (Chapter 8), or the Indian peasant women described by Sharma (Chapter 10), we have a situation that more correctly falls into the last model described above: precapitalist social configurations with developed forms of property relations. The Maasai constitute an enclave of subsistence production (pastoral nomadism), within the context of a nation (Kenya) with a developed market economy. The Indian peasants are agriculturalists producing a surplus for exchange on the world market. In both these cases, the domestic unit is the productive unit and hence domestic labour is incorporated into subsistence production. The women's labour is significant within this contextual unit, although its product is alienated by the owners of the relevant productive resources (cattle or land).

In two cases described – the peasant women of China (Chapter 2) and the women beer brewers of Nairobi (Chapter 3) – women are independent producers, in control of the product of their own labour. Significantly these are also both instances where female solidarity is well in evidence. Although these women continue to be domestic labourers as well, this is mitigated by a degree of socialization of domestic tasks. This is organized either as a product of women's mutual support, or additionally in the case of China, as a consequence of wider social developments. This is not to say that such sharing of domestic labour is not evidenced in our other examples of female solidarity – indeed the most common form of mutual co-operation among women would appear to be directed at the 'communalization' of certain aspects of domestic labour. Nevertheless, it is only where this is linked to the increasing independence of women, both from such tasks, and from control by and dependence on males, as property owners or income-earners, that it entails a radical restructuring of gender relationships.

In the second part of this essay I propose to consider the character and basis of female solidarity as it manifests itself,

first in capitalist society and then in pre-capitalist social formations. I conclude by considering the socio-economic conditions
within which female solidarity goes beyond a merely defensive
position actively to question the basis of gender hierarchy. This,
I would argue, comes about as a product of the 'disarticulation'
of domestic labour with the prevailing mode of production.

Female solidarity, domestic labour, and class struggle

Radical feminists, and those engaged in the Wages for Housework campaign, have often suggested that a material basis for
'sisterhood' exists in the common domestic oppression of women
(for example, Dalla Costa and James 1972; Delphy 1977). Arguing that domestic labour is essential to capitalism, they strive to
politicize housewives to demand material recognition of this
claim, in the belief that the withdrawal of domestic labour will
mean the collapse of capitalism.

Secombe, however, has argued that in western capitalist
societies, women, as domestic labourers, have no basis on which
to unite, because domestic labour in capitalism is 'privatized'.[6]
Privatization has both structural and ideological implications.
At a structural level housewives are physically isolated from
each other and therefore not in a position to organize themselves. Ideologically their labour manifests itself not in its
'true' form as indissolubly linked to processes of capitalist
reproduction, but as an individuated service. Its link with
capitalism thus fails to find an echo at the level of consciousness, and the discontents of housewives are dissipated in
'interpersonal contestations' within the family. Secombe goes
on to argue that it is only when women move into the external
economy that they enter, 'the arena of collective struggle ...
[where] the power of collective action is discovered and the
practical talents of political organization are developed'
(Secombe 1974:22).

While I would accept Secombe's rejection of the radical
feminist position, his own argument is also inadequate in two
respects. First, he fails to take into account the disabilities
suffered by women in the sphere of wage work, which stem
directly from their primary status as domestic labourers. These
disabilities directly inhibit women's activism in the work
context.[7] A crude measure of this can be seen in the fact that

in Britain in 1968 only 25 per cent of women workers were unionized as compared to approximately half of male workers (HMSO 1971). Women may, in becoming wage labourers, enter the 'arena of collective struggle', but they do so with their primary identification as domestic labourers largely unquestioned.

The second point relates to Secombe's view of domestic labourers as ideological reproducers of the capitalist system. Writing specifically of the proletarian family, Secombe argues that: 'it is the family, and above all the mother, that produces willing participants for the social order' (Secombe 1974:15). 'The social order' in this formulation must be taken to mean not only capitalist social relations, but also, and embedded in these, the *sexual* division of labour. The contradictions inherent in this argument can be seen when we contrast it with Smith's assertion that this function of socio-ideological reproducion is only relevant at the level of the middle- or ruling-class family. This is because it is only the middle-class family that finds its interests in line with those of the ruling-class (Smith n.d.).

Granted that domestic labourers perform a socialization function and that this entails the transmission and imposition of 'ideology', it does not necessarily follow that this ideology is a homogeneous whole or that it bolsters the social order. In class society ideology has two aspects. It expresses ruling-class hegemony (dominant ideologies), but also reflects antagonistic class relations. Class struggle also has its ideological echoes; as Marx and Engels argued: 'Consciousness can never be anything else than conscious existence, and the existence of men [*sic*] is their actual life process' (Marx and Engels 1935:212). 'Men' may be taken here to include women, whose existence as domestic labourers reflects both their covert relationship to capital and their economic and social dependency on their husbands. Domestic labourers occupy a *common* position as socio-ideological reproducers, at the same time as they are *divided* among themselves on class lines. Their consciousness will reflect this ambiguous location in the social formation: as domestic labourers and as wives of men of a particular class.

It is only when we begin to understand the relationship *between* domestic labour and the mode of production of which it is a part that we can comprehend the emergence of *feminist* consciousness and its class limitations. The first stirrings of feminism in Europe, for example, in the seventeenth and eighteenth centuries, came at a period when bourgeois women began to be divested of their productive usefulness. The prosperity of the new bourgeoisie allowed it to dispense with family labour and to hire servants to perform domestic drudgeries. A transformation, both of productive and domestic labour, thus took place at this class level, leaving bourgeois women to be little more than ornaments to their husbands' success. Isolated women, such as Astell, Wollstonecraft, and Hays, rebelled and articulated their dissent.

Nineteenth century feminism was less to do with individual rebellion against the unequal rights of women and more a matter of organized dissent. However, it remained a largely middle-class phenomenon, engendered by what Olive Schreiner called the 'social parasitism' of women at this class level.

The suffrage movement of the early twentieth century was a product of such processes at both levels of bourgeois and petty bourgeois women and of the organized strength of working women (textile workers particularly). Often these latter women had to come to terms with the problem of combining domestic labour with wage labour, and in the context of working-class communities organized themselves, often on a kinship basis, to combine child-care with factory employment.

As for the modern wave of feminism, it would appear to be a product as much of developments in domestic and reproductive technology (which have given women potentially more leisure and control over their own destinies) as it is of the increasing demand of capital for female labour.

Female activism of the type just described has entailed women becoming conscious of their specific oppression *as women* – or has it? In fact there are very few instances in a class-divided society of women *per se* – as opposed to bourgeois women or proletarian women – acting together. Even the suffrage movement was unable to submerge class differences in a united front for more than a brief period (roughly five years) before it began to splinter into opposing fragments.

The form taken by women's oppression is not only historically specific, but also class specific. Within any stratified society it is clear that some women are more oppressed than others, and indeed some women may themselves be engaged in oppression. As Suzanne Lowry has recently remarked, we live in a

27

society 'which may be male dominated, but has plenty of women quite wittingly holding it up' (*The Guardian* 1977). The view that women are inextricably bound together in subjection to a common and unchanging oppression is a patent oversimplification.

This comes out very clearly from some of the case studies presented in this book. It is clear that the activism of some of the women described is as much a function of their class position as it is of their position as women. When the Creole women of Sierra Leone, or the women on an English housing estate (Chapter 5), seek, along with other women, to improve the chances of their children within the educational system, or when middle-class Indian women organize for the social welfare of the poor (Chapter 4) they are engaging in the practice of social reproduction of their own class relations. This is brought out vividly in Caplan's account (Chapter 4) of women's organizations in Madras, where appearances suggest women actively pursuing their emancipation. Women's associations here echo the hierarchical structures of male assemblies, and to some extent offer an independent or alternative route to a political position for women. However, as Caplan suggests, they can also be seen as manufacturing the cultural elaboration of class position. For example, in their major manifest function – that of administering charity to the poor – they are both defining and protecting their own class positions. Some women, as Caplan notes, 'do not even pretend to an altruistic motive for their social work – they openly voice their fear of revolution'.

I would argue that this is by no means an isolated example. A good many women's organizations – particularly in the Third World where class contrasts are so stark – would seem to serve the class interests of the bourgeoisie, rather than feminist interests (Jahan 1975; Wipper 1975).

To find the perpetuation of class privilege disguising itself as female solidarity may be ironic. However, we still have to explain why it is *women* who have consciously sought out other *women* to further these goals, rather than members of either sex indiscriminately. That they have done so is a reflection not only of their common class membership, but also of their common position in processes of social reproduction and of the contradictions to which this gives rise. The class membership of these women derives in large part from the class position of the spouses on whom they are dependent. This individual dependence finds ideological expression as 'conjugal solidarity', with its injunction that a woman's primary loyalty is to her husband, not to other women. Contradictions here, however, give rise to some of the instances of female solidarity we discuss in this book. Studies by Stivens (Chapter 6) and Cohen (Chapter 5) lay bare the credibility gap between the promise of conjugal solidarity and what Stivens calls 'the structural isolation of housework'.

Writing about an English middle-class housing estate, Cohen notes that the ideal of conjugal task sharing is undercut by the reality of men's occupational careers which necessitate frequent absences. Among the Australian middle class, described by Stivens, 'conjugal solidarity' is placed in a wider context, that is, 'the vociferously oppressive Australian version of the "women's place" ideology'. Dominant ideology promises Creole women monogamous marriages, but they must contend with the reality of 'outside wives'. In each of these situations (and perhaps atypically) women respond as much to their *actual* situation as to the dream world which they are promised. They react by reaching out to other women in the same position – an initially defensive response, but one that creates for them a political base. (Thus, for example, in the English housing estate described by Cohen (Chapter 5), women use the confidence engendered by female solidarity to put pressure on their husbands to behave in ways more congenial to them.)

One can see parallels here with the response of women in traditional working-class communities in Britain, as described, for example, by Young and Willmott for Bethnal Green (1959), or Rosser and Harris for Swansea (1965). In Bethnal Green:

> 'nearly all men were at some time unemployed ... even when they were in work they frequently kept their families short of money. So the wife had to cling to the family into which she was born, and in particular to her mother, as the only other means of ensuring herself against isolation. The extended family was her trade union, organised in the main by women and for women, its solidarity her protection against being alone.'   (Young and Willmott 1959:189)

The co-operating group of women is here made up of women and their adult daughters, all of whom belong to the same local community, even though they may not share the same roof. Their solidarity is directly related to the weakness of the conjugal bond, both emotionally and as a source of economic security – in this sense it is a 'defensive' mechanism (Morpeth and Langton 1974). However, it is also linked to the fact that women have access to independent sources of income (in this case petty employment made possible by mutual help in child-care). In this sense female solidarity is more clearly an 'offensive' activity, designed to provide female alternatives to dependence on male breadwinners. This is where it differs from the female kin solidarity described by Stivens (Chapter 6) for Australian middle-class women. There the solidarity was much more a response to the need for mutual moral support than to the necessity of providing alternative arrangements to dependence on males.

My argument is, then, that in the capitalist mode of production a common position as domestic labourers is, of itself, not a sufficient basis for female solidarity. As a sphere of *reproduction* rather than production, domestic labour mirrors the divisions of the wider society. Domestic labourers do not form one class, as Delphy (1977) would have it; they are themselves divided on class lines. Female solidarity only over-rides class divisions in very exceptional circumstances and it may indeed contribute to the perpetuation of those class divisions. In capitalist society female solidarity may perhaps more realistically be seen as the product of contradictions *within* classes. One basic contradiction of this kind is indicated by the ideology of conjugal solidarity. This masks both the inequality built into the relationship between domestic labourer and income-earner, and their asymmetrical relationship to the economic structure (the income-earner's direct, the domestic labourer's indirect). A further contradiction lies in the situation of workers who are also domestic labourers, and whose primary location as domestic labourers is reflected in their inequality in the labour market. Female workers are not, by and large, equivalent to male workers since both male and female wage levels assume female dependence. As Angela Phillips put it: 'men are paid a family wage, women are paid pin money' (*The Guardian* 1978).

Intra-class contradictions at either of these levels may engender female solidarity, though it is clear that in general such solidarity is structurally inhibited.

Female solidarity, domestic labour, and sexual segregation in precapitalist economies

In precapitalist society it is rare for domestic labour to be such a privatized activity as it is under capitalism. Productive relations in such societies are generally built on the scaffolding of kinship. A group of related people form the unit of production and consumption, and often co-operate with other similar groups in economic activities. Generally such groupings are wider than the nuclear family and hence contain groups of co-residing women. In such situations does there exist a firmer base for female solidarity? The evidence is contradictory.

In several of the instances we discuss in this book 'female solidarity' is merely an organizational expression of the 'relations of reproduction', in other words women getting together to carry out the tasks associated with biological and social reproduction. In so doing they help to perpetuate an order within which they are very often unequal participants. This is brought out rather vividly in the Maasai folk tale related by *women* to explain their status as non-property owning dependents (Chapter 8). They relate that in the mythical past women were so concerned about their *children's* welfare that they let their cattle wander off into the bush to become wild. Maasai women's solidarity and mutual support are mainly directed to promoting reproductive ends, but even this passive solidarity may, in certain conditions, be a source of strength, a political base from which women can take the offensive in their relations with men. Thus Maasai women also stand firmly beside each other in activities designed to assert their own sexual freedom in relation to their husbands, the elders, by adulterous affairs with their contemporaries, the moran 'warriors'.

It is important, however, to ask ourselves whether the 'solidarity' exhibited by women in these situations is merely a 'forced solidarity' based solely on women's mutual exclusion from male society, in other words, sexual segregation. Sexual segregation may take many forms, from the highly ritualized avoidance techniques of *purdah* situations, to what some contributors refer to here as the '*de facto* segregation' of men from women in work and home. Even a sexual division of labour in the productive sphere can effectively segregate the sexes.

When we speak of 'segregation' we normally mean the segregation of women from men, but the segregation of women from each other is also relevant. Both represent modes of social control over women, but whereas the former throws women into each other's company and creates the preconditions for female solidarity, in the latter case such solidarity is effectively inhibited.

It is clear that extreme forms of sexual segregation reflect a situation of marked female dependence characteristic neither of simple subsistence economies nor of developed capitalist society, but of intermediate economic forms. In such situations women are withdrawn from productive labour and restricted to purely domestic activities. The irony of this in general terms is that it usually reflects an expansion of the productive forces such that female labour is no longer required (note the suggestive linking of 'the veil and the plough' by Boserup (1970), Women, as domestic labourers, become appendages of a structure of property relations in the productive sphere. Thus Saifullah-Khan notes that a prerequisite for female seclusion is 'a strongly patrilineal and virilocal society' (Saifullah-Khan 1976:236).

The formal powerlessness of women in such a context may be marginally offset by the existence of a compensatory 'women's world' within which women have 'exclusive responsibilities' (Saifullah-Khan 1976). The women's world has its focus in the extended or joint family household within which groups of women carry out domestic tasks conjointly. Such domestic clusters of women are linked together – usually by relations of kinship and affinity – into what Maher has called 'women's networks' (Maher 1976). Recent research has suggested that with the confidence born of mutual support women can exercise some informal influence on the extra-domestic sphere, even from this restricted base (Maher 1976). The urban Sudanese women, described by Constantinides (Chapter 7), have responded to an extreme form of segregation (the physical seclusion of women from unrelated men) by creating women's groups. By focusing on 'women's illnesses' these groups address themselves to the primary function of the domestic labourer – reproduction. While limited in its effect, such female solidarity can be exerted to pressure men into activity on their wives' behalf. Compare the situation existing in Désirade where women are not only effectively separated from men by lack of employment and norms of modest behaviour restricting them to their homes, but also from each other by the privatization of domestic labour within the nuclear family.

On the other hand, as I have already noted, the simple existence of a group of females carrying out domestic labour together does not necessarily make for female solidarity. The conditions of that labour are often beyond women's control, and may actually be inimical to the development of solidary ties. The women grouped together in a household have not necessarily chosen each other's company – they may co-exist solely in consequence of their separate conjugal ties with the males who make up the household. 'Women under separate masters are the most divided of oppressed groups' (Guettel 1974:5). In a general way women's relations to each other are determined by their relations to men, and by the property relations between men. These relations may dictate not only the composition of the household group but also that of the local community. Let us take the second point first.

Where the local community is made up of one or more groups of related men, and where the preference is for marriage outside the local group, the women who make up the inhabitants of a local settlement will be inmarrying strangers. In such circumstances solidarity is a genuinely political act in which women overcome the divisions between them in a wider realization of their common situation *vis-à-vis* men. Not surprisingly, though, female solidarity often fails to emerge in this situation. For example, it is not realized in the Indian village described by Sharma (Chapter 10). By contrast the Moroccan women described by Maher were generally kinswomen, since the preference here was for endogamy within the local community, and it was actually women who arranged such endogamous marriages (Maher 1976).

Relations between women in the household may be a reflection in microcosm of relations between women in the community. Whereas matrilocal marriage residence constantly renews the 'natural group' of a mother with her grown daughters and grand-daughters, virilocal residence divides this group, and creates the potentially hostile diad of mother-in-law and daughter-in-law. Structurally these two roles are ones of competition: whereas the mother-in-law aims to retain the

33

affection and material interest of her son, the daughter-in-law attempts to attain it. The normal solution to such a conflict of interests is to place the elder women in an unequivocal position of authority over the younger. This authority is not intrinsic to women's relations, but rather derivatory, since it represents, in feebler form, the terms of control of the father over his son.

The old adage of 'divide and rule' takes on a new guise here, for as Sharma notes : 'There is no better means of social control than the devolution of internal control onto the group that is to be subordinate'. In the Indian village that she describes in Chapter 10, co-operation between women is important in the performance of domestic tasks, but it does not lead to the formation of solidary groups of women. The interaction of women ensures only an effective policing of their role as domestic labourers. Even 'solidarity' can assume this form, however, as is indicated by the Maasai case (Chapter 8), where women may organize themselves to punish *other women* for ritual offences relating to procreation.

Female solidarity and petty commodity production

In the cases described above women's consciousness is muted, and female solidarity, where it occurs, is largely restricted to restating women's primary role as domestic labourer. Even where women's labour is vital to subsistence production they labour for the males to whom they are espoused; the product of their labour is alienated. Where women control the product of their labour, however, a much more favourable climate for female solidarity exists.

Sanday has argued that female solidarity is one dimension of high female 'status' in the 'public domain'. Comparing societies one with another she argues that three other dimensions are related to high female status. First, women must control the products of their own labour; second, these products must find a market outside the domestic subsistence sector; and third, women must participate in public political activities (Sanday 1974).

As I have indicated, I do not regard 'the problem' as being one of 'female status', but of delineating the relationship between domestic labour and particular modes of production. I would therefore argue that it is impossible to devise an ahistorical measure of only one term of the equation.[8] Indeed, if I understand Sanday's argument correctly, it would itself seem to be historically specific, and to apply only to economic systems characterized by petty commodity production – that is, independent individual or family production on a small scale for the market. This at least is what I would take to be entailed in her second dimension of high female status: 'Demand for female produce. Female produce has a recognised value either internally – beyond the localised family – or in an external market' (1974: 192) – when taken together with the first dimension, women's control over the products of their labour. Petty commodity production is specific either to pre-capitalist modes in transition to capitalism, or to areas on the periphery of the capitalist economic system.

Sanday's model would thus be inapplicable to societies based on communal appropriation (for example, hunting and gathering communities), and yet it is such societies that are most strongly urged by many writers to have egalitarian or complementary sexual relations (Aaby 1977; Engels 1972; Rohrlich-Leavitt 1975). On the other hand, with the triumph of capitalist social relations the very terms of this formula of high female status become inapplicable. Not just women, but also most men lose control over the products of their labour, and gain no power by these products being in demand.

Could it be, however, that petty commodity production in fact offers the most favourable context for women, as domestic labourers, to improve the terms of their situation? Of course it does not necessarily follow that in a system of petty commodity production women are producers, or that they produce on their own account, or that their products find a market (Désirade, see Chapter 9, is a good example of this). On the other hand petty commodity production is likely to be production *within the context of the domestic unit,* and is, therefore, the form of production most compatible with domestic labour.

Petty commodity production does not, of itself, engender female solidarity. On the contrary, the essence of such a productive system is that it is individualistic and competitive. However, the evidence would seem to suggest that where female solidarity is manifested in such a context, it is not as an aspect of women's participation in the public political arena (as

Sanday implies), but related to the *exclusion* of women from the public domain. It is being *both* producers and domestic labourers to which women are responding.

A good example of the significance of female solidarity in this context is offered by the 'women's war' among the Igbo of Nigeria in 1929 – though a good deal depends on how one interprets the events that took place on that occasion. In this instance women's subsistence products had found an external market, and a great many women had turned to trade and begun to accumulate small-scale capital. In an economy generally characterized by petty commodity production and with the development of a commercial class, women's position was equivalent to men's – indeed, in some cases, even superior.[9] However, formal (political) power relations did not take cognizance of women's enhanced economic power. Indeed, in the colonial context, even women's secret societies, their traditional locii of solidarity, were given no public recognition. When rumours began to circulate that women were to be taxed they rebelled. In the course of their revolt they behaved in ways that were shaming to their men, exposing their nakedness, making obscene gestures, and the like. My interpretation of these events would be that women, denied public recognition of their undoubted economic power, and denied any 'legitimate' political means by which to protect their interests, turn back on their only publicly accepted role, that of reproducers. By making a mockery of that role they threaten the authority of males, *because males have here connived in their lack of political representation*. In protesting an issue that affects *material* and *political* interests, women are caught up in the contradictions of their position, in which, in the last analysis, they remain domestic labourers, irrespective of any other additional extra-domestic relations they may have forged.[10]

In one of the case studies, described in Chapter 3, female solidarity is evidently a vital *precondition* for petty commodity production. The female beer brewers of Nairobi are self-reliant women, no longer dependent on husbands or other male kin in order to survive. Although they operate individually they have created effective networks of mutual support to share out their domestic tasks and to ensure the success of their businesses. While these women scorn men (in the guise of husbands, or as agents of wider social disapproval, for example,

36

policemen) they cannot be entirely independent of them, for it is largely males who purchase their products.

Would female solidarity inspired by feminist consciousness necessarily lead to separatism? Does awareness of gender inequality and the determination to abolish it necessarily dictate an anti-male attitude? The Chinese do not appear to think so. As a Peking factory worker commented: 'I'm not for what is called women's rights in and for itself, as opposed to men's rights. We cannot make the men our target of struggle ...' (Croll 1974:ii).

Female solidarity and social revolution

We may now consider what lessons are to be learnt (if any) from the one case here – that of China – that can be decisively described as active solidarity. It is active since such solidarity is consciously motivated to change the relationship between reproductive and productive activities. As Croll shows (Chapter 2), the situation of rural Chinese women in the pre-liberation period was not unlike that of rural Indian women today, though a good deal harsher. Among the semi-feudal peasantry, women were pawns in a system of male property relations. Virilocal marriage residence and village exogamy created extended households to which women came as strangers and within which they were subject to the authority of senior women.

'In the women of China', Jack Belden asserts, 'the Communists possessed, almost ready made, one of the greatest masses of disinherited human beings the world has ever known' (Belden 1949:421). This is true, but disguises the fact that the success of the Chinese Communist Party in winning over women to their cause was in some measure dependent on their 'exploitation' of divisions among women themselves. It was, as Croll remarks, 'the younger generation, the daughters-in-law who had no support or power base even of the most informal kind within the household', who flocked to the Communist cause. Older women, particularly if they occupied the position of mother-in-law, felt almost as threatened by the new women's associations as did men, and they did what they could to inhibit their success.

There is a good deal of current debate on the implications

for women of a socialist revolution. Elisabeth Croll here approaches the issue from a slightly different vantage point. She examines the extent to which women are able to *create* their own 'revolution within the revolution' by standing together. In China the women's associations initiated the politicization of women, and mobilized them in order to carry out new productive tasks. In so doing they contributed to the revolutionary transformation of the relations of production, and threw into question the 'natural identification' of women with domestic labour. Assuming the continued militancy of women, the limitations to this developing revolutionary transformation are two-fold. The first is technical – the lack in an under-developed economy of adequate resources for effectively socializing the major tasks of domestic labour. The second is ideological – the continuing reluctance of men to contribute their fair share to household labour. Both are political questions and their solution will depend on the continued pressure brought to bear by militant women.

Must we conclude, then, that for female solidarity to effect real changes in women's position, it must take place within the context of general social upheaval? Alternatively, is the success of the women's associations in China related to their promotion by powerful and exogenous forces dedicated to revolutionary transformation? Both of these conclusions would seem to carry some conviction, as Rowbotham remarks: 'It is only in the abnormal circumstances of political revolt that it is possible for women to take uncustomary action' (Rowbotham 1972:204). The fact that the radical feminist activity engendered by political upheaval can dwindle into forms of bourgeois feminism or even anti-feminism (which is what seems to have happened to the women's rights movement in India) testifies merely to the limited nature of the political struggle. According to Rowbotham: 'It is only when national liberation movements have become revolutionary movements that the real problems of women's liberation have even begun to be considered' (Rowbotham 1972:205). The danger here lies in the scope that the revolution allows (or does not allow) for women to transform their own situation, as domestic labourers and super-exploited producers. The history of the women's movement in China (and of its counterpart in Russia) is one of subjection to the over-riding concerns of official policy, and hence the chequered careers of each movement. However, where such a movement has once been brought into being, it is impossible to silence it fully.

Conclusion

I began this essay by questioning the common assumption that 'the problem of women' is a problem of 'women's status'. To suggest that it is, is equivalent to arguing that the central problem of the working class is the low status attached to the occupational roles it plays. This position would then entail the conclusion that all that is required to improve the situation of the working class is to 'educate society' as to the intrinsic 'value' of, say, refuse collection, assembly line work, or mechanical drilling. Yet 'status' does not derive from the intrinsic value of an occupation, but rather from the power (or lack of power) of its personnel. Power is in turn a reflection of control within the economic structure, of collective awareness of position, and the organizational ability to uphold or transform it. Women, I have argued, are anchored in domestic labour because of their physical capacity to reproduce. The character and conditions of domestic labour vary according to the total mode of production of which it is a necessary constituent. So too does the definition of its personnel: women may be determined by it to a differential degree. There is a complex and dialectical interrelationship between the spheres of production and reproduction, though the latter is, by its nature, a sphere of conservation rather than innovation. It is rare for domestic labourers to be able to exert control within the economic structure, though this capacity too is a reflection of the mode of production within which they operate.

In technologically underdeveloped economies women have little power to control their reproductive cycle. Among the Mundarucú Indians of Brazil:

> 'Women are resentful of the continued cycle of pregnancy and birth, regarding it as an encumbrance and physical handicap and the source of their principal occupations and labours ... After three or four live births ... their desire for more children declines markedly ... Their own contraceptive techniques, they claimed, had only variable success.'
>
> (Murphy and Murphy 1974:161)

In Russia today the one child family is becoming the norm, evidence, one would suppose, of women protesting with their bodies against the dual burden of work and housework which is placed upon them. Clearly the degree to which women can influence the reproduction of the labour force will depend both on the technological level (especially in medicine) and on the structure of production (its labour intensity, for example).

If women, as domestic labourers, generally lack control within the economic structure, they also frequently lack a collective awareness of their common position and the contribution that they make to processes of production. One may draw a parallel, perhaps, between the development of class consciousness and the emergence of feminist consciousness. A class exists in an objective sense when its members share a common relation to the means of production, but its objective existence does not automatically generate a subjective realization. A class, as Marx observed, may be *in itself*, but is not necessarily *for itself*. The development of a *revolutionary* consciousness, as opposed to a merely economistic or 'trade-union consciousness' (to use Lenin's distinction) only occurs in very special circumstances.

As domestic labourers, women share a specific common relation to the means of production – namely they perform the socially necessary task of reproduction, social as well as biological. This common situation is not necessarily an oppressive one: the tasks of domestic labour may not be very onerous, or they are performed overtly for the common good, or they are not specifically confined to women. Even where none of this is true, and where women are pawns in a system of male property and productive relations, they do not necessarily become conscious of their common position and organize to transform it. Social relations may be structured in such a way as to inhibit the development of a collective consciousness among women: the privatization of domestic labour, the dispersal of female kin groups, the inequalities of class and status among women themselves, may all act towards the suppression of common feeling. Alternatively women's organization may simply reiterate the terms of their relations to men, and reinforce women's identification with domestic labour. It is only where women have independent resources (and not always then) that their organizations challenge the terms of the gender relationship. They can then begin effectively to communalize the sphere of social reproduction, making it a task of society at large, rather than one dictated by sexual identity.

In any class divided society the objective similarity of function of domestic labourers cannot be effectively translated into subjective consciousness because domestic labour is not specific to the reproduction of one class but to the reproduction of opposing classes. Differing class situations change the very terms on which domestic labour is performed. Only a revolutionary movement dedicated to the destruction of classes can thus erase the divisions among women themselves. In lieu of such a revolutionary context, the consciousness exhibited by women in solidarity is more often of the 'trade-union' variety, devoted to the amelioration rather than the transformation of existing sexist relations of production and reproduction.

Notes

1 I have deliberately chosen these titles from works purporting to discuss the issue of women in a cross-cultural perspective. One should add, however, that Reiter justifies her position in terms that I have ignored here: 'we need new studies that will focus on women; it cannot be otherwise because of the double bias which has trivialized and misinterpreted female roles for so long. Yet the final outcome of such an approach will be a reorientation of anthropology so that it studies *humankind*' (Reiter 1975:16).

2 This task is, of course, shared with more formal agencies of social reproduction, particularly the education system. In other words I use the term domestic labour here to designate that labour devoted to reproductive processes only within the context of the domestic unit. Although women also predominate in the labour force assigned to social reproduction outside the home it is not this labour that defines their ideological status.

3 Secombe goes into this at length, and my exposition here owes much to his article of 1974. Edholm, Harris, and Young (1977) have argued that domestic labour is an analytical category only properly applied to capitalist social formations because it is only there that it is distinct from other forms of labour. Whereas in the capitalist mode of production labour power in general becomes a commodity, domestic labour does not. Whilst I would not deny this characterization of the distinctiveness of domestic labour in capitalist society, I would not agree with Edholm *et al.*'s argument that: 'To treat as domestic

41

labour the superficially similar tasks performed by women in other productive systems, in which little or no labour is valorised, is confusing ...' (1977:104). Domestic labour is not, I would argue, defined either by 'superficially similar tasks' or by its subjection or non-subjection to the law of value. It is rather defined by its relation to the universal process of social reproduction, being labour devoted to that process in the context of the domestic unit.

4 This does not lead to any necessary conclusions concerning the 'status' of women. Note Marshall, who, writing before the rise of the women's movement renewed interest in these questions, remarks of the !Kung Bushmen that: 'Although the hunters supply only about a fifth of the people's food, and the women four-fifths, the women play a dependent role in !Kung society. Nevertheless the men do not ill treat the women and require no extreme form of obedience or subservience of them'. (Marshall 1965:255). Men in this communally organized society hold the only political office, that of headman of a band, but membership of a band is dicated by choice and availability of food, as is marriage residence. Marirage entails no 'property entanglements' so divorce is uncomplicated.

5 Note that among the !Kung, for example, the wild plant food, 'that each woman gathers belongs to her and with it she feeds her own family, sharing with whatever relative or friend she wishes' (Marshall 1965:250). Marshall notes that the habit of sharing is deeply embedded in the social practice of the !Kung. Among the Mundurucú Indians of Brazil, hunting, gathering, and fishing is supplemented by semi-communalized horticultural production. Within this system it is women who control the communal distribution of garden products, and 'even the distribution of game [hunting is a male activity] eventually falls under female control. The man brings his kill to his wife ... and she and her housemates butcher it. They send pieces to other houses but they determine who gets which parts' (Murphy and Murphy 1974:131).

6 One may note the parallel with a set of arguments very much in vogue within mainstream sociology relating to class consciousness, and associated with the 'end of ideology' thesis. 'The emphasis [in this position] is on a postulated increasing isolation of workers from one another; a realignment of their aspirations towards individual and family goals rather than to collective and class objectives' (Westergaard and Resler 1975:26). 'The "privatised worker" can indeed hardly aspire to a class consciousness: concerned [as he is said to be] only with consumption and his own private life' (Swingewood 1975:131–2). Other parallels can be drawn between studies of class consciousness and of feminist consciousness, though the former may more usefully be seen as a *metaphor* for

the latter rather than as a statement of identity. I shall return to this point later.

7 Many employed women are merely casual workers, whose level of unionization is low. Low wages, lack of skills, and women's domestic responsibilities do not, on the whole, make for a committed female work force.

8 Although she recognizes the biological basis of women's position Sanday decides to exclude discussion of 'the domestic domain ... since it is conceivable that status in one domain may preclude status in the other' (Sanday 1974:192).

9 See the excellent and stirring account by Ifeka-Moller. She notes the transformation of a subsistence economy into one characterized by petty commodity production as being crucial to the, 'radical changes in the sexual divisions of labour and in the distribution of wealth'. Nevertheless there were limitations to women's growing economic power: 'men still controlled the bulk of the economy's capital assets – land and labour' (Ifeka-Moller 1975:137).

10 Ifeka-Moller's analysis coincides with mine insofar as she sees a 'contradiction' here between women's productive role and their 'biosocial functions in reproduction' (Ifeka-Moller 1975:144). However, she interprets this in symbolic terms, arguing for 'women's "inner belief" that reproduction brings them full maturity and satisfaction' – an 'inner belief' which she claims these women saw as threatened. Hence their obscene actions were, 'symbols for demonstrating their fear that they had become as men' (Ifeka-Moller 1975:144). This seems to me to be twisting the facts, as no evidence is presented of women being involuntary participants in commerce or petty commodity production. Indeed their behaviour implies that they desired to become *more* like men, by moving into the public political arena.

References

AABY, P. (1977) Engels and Women. *Critique of Anthropology 3* (9) and (10):25–54.

ARDENER, E. (1975) Belief and the Problem of Women. In S. Ardener (ed.), *Perceiving Women*. London: Malaby Press.

BEECHEY, V. (1977) Some notes on Female Wage Labour in Capitalist Production. *Capital and Class 3*:45–66.

BELDEN, J. (1949) *China Shakes the World*. New York: Harper Bros.

BENSTON, M. (1969) The Political Economy of Women's Liberation. *Monthly Review 21*:13–27

BOSERUP, E. (1970) *Women's Role in Economic Development*. New York: St. Martin's Press.

CROLL, E. (1974) *The Women's Movement in China*. Anglo-Chinese Educational Institute. Modern China Series No. 6.

DALLA COSTA, M. and JAMES, S. (1972) *The Power of Women and the Subversion of the Community*. Bristol: Falling Wall Press.

DELPHY, C. (1977) *The Main Enemy: A Materialist Analysis of Women's Oppression*. WRRC, Explorations in Feminism No. 3 London.

DEPARTMENT OF EMPLOYMENT AND PRODUCTIVITY (1971) *British Labour Statistics: Historical Abstract 1886-1968*. London: HMSO.

EDHOLM, F., HARRIS, O., and YOUNG, K. (1977) Conceptualising Women. *Critique of Anthropology* 3 (9) and (10):101–30.

ENGELS, F. (1972) *The Origin of the Family, Private Property and the State*. New York: Pathfinder Press.

GUETTEL, C. (1974) *Marxism and Feminism*. Toronto: Canadian Women's Educational Press.

IFEKA-MOLLER, C. (1975) Female Militancy and Colonial Revolt: The Women's War of 1929, Eastern Nigeria. In S. Ardener (ed.), *Perceiving Women*. London: Malaby Press.

JAHAN, R. (1975) Women in Bangladesh. In R. Rohrlich-Leavitt (ed.), *Women Cross-Culturally: Change and Challenge*. The Hague: Mouton.

LEACOCK, E. (1975) Class, Commodity and the Status of Women. In R. Rohrlich-Leavitt (ed.), *Women Cross-Culturally: Change and Challenge*. The Hague: Mouton.

LENIN, V. (n.d.) *What is to be Done?* Moscow: Foreign Languages Publishing House.

LOWRY, S. (1977) *The Guardian*. August 19.

MAHER, V. (1976) Kin, Clients and Accomplices: Relationships amongst Women in Morocco. In D. L. Barker and S. Allen (eds.), *Sexual Divisions and Society: Process and Change*. London: Tavistock Publications.

MARSHALL, L. (1965) The !Kung Bushmen of the Kalahari Desert. In J. Gibbs (ed.), *Peoples of Africa*. New York: Holt, Rinehart and Winston Inc.

MARX, K. (1930) *Capital 2*. New York: J. M. Dent & Sons Ltd.

MARX, K. (n.d.) *The Poverty of Philosophy*. Moscow: Foreign Languages Publishing House.

MARX, K. and ENGELS, F. (1935) The German Ideology. In *Handbook of Marxism*. London: Victor Gollancz.

MITCHELL, J. and OAKLEY, A. (1976) *The Rights and Wrongs of Women*. Harmondsworth: Penguin

MORPETH, R. and LANGTON, P. (1974) Contemporary Matriarchies: Women alone—Independent or Incomplete? *Cambridge Anthropology* 1(3):20–38

MURPHY, Y. and MURPHY, R. F. (1974) *Women of the Forest*. New York: Columbia University Press.

44

NADEL, S. F. (1951) *The Foundations of Social Anthropology*. London: Cohen and West.

PHILLIPS, A. (1978) *The Guardian*. March 7.

POWER OF WOMEN COLLECTIVE (1975) Foreword to M. Dalla Costa and S. James, *The Power of Women and the Subversion of the Community* (3rd ed.). Bristol: Falling Wall Press.

REITER, R. (1975) *Toward an Anthropology of Women*. London and New York: Monthly Review Press.

RICHARDS, A. (1974) The 'Position' of Women – an Anthropological View. *Cambridge Anthropology* 1(3):3–10.

ROHRLICH-LEAVITT, R. (1975) Conclusions. In R. Rohrlich-Leavitt (ed.), *Women Cross-Culturally: Change and Challenge*. The Hague: Mouton.

ROSALDO, M. Z. (1974) Women, Culture and Socitety: A Theoretical Overview. In M. Z. Rosaldo and L. Lamphere (eds.), *Women, Culture and Society*. Stanford, California: Stanford University Press.

ROSSER, C. and HARRIS, C. (1965) *The Family and Social Change*. London: Routledge & Kegan Paul.

ROWBOTHAM, S. (1972) *Women, Resistance and Revolution*. London: Allen Lane.

ROWBOTHAM, S. (1973) *Women's Consciousness, Man's World*. Harmondsworth: Penguin.

SAIFULLAH-KHAN, V. (1976) Purdah in the British Situation. In D. L. Barker, and S. Allen (eds.), *Dependence and Exploitation in Work and Marriage*. London and New York: Longman.

SANDAY, P. (1974) Female Status in the Public Domain. In M. Z. Rosaldo and L. Lamphere (eds.), *Women, Culture and Society*. Stanford, California: Stanford University Press.

SCHREINER, O. (1911) *Women and Labour*. New York: Frederick Stokes Co. (reissued by Virago 1978).

SECOMBE, W. (1974) The Housewife and her Labour under Capitalism. *New Left Review* 83:3–24.

SMITH, D. (in press) Women, the Family and Corporate Capitalism. In M. Stephenson (ed.), *Women in Canada*. Ontario: New Press.

SWINGEWOOD, A. (1975) *Marx and Modern Social Theory*. London: Macmillan.

WALLMAN, S. (1976) Difference, differentiation, discrimination. *New Community* 5(1) and (2):1–14.

WESTERGAARD, J. and RESLER, H. (1975) *Class in a Capitalist Society*. Harmondsworth: Penguin.

WIPPER, A. (1975) The Maendeleo ya Wanawake Organisation: The Cooptation of Leadership. *African Studies Review XVIII* (3):99–120.

YOUNG, M. and WILLMOTT, P. (1959) *Family and Kinship in East London*. Harmondsworth: Penguin.

TWO

Rural China: segregation to solidarity

ELISABETH CROLL

In theorizing the status of women or indexing the number of economic and political rights that accrue to women, it has only recently been emphasized that female solidarity groups devoted to female political and economic interests constitute an important criterion of female status in any society. Previously it has often been assumed that there is a direct correlation between women's participation in social production and their degree of participation in political decision-making. That is, where women are in social production long enough and in sufficient numbers it was thought that they would automatically move from dependent to independent and from powerless to powerful roles. Cross-cultural analyses of the position of women have qualified this interpretation by suggesting that although female productive labour is a necessary condition for female status, it is not a sufficient condition. Other factors discourage access to and control over the strategic resources of society. In her cross-cultural analysis of the position of women in society, Sanday (1975) found a high correlation between the presence of female solidarity groups (devoted to female economic and political interests) and female control of produce, demand for female produce, and female participation in political activities.

An interesting question in any analysis of the position of women is under what conditions do women form their own solidarity groups? That is, what factors contribute to female co-operation and consciousness of themselves as a separate and significant social category of economic and political import, with interests in opposition to those of men? In examining this question the experience of China in the last few decades is of great significance. In China, the strategy used to redefine the sexual division of labour and alter the balance of power between the sexes in favour of women has increasingly taken account of factors, other than separation from social production, which discourage and discriminate against the acquisition of female status. The experience of Chinese women confirms the qualified assumption that although participation in social production is a necessary condition for improving female status, it is not a sufficient condition. Moreover, the establishment of female solidarity groups has been an important component of the strategy redefining the position of women. Since the establishment of the nationalist and socialist revolutionary movement in the early 1920s, the Communist Party has argued that the presence of female solidarity groups is necessary in order to draw women into new economic and political activities. They help to facilitate women's access to and control over, not only the products of their own labour, but also the economic and ideological resources of society. The experience of China suggests that female solidarity groups can play a crucial role in redefining the position of women in society. At the same time, though, the uneasy alliance between the national revolutionary movement and the women's movement has sometimes brought competing claims on the identity of women as both members of social classes and their separate gender. The balance of these class and separate gender interests has directly affected the history of solidarity groups, causing certain ambiguities to surround their role within the strategy used to redefine the position of women.

In China the new ideology of solidarity was designed to

substitute one in which women were conceived of as a separate and inferior social category, segregated by the division of labour separating the domestic from the public sphere of activities. This short study sets out to examine the foundations and functions of female solidarity groups and assess their contribution to the redefinition of the role and status of women in rural China.[1]

Segregation

In the social, political, and economic affairs of the country, the most important distinction for all social classes in the nineteenth century was between household or domestic and non-household or public spheres of activity. The classical codes of feminine conduct ruled that women were as different from and secondary to men as heaven was from earth, and that women were to take no part in public affairs. Over the centuries these codes were elaborated to include the practices of segregation and relative seclusion. From the earliest times women were taught by the classics and folklore that they should not concern themselves with public affairs. The Book of Rites (compiled in the second century AD and later to become one of the venerated Confucian classics containing rules of correct conduct) clearly stated that women should have no public influence or knowledge of affairs outside the home. 'A wife's words should not travel beyond her apartments', and 'a woman does not discuss affairs outside the home' were common folk sayings (*New Youth* 1916). Women were denied participation in any government or local community institutions and all the significant ceremonial roles in society could only be fulfilled by men. The confinement of women to the domestic sphere was further reinforced by the concern for or almost obsession with the preservation of their virtue, honour, or chastity.

Perhaps the most striking feature of social life was the segregation of the sexes. It was deemed desirable that women should have no public social relations with men, and at the turn of the century Peking was described as 'a city of men' (Conger 1909 : 2). Even within the household, relations between the sexes from adolescence onwards were supposed to be marked by avoidance (*New Youth* 1916). The cult of feminine chastity and the ideology of segregation were reinforced by the practice of footbinding, which acted as a physical constraint on the mobility of all but the poorest women and those in the southern-most provinces, and the absence of any available independent economic role in society. A combination of such factors led to the increasing seclusion of women and girls from everyone except their own female family members. Indeed, the very word for wife, *neiren*, literally meant 'inside person'.

If ideally women were confined to the domestic sphere, in reality it was the prerogative of the richer social classes to live up to these norms. Among the poor, economic factors interceded to varying degrees and modified these standards in practice. In peasant households of the villages, women customarily had more freedom of movement. Their living quarters afforded them less seclusion than the rambling courtyards of gentry dwellings. The very size of the peasant household allowed less segregation and where the light inside was poor, peasant women frequently sat and worked on their doorsteps. In the village, women sometimes gathered water from the well, did the washing at the river, and had no servants to shop and market on their behalf. They had some contact with local shopkeepers and pedlars and in some areas of China such as the southern provinces, women traditionally worked in the fields alongside their menfolk during the busy seasons. Despite this the movements of most village women, especially those of child-bearing age, were still restricted, and they were often not permitted to leave their courtyards for the first three years of marriage. One traveller in nineteenth-century China observed that tens of thousands of women had never been more than two miles from their village and this was often only on the occasion of their marriage (Smith 1900). One such woman described her existence as that of a 'frog in a well' and common sayings, 'man travels everywhere while a woman is confined to the kitchen', and 'an incompetent man can get around nine counties but, a competent woman can get around her cooking stove' arose because women appearing outside their courtyards and houses was a rare event (Myrdal 1967). In her autobiography a working woman recalled how she and her sister were not allowed on the street after they were thirteen years of age. She also recalled that, when a family who wanted to know more about a girl who had been suggested as a prospective daughter-in-law asked neighbours for an opinion, the highest praise and compliment in response was 'we do not know, we have never see her' (Pruitt 1967:29).

The peasant family was the chief organizational unit of production and consumption and to a large degree self-sufficient. It was, therefore, difficult for women to find an alternative viable source of economic support. Women ordinarily could not produce or consume without the sanction of the male members of the household. Within the patrilineal, patrilocal, and patriarchal household, women generally played a subservient role until they became the sole surviving representative of the senior generation. A woman's life-cycle was dominated by two states: first, she was a 'temporary' member of her natal family destined to leave her family and usually her village on marriage. Second, as a new bride chosen by her husband's parents, she became an 'outsider' or 'stranger' in the household of her husband. In the daily household routine she was normally under the constant surveillance and discipline of her mother-in-law. It was by forming and nurturing ties with her son which were personal and exclusive that women cultivated a source of power in a social structure dominated by men. Any potential threat to this relationship by the daughter-in-law was felt deeply. Trapped all their lives, women, with the authority of being the mother-in-law, appeared to compensate for their own former suffering and impotence as outsiders by repeating the very same process of domination.

In effect the structure of the Chinese family was based on a hierarchy of the generations and sexes that were divided in interest from each other. Outside the household ideological and economic factors interacted to deprive women of the opportunities for independence or association which might have arisen from participation in political, social, and economic activities. Their confinement to the activities of the household ensured minimal co-operative links with other women which might have reduced the hierarchy within the ranks of women and mitigated the effects of male dominance.

The women's community

Traditionally tied to the family and separated from her own kind, women in organizational terms formed one of the most underdeveloped social categories. However, it could not be said that they were entirely powerless individually or collectively. Individually they could influence domestic and village affairs through initiating gossip in the women's community, threatening suicide, or by manipulating intra-familial bonds to suit themselves. These activities, though, were usually interpreted in terms of the nature of woman being given to hysterical, disturbed, or disruptive behaviour. In village affairs the women's community, composed of loose and overlapping groups of women, was at its most visible when women of neighbouring peasant households gathered to wash their clothes, perform other domestic chores, talk and exchange information. An anthropologist said about women of his native village in Shandong province:

'Women of neighbouring families gather before their front doors to talk and gossip. Especially in the summer time when men are eating at home, the women come out to have a breath of fresh air under the trees. A spontaneous and informal group is formed and the talk ranges from discussion of the daily work to gossip about the marriage of a family at the other end of the village.' (Yang 1945:153)

Margery Wolf used her experience in Taiwan to draw attention to the informal role of the women's community and emphasized the mutual interests of its members (Wolf 1974). She suggested that in traditional China, too, each woman valued her standing within the women's communities because at some time in her life she might need their support. Women could and did affect the affairs of individual households and the village: by merely talking about their affairs they could influence men's behaviour by drawing attention to unfavourable aspects of their behaviour and causing the victim of gossip to 'lose face'. She thought that in this way the women's community did exercise a certain degree of power and the women who had the most influence on village affairs were those who had worked through the women's community.

However, the formal establishment of female solidarity groups in the villages of twentieth-century China required more than the institutionalization of the women's community. They required that women conceive of themselves as a separate social category whose common interests were not always coincidental with those of the men; that they speak out in defence of their own interests and openly and directly participate in village affairs.

The formation of solidarity groups

Since its establishment in 1921 the Communist Party has nurtured separate organizations of village women on the basis of their special experience of oppression and the necessity to form an independent power base, from which women would be able to conduct their struggle for the protection and expansion of their new rights and opportunities in negotiating a new role and status. The special oppression of women, which was identified as different from that of the political, clan, and religious oppression shared by the men of their own social class, distinguished them as a separate social category. The common identity of women was based on the sexual division of labour and the inheritance of male supremacy. These were responsible for the low jural status assigned to women, their economic dependence, their exclusion from the public sphere, and certain beliefs and thought patterns peculiar to women. The Communist Party also forecast that while a government could provide the legal and material conditions favourable to improvements in female status it was the women themselves who must recognize their common interests and negotiate a new collective role in society. Female solidarity groups were to be assigned a major role in encouraging women to evolve a collective sense of identity, translate the individual experience of oppression into a coherent analysis of oppression, and redefine their position within individual families, villages, and factories.

Women's groups were first established in the villages of rural China in the wake of the 'liberation' of the village by the Communist Armies (in the late 1930s, 1940s, and early 1950s) as part of the nation-wide construction of the women's movement.[2] Specially trained women leaders or cadres entered the villages to encourage the women to meet together and identify common grievances. They normally approached individual women known to be influential in the women's community, as well as socially oppressed women like adopted-in daughters-in-law, or those recruited into their husband's households in early childhood, and deviant women who earned a living in one of the few occupations available to women, such as mid-wifery or sorcery. Many months might pass before the village women were persuaded to meet together to share their personal experience or 'speak their bitterness' (Selden 1971:116). The very sight of the young uniformed and free-striding girl cadres was often enough to frighten local women indoors. 'Here come the terrible women soldiers' they were heard to mumble to each other in awe and fear (Epstein 1939:249). It was only after the young girls discarded their uniforms, donned peasant clothing, and at first contented themselves with offers to help with washing and babysitting that the peasant women could be encouraged to talk about their lives and admit their suffering and oppression (*China Reconstructs* 1973).

Women had to be persuaded that it was only when they became aware of their common grievances and formed a group of solidarity would they be able to effectively introduce and defend their new rights (Epstein 1939). However, when they first held meetings peasant women responded to the new idea of common interests and new rights with a certain amount of scepticism. They argued that it would be wonderful if women were the equals of men, but what chance did they have if from ancient times till now 'man has been the heaven and woman the earth'. One of the leaders of the movement establishing local groups noted that in these early years the fight to conquer the idea that women knew nothing but household affairs was particularly difficult. She said that it was not easy to give women a sense of collective identity of their importance and arouse an awareness concerning their collective interests (Cusack 1958). In more isolated rural areas it was many months before local groups were established.

The expansion of the women's movement from the urban into the rural areas brought many young urban educated and professional women into contact with more female peasants, factory women, slave girls, and prostitutes than ever before. There was much suspicion of their motives, and misunderstandings on both sides. Within the rural villages women were divided by social class and generation. The first women's groups often became identified with and reflected the interests of one group to the disadvantage of the others. For example, poor peasant women such as adopted-in daughters-in-law found their interests to be neglected. Alternatively, the richer women boycotted the groups and sent their menfolk instead, thus implying that these meetings were attended by women of ill-repute or prostitutes (Smedley 1944).

There was also a tendency for the women's groups to become the monopoly of the younger generation: the daughters-in-law who had no support or power base, even of the most informal kind, within the household. Not surprisingly the older generation, the mothers-in-law who had at last gained a position of relative respect and authority in the household, felt threatened by the women's unions to whom defiant daughters-in-law and slave girls could turn for protection. Thus, the leading activists in the female solidarity groups often tended to be young wives who had been adopted into their husband's families at a very early age. While the younger members might be concerned with free-choice marriage, the elder women saw this as a direct threat to their control over their daughters and daughters-in-law. Notions of courtship and free-choice of marriage partner directly threatened their position in the household and horrified them. This conflict of interests widened the generation gap and the older women attempted to bar the younger ones from attending meetings by denigrating their cause. 'They're a pack of wild women. Their words are not for young brides to hear' (*China Reconstructs* 1973). The opposition of the mothers-in-law was often as adamant as that of their sons.

In establishing the early solidarity groups, women individually and collectively within the village found it difficult to counter the resistance of the men of the household when they tried to extend their activities beyond the domestic sphere. Husbands, fearing their wives might go astray, objected to their attending public meetings. Very young wives who insisted on such attendance braved the inevitable domestic crises on their return, usually a beating or scraps of food instead of the usual meal. Individual women said they found the road as 'rough as stones' when their elders did not approve (*People's China* 1954). The women of one village found that as they organized themselves into a separate association, attended public meetings, and entered political life they encountered more and more opposition. In the late 1940s William Hinton observed that opposition from the men within their own households, most of whom regarded any activity by their wives and daughters-in-law outside the home as 'steps leading directly to adultery', took a particularly virulent form (Hinton 1966). In Ten Mile Inn village at the same time, men cadres forbade their wives to attend the women's associations which they nicknamed the Prostitutes' Meetings' (Crooks and Crooks 1959).

In the areas governed by the Communist Party before 1949, the anti-Japanese and civil war undoubtedly contributed to the early establishment of female solidarity groups. Women were incorporated into programmes of war work which necessitated collective action and they appropriated new economic roles in the absence of their men. Local groups were more easily founded if they were linked to practical objectives such as agricultural work teams, co-operative handicraft ventures, or literacy classes. These could gradually play a supportive role in meeting the practical and emotional problems of the members before raising their consciousness concerning common grievances and interests.

In villages in the 1940s where the women's associations had taught the girls of the village a number of productive skills, the village elders began to admit that 'the Women's Association doesn't seem to bad after all! They're learning quite a lot that's useful there' (*People's China* 1954). In Liuling village in the 1950s the local group of women combined study, labour, and consciousness-raising. Their leader Li Guiying had attended a Party school in 1951 and learned to read and write. On her return to her village she formed a local group of women to teach them her newly acquired skills. Many came to the winter classes and learned to read and write enough characters to keep simple accounts, receipts, and notes. The group became a labour group in 1953 and learned to make shoes, clothes; improve their agricultural tools; feed poultry; and spin. However, Li Guiying still felt that they had not really broken away from the past, and accordingly she encouraged the village women to meet together for discussions after winter school. 'We tried to get the women to tell us themselves what things had been like before, how it was now and how it ought to be in the future.' They contrasted the old practices of seclusion, arranged marriage, and bound feet with the new opportunities. The question of equality posed more problems. 'We discussed whether women are men's equals or not, and most felt that within the family, men and women are equal. We help the men when they work in the fields and they should help us in the house.' However, many of the older women relaxed in the belief that 'women are born to attend to the household'. 'A woman cannot work in the fields! That can't be helped. It is just that men and women are born different. A person is born either a man or a woman. To work in the fields or in the house.' Li Guiying said that they had long discussions on these and similar questions (Myrdal 1967).

Since 1949 the formation and functioning of women's solidarity groups as active agents in the redefinition of their individual and collective roles has been encouraged by the assignment of certain functions to the groups based on their common grievances and separate interests in the jural, economic, and political spheres of activities.

Strategies of solidarity

The separate interests of women were partially based on the new jural status assigned to women as a result of the new legislation passed in 1950 and 1951, such as the Marriage and Labour Laws for the equality and protection of women and children. In offering women an alternative power base and providing institutional access to legal sanctions, these laws defined the interests of women as separate from those of men. They allowed women the first opportunity to defy the authority of the household head, and directly contend his patriarchal authority.

The Marriage Law was designed to reduce the power of the men of the family by altering patterns of inheritance and control over children in favour of women, and prohibiting the exchange of women as a commodity. It increased the standing of the young bride both *vis à vis* her husband and her mother-in-law by introducing free-choice marriage. This strengthened the conjugal bond and protected the rights of women and children in the event of divorce. The Agrarian Reform Law gave rural women the right to own land and property in their own name. The Labour legislation provided for employment opportunities for women in the labour force equal to those of men and made allowance for maternity leave and benefits. The promulgation of these laws was followed by extensive campaigns to make the new legal provisions and

56

facilities widely known and available throughout the country.

In each of these areas of legislation, the women's leaders used the new rights to arouse an awareness of common grievances and helped women to exercise those new rights. In the implementation of the Marriage Law, women's groups arranged for their members to study the law, and share their own experience. They also gave support in the village and in the law courts to women who wished to choose their own marriage partner in the face of parental opposition (Yang Yu 1952), marry again after the deaths of their husbands, or apply for a divorce (*People's China* 1951). In the implementation of the Agrarian Reform Law, the women's groups supported the interests of women and very often prevented the men from disregarding their new rights. In one area the attempt by the men to redistribute the land without involving the women of the village was halted by their collective criticism and action. At a meeting of the Peasants' Union, the women's union was not invited to participate. The all-male meeting ruled that girls under the age of eighteen should not be eligible for their share of the land. It was the Women's Association that drew attention to the law and demanded a fresh discussion at which they be present, and the old decision was rescinded (All-China Democratic Women's Federation 1950). Time and again instances are recorded in which individual women turned to the newly formed solidarity groups for support in resolving a particularly difficult and oppressive personal and domestic problem. Without the apparent support of their sisters, few women reckoned that they personally would have dared to take the struggle into their own families, villages, and factories.

Women were encouraged to identify their separate interests in terms of their necessary entry into the public domain and especially into social production. In the tradition of Marx, and Engels, the Chinese Communist Party assumed a direct correlation between participation in social production and the redefinition of the roles and status of women. In anticipation that women would acquire an economic independence and would move from dependent to independent and powerless to powerful roles, the Party strategy was based on women acquiring the requisite skills and overcoming opposition to the redefinition of their economic roles. The local groups undertook the introduction of women into social production in the villages.

During the successive government policies to increase production and substitute individualized peasant production with collectivized agriculture through land reform, the collectivization and communization of agriculture, the establishment of rural industries, and projects of capital construction in the country-side, it was the local women's groups which encouraged their members to take advantage of the new opportunities and take a full and wide-ranging part in production.

Through their membership of local women's associations women had acquired raw materials and been introduced to handicraft and productive skills. Small co-operative production units of rural handicrafts and all-women work teams in agriculture have often coincided with the local women's groups. They made arrangements for and encouraged women to learn new skills and break into new spheres of work which were traditionally male preserves. This helped to adjust the division of labour within agriculture and between agriculture and other sectors of the rural economy, such as rural industries and construction projects.

Out of the women's groups, for example, came the impetus to form all-women fishing teams to challenge traditional taboos and prohibitions. For generations it had been believed that their reputation as polluting agents and their inherent bad-luck meant that 'if a woman gets in a fishing boat it will capsize' and if 'she casts a net the fish will step out of it' (*People's Daily* March 30, 1974). The women's groups have also acted as pressure groups to expedite the implementation of government policies to accommodate women's biological roles (*Women of China* August 1, 1961), introduce public health measures to reduce infant mortality (*People's China* 1953), give women control over reproduction (*People's China* 1957), and end discrimination against women in favour of the policy of 'equal pay for equal work' (*Women of China* November 1, 1961).

The legitimization and institutionalization of women in political affairs required the direct participation of women in political activities, and the meetings of production units to decide the allocation of labour, and the distribution of the produce and other resources. The value of separate women's groups in defining the separate interests of women and establishing their own power base from which they could confidently and collectively participate in the political affairs of the villages had been definitively established by a document published in 1948. This reported that in areas where there was an absence of female solidarity groups, women felt uncomfortable in the presence of men and few had spoken at any of the village meetings. The women themselves had admitted that if 'we are speaking with men present those who ought to say a lot say very little'. In contrast it was found that only in those areas where solidarity groups had been established did women attend meetings enthusiastically, lose their reserve in speaking publicly, and participate in political affairs. Their establishment had encouraged women to speak out for themselves and openly and directly participate in village affairs (Davin 1973).

One resident in a newly liberated village in the north of China in the late 1940s observed that the women's associations worked to bring to the village-wide gatherings the strength of 'half of China' (Hinton 1966). Their association enabled them to defend the newly won political rights of women to participate in village affairs. In one village where women were excluded from the first village elections, the women's associations refused to recognize the newly elected head of the village. They only gained recognition of their voting rights after the women's groups encouraged all its members to boycott their husband's beds. In the repeat election a woman was elected deputy-head of the village (Belden 1951). During the expansion and reorganization of production in the Great Leap Forward (1958 to 1959) women were not always involved in the discussions taken by the productive units. When they did attend meetings only their prior collective discussions and actions encouraged them firmly to challenge opposition to their rights to contribute opinions (Myrdal 1967).

The solidarity of women was also encouraged by raising the consciousness of women as members of their sex suffering a particular form of cultural suppression. The manipulation of their self-image and expectations by the traditional ruling ideology, which for the illiterate had become the forces of fate, had caused certain beliefs and thought patterns to continue to be peculiar to women. They required a separate consciousness that was not the automatic result of new jural, economic, or political positions in society. Indeed it was the wide-scale entry of women into social production or into the labour force

59

in the Great Leap Forward in the late 1950s, and the initial establishment of new social institutions such as creches, nurseries, and those for socializing laundry, sewing, mending, dining, and food préparation, which were said to be responsible for highlighting the fundamental problem that confronted women. That is, the removal of a whole history of cultural oppression or institutionalized and internalized subordination.

Beliefs elaborated on women's supposed inferiority, self-abasement, and dependence survived transformations in the mode of production. At the end of the first decade an editorial in the national newspaper concluded that 'only by enabling women to obtain their ideological emancipation will it be possible for them to develop their infinite source of power' (*People's Daily* 1958). The Peking Women's Federation also made it clear that it was the ideological aspects of women's emancipation that demanded the continuing separation and solidarity of women:

'Now that the broad masses of women have taken part in productive labour can one say that there is no more work to be carried out among women? No, on the contrary, the contents of woman work are now richer than before, and we are now required to carry out this work more pene-tratingly, carefully and solidly. For instance, though the broad masses of women have taken part in production, they still have many special problems in production, living and thought. The thought that women are inferior and depen-dent is present to a greater or lesser degree among the women themselves, and, in society the vestiges of feudal thought that women are contemptible cannot be thoroughly elimin-ated within a short time ... For this reason, it is not true to say that, there is not more work to be carried out among women, on the contrary the work in this respect must be reinforced.'   (*Women of China* 1962)

In the 1960s the women's movement embarked on a 'conscious learning process' to arouse a common awareness of these pro-blems and ways in which the traditional ruling ideology con-tinued to circumscribe women's lives. 'Without self-awareness', they said, 'women will be unwilling to fly though the sky is high' (*Women of China* 1963a). The consciousness-

60

raising movement was organized on the twin premises that the continuing social secondariness of women had ideological foundations and that 'first we [women] must begin with ourselves' (*Women of China* 1963a). On the basis of the first premise many articles were published that defined the individual and collective problems of women in ideological terms. For instance, the problem of combining the demands of child-bearing and rearing, the maintenance of the household and involvement in social production (*Women of China* 1963b) or of receiving an equal remuneration for equal work (*Women of China* 1961b) could be overcome by simply identifying and then eliminating the continuous influence of old beliefs and attitudes.

One article in the national Women's Magazine outlined what this process of consciousness-raising should entail for local groups in the villages. In reply to the question, 'in what respects should we women be self-conscious?', it made several recommendations in order to bring the unconscious to the conscious level. Women's groups should meet and study their own individual life-histories and the collective history of women, analyse the foundations of past subordination, and compare it to their present and potential positions in society. Such a self-examination, it suggested, would reveal the thought patterns that governed the daily practice of their lives and the continuing, but often quite unconscious, influence of beliefs. For example, beliefs such as 'the household is responsible for supporting a family, while the wife is responsible for household chores', or a 'man is superior to a woman', underlay the sexual division of labour and the evolution of the sexes into superior and inferior categories (*Women of China* 1963a). As a first step women were encouraged to 'begin with themselves', by articulating their individual experiences and learning from each other in an 'exchange of experiences' in their local groups. On this basis, the necessity of separating women into their own solidarity and study groups was reiterated in the early 1960s and defended on the grounds that although men and women workers might view many questions in the same light, there were also questions specific to women. For example, issues concerning the role of the Communist Party and the working class in the revolution, the question of who is working for whom, the relationship between individuals and the State, and between production and livelihood were all said to be of common concern to both sexes. On the other hand the traditional ruling ideology, different physiological conditions, and different social obligations in the past separated women from men. To overcome these factors women still required their own solidarity groups (*Workers' Daily* 1959)

The Communist Party, both before and after 1949, has encouraged an ideology of solidarity among women and taken practical steps to encourage the formation and functioning of local solidarity groups on the basis of their common and separate identity, grievances, and interests.[3] It is an inherent component of the wider strategy to redefine the role and status of women and many observers of local groups in action recognized their value to the women of the village. One foreign resident in a newly liberated village in the north of China in the late 1940s observed that within the women's associations 'brave wives and daughters-in-law untrammelled by the presence of their menfolk could raise their own bitterness and encourage their sisters to do likewise' (Hinton 1966:157). An anthropologist undertaking fieldwork in a south China village in the early 1950s noted that 'the very presence of an independent organisation of women dealing with public affairs was itself a new phenomenon of considerable importance, something entirely out of context of the social order based on the sexual division of labour and the seclusion of women from public affairs' (Yang 1959:157).

In the last twenty-five years since their creation, case study after case study illustrates the importance of solidarity groups in translating the individual experience of oppression into a collective consciousness. They act as mediators between their members and other social institutions and organizations, and attempt to legitimize and institutionalize women's participation in political decision-making bodies. The value of solidarity to women individually and collectively has continually been reiterated throughout each phase in the government policies to redefine the position of women, jurally, economically, and politically. However, the promulgation of legislation and the new opportunities created to allow women to work together in social production did not automatically make for solidarity in defence of their interests. At each stage the ideology of solidarity establishing a common consciousness and power base has been actively fostered by the government and the national women's movement.

Although the consciousness of women as members of a separate group with their own interests has been carefully nurtured in the People's Republic of China, they have not always acted to defend their own interests. Women in the rural sectors of the economy still tend to be found predominantly among the less skilled and lower paid members of the work force. They have also been largely employed in agriculture while their male counterparts are recruited into rural industries and projects of capital construction. In politics women's very participation was innovatory, and even in the 1970s they were still likely to constitute only 20 to 30 per cent of the representatives in leadership groups, a figure well below their proportion represented in the population and social production.[4] They continued to be influenced by the traditional division of labour grounded in the separation of the domestic and public spheres and the subordination of women. This has resulted in the uneven accommodation of their reproductive and domestic roles and the prevalence of traditional thought patterns. For example, folk sayings such as 'just as a mare can't go into battle, a woman can't go into politics', 'the horse is the leader and the donkey runs between the traces', and 'when a woman rules the roost everything is in a mess' can still be heard (*China Reconstructs* 1975).

Within the domestic sphere the function of the household as a unit of production in rural areas, the persistence of the private sector based on vegetable plots and livestock, and the organization of labour within the household tends to balance the distribution of women's labour power for all but the younger and unmarried in favour of the domestic and private spheres. The community services to reduce the functionality of the household and share in its maintenance are very unevenly implemented. The traditional customs of surname exogamy and patrilocal marriage lead to a marked preference for male children and the elaboration of male kinship groups (Diamond 1975). For much of their lives, then, women still remain 'temporary' or 'outside' members of their households. The media has constantly exhorted women to act in defence of their interests in most of these matters. The failure of women to do so at all times is not necessarily due to lack of perception regarding the anomalies in their position (although at times this may be so), but due to the sometimes conflicting demands inherent in the very definition of a separate solidarity for women in a class society.

Female versus class solidarity

The ideology of solidarity demands that differences between women due to age and position in household hierarchies and social class be de-emphasized in favour of the ideal of unity within the female group. However, at the same time in China continuous class struggle has demanded that women be divided into social classes with their attendant consciousness and solidarity. Indeed the history of female solidarity groups is marked by certain ambiguities that surround their position as an independent power base in a society in which the division between the classes and class struggle is viewed as the motivating force generating social change. The history of women's subordination did call for their separation into their own solidarity groups and they had proved invaluable as a source of confidence and collective strength in redefining the domestic and public roles of women. But it was also argued that 'women did not form a social class however the term was defined' (*Red Flag* 1964). That is solidarity could not be based on the premise that there were in existence 'abstract above-class women'. Rather each sex was seen to be divided into classes the nature of which *primarily* determined their social attitudes and priorities. Hence the Communist Party, before and after it became the national government, has always demanded from the separate women's groups that in addition to creating solidarity among women, they also arouse a consciousness of class interests and class struggle in contemporary China and respond to all forms of subordination, class as well as gender.

In cases of conflict between the interests of class and sex, the former was to take priority. While in theory the achievement of the goals of class and women's solidarity are seen to be mutually interdependent, in practice the uneasy alliance between the national revolutionary and the women's movement has sometimes brought competing claims on the identity of women. The balance of these dual demands has directly affected the local history of the solidarity groups in the villages.

64

At certain periods during the last few decades local conditions have favoured a strong group identity among women and their groups have forwarded their interests in a policy of direct confrontation with the rest of the village. In the 1940s when the initial acquisition of jural, economic, and political rights immediately affected the balance of power in every household, and where husbands and mothers-in-law persisted in their opposition and ill-treatment, there was some open and direct struggle between the sexes. Women felt that unless they actively struggled against the men of their families they would not acquire their new rights. Indeed, many a recalcitrant or chauvinist husband was brought before the village women's groups and publicly asked to explain his behaviour (Belden 1951; Hinton 1966). However, in 1940 a resolution of the women's movement on 'woman work' warned against isolating the cause of women's liberation and alienating potential support (All-China Democratic Women's Federation 1949). In 1953 a general government directive criticized the work methods used by many local groups in their implementation of the Marriage Law of 1950. It accused them of interpreting the law almost exclusively in terms of women's rights and adopting an attitude of separatism and autonomy directly generating antagonism between the sexes. The ensuing conflicts between the apparently divided interests were reported to have caused disruption in village life, brought the new law into disrepute, isolated the active members of the women's groups, and in some cases led to the deaths and suicides of individual women (*New China News Analysis* 1953). In the mid-1960s the women's movement was criticized for attempting to create an all-inclusive solidarity among its members on the basis of the individual experience and oppression of women, without translating it into a coherent analysis requiring the recognition of class identity and class consciousness (*Red Flag* 1964; *Women of China* 1966).

A more common trend in the villages, however, has been for women to display a weak group identity in the face of competing claims. Activists in the local women's groups often found themselves on the defensive, arguing for the continued need for active solidarity collectively to give expression to their aspirations, protect their rights and interests, and supervise the implementation of decrees and policies regarding the equality of men and women (Teng Ying-chao 1956; *Women of China* 1962). The continuing obstacles to the implementation of their rights, and the sometimes limited definition of 'emancipation' or 'liberation' to mean mere entry into social production, had caused some village groups to conclude that their goals had all but been achieved. The groups either lay dormant through lack of vitality and purpose and continued to give instrumental support to individual women members in problem-solving, but did little to further women's interests *vis-à-vis* men (Crooks 1966), or alternatively they were abolished when thought to be 'no longer needed' as in Liuling village (Myrdal 1967). It was not unknown for local women leaders and activists to prefer to work in class associations or what they considered to be the mainstream of economic and political activities rather than in the apparently secondary or even diversionary women's groups concerned exclusively with the complications of the personal lives of women (*People's Daily* 1962). Resolutions on 'woman work' have campaigned against the tendency to think that all would be well for women so long as general revolutionary aims were fulfilled and that solidarity among women was at best secondary and at worst unnecessary. This attitude towards the work of separate women's groups received a substantial blow during the Cultural Revolution in the mid-1960s, which has been responsible for a new reappraisal and re-evaluation of solidarity among women in the 1970s.

There is every evidence to conclude that following the movements to improve the jural, political, and economic status of women in the 1950s and the substantial improvements in their position, many productive units had indeed come to think that so long as the construction of socialism persisted and was achieved there was no need to pay particular attention to solidarity among women. Prior to the Cultural Revolution, the women's movement itself was divided around the question of whether women should primarily identify with their sex or with their class associates. An article written in the Party magazine in 1964, entitled 'How the Problem of Women should be Viewed', analysed the present state of the women's movement and revealed that there was an acute internal struggle between those who thought that solidarity among women was paramount and those who thought that priority should be accorded to class solidarity. The controversy centred around whether the divisions between the sexes or those between classes were the primary divisions in society. Was it possible to distinguish a single female or woman's as opposed to male or man's conception of life and, if so, were the widely disparate social attitudes of different classes of women sufficient to divide women one from another and cancel out the factors working for unity (*Red Flag* 1964)? The controversy between the two points of view threatened the very fabric of the Women's Federation and this, plus the tendency to think that it had outweighed its usefulness, almost brought it to a standstill as a national and local functioning organization. During the Cultural Revolution most of the local solidarity groups fell into abeyance.

During the Cultural Revolution there was no attempt to foster solidarity among women, rather the very definition of class terms was elaborated to include attitudes to and by women. Women were encouraged to raise their class consciousness through political study and participate in the current class struggle. The organization of women in the exclusive pursuit of their own rights, interests, and ideas, such as, 'if men earned more women needn't work' and 'somebody has to maintain the household, why not the women, for men already have enough responsibility outside the home', were associated with the bourgeois class viewpoint and hence to be struggled against. There is some evidence that in the direct incorporation of women into the same political and vocational framework as men, women did play a more significant part in the events of the Cultural Revolution on a national and particularly at local levels than hitherto (*People's Daily* 1969). When Myrdal in one of the nearest approximations to an anthropological fieldwork study since 1949, returned to Liuling village in 1969, seven years after his previous visit, he found that one of the greatest changes in the village was the attendance of women at political meetings (Myrdal and Kessle 1973). However, there is much more evidence to suggest that in incorporating women's interests into broader class definitions and the wider class struggle, the special interests of women were neglected.

At national and local levels there was little attention given in the media to the position of women in society after the suspension of the Women's Federation and its magazine. Articles published in the media after the Cultural Revolution and my own interviews conducted in China in 1973 substantiate the impression that many individuals, associations, and enterprises gave little attention to furthering women's interests. When the revolutionary committee assumed overall responsibility for the affairs of Lochang *xian*, for example, they thought that cadres representing the interests of women's groups were unnecessary. They assumed that they would involve women in all their work, but as a result the latter found their special interests ignored. The revolutionary committee had more work than it could possibly manage and there was no one person who was specifically charged to remind them of their responsibility to women (*Red Flag* 1971a). Again from Hunan province it was reported that local revolutionary committees either thought that anything they could do would have little bearing on the general position of women or they tended to assume that their work would automatically include the interests of women. They tended to generalize that 'since work in every field included women there was no need to grasp "woman work" as a separate task' (*Red Flag* 1971b). In 1968 an article in a Shanghai newspaper warned revolutionary committees generally against the new tendency of 'showing concern' for women without involving the latter themselves (*Wenhui Newspaper* 1968). My own interviews with national and local leaders of women's groups in the summer of 1973 also suggested that revolutionary committees had tended to ignore women's interests (Croll 1978). As a result many of those interviewed said that they had come to recognize that although every field did include women, it was not enough to include women in every field and neglect their special difficulties inherited from the past or their reproductive roles. It seems that their experience at the hands of the revolutionary committees had re-established the value of solidarity among women, and led to the rebuilding of local groups in the late 1960s and early 1970s.

Solidarity reappraised

In turning its attention to the creation of new solidarity groups, one commune described how it was responding to the demands of women and a recent instruction from Mao Tse-tung who recommended anew that 'it was still necessary to struggle against the concept of despising the women's movement because the people holding this concept fail to see its importance in re-defining the role of women and the importance of their partici-pation in the revolution' (*Red Flag* 1971a). In a production brigade in another province, leaders reported that Mao Tse-tung had also recommended three points for communities to keep in mind when rebuilding the women's groups. The first maintained that the question of women's position in society must be analysed from a class point of view and was not an area exempt from class struggle. Second, the revolution could not continue without the support of half of the population and therefore 'woman work' was a serious matter. Third, the women's groups were to make political study their priority so that their members could participate in political decision-making and represent the interests of their groups (*Red Flag* 1971c). In the same article the leaders of this model brigade described how they and the women put these recommendations into practice. Initially, the leaders had met to discuss their own attitudes towards women's groups. In retrospect they thought that they had been too pre-occupied with the general class struggle to pay attention to the interests of women. They revealed that they had thought that since they were busy with work of central importance they 'must not allow women to drag their legs' and that 'woman work really had no bearing on the general situation within the brigade'. They held a meeting to criticize their tendency to slight or neglect the interests of women and to encourage the re-establishment of local women's organizations. At the same time the women of the brigade met to discuss their experience of the last few years, to reform their own groups, and draw up their demands.

These debates and discussions were published as an example to other brigades who were also re-establishing their local women's groups, but how far they were followed it is difficult to ascertain. Certainly by the time of my visit to China in sum-mer 1973, the separate groups of women had been reformed at local levels, with the avowed aims of developing both women's class interests and their interests as women. The dual demands stemming from class and sex membership were combined with top priority given to the encouragement of political study, political participation, and the development of class consciousness. Women leaders of local groups without fail isolated this aspect of their work as constituting the major change since the Cultural Revolution. Only after this aspect of their work had been discussed did they go on to detail the other main categories of interests of the groups.

In a production brigade near Jinan city in Shandong province, women of the brigade met in their groups for two days and two to three evenings a month for political study and to exchange their own personal experiences. At one evening meeting a woman talked about her reluctance to attend meetings. At another meeting, held during the day, the women discussed the problem of housework and in small groups studied and assessed the experience of those who had appeared to have solved this problem. In addition on one half-day a month, all the women of the brigade met to discuss and formulate their opinions on the affairs of the brigade and they elected a number of representatives to report their opinions at higher administrative levels.

In a number of brigades on the outskirts of Shenyang in northeast China, the women met three times a month for political study and three times a month to discuss their own problems. In one brigade they had a special meeting to discuss ways of improving their productivity without jeopardizing their interests. At another meeting they invited the men to discuss ways of distributing housework. In a commune near Peking the women requested that their local groups be re-established in 1969. They now hold their own separate meetings for political study and also discuss their ideological and practical problems twice a month. They felt that their interests were better served by their own organization. At recent meetings they had put forward suggestions on ways to advance their own particular interests at higher administrative levels, invited the men in order to remind them of the role of women in history and the importance of sharing housework. They also mediated a quarrel between two women, one of whom always took the easy work in the fields to the chagrin of the other. Men were occasionally criticized at their meetings, but they said it was more common for the women to take their complaints to joint class organizations for further discussion than to take direct action themselves. Among the problems that the group faced was the continuing divisions between the generations. The support and level of participation of the younger members was not shared by married women once

70

they had their own households to maintain, and older women still tended to disapprove of the breakdown in segregation and the mixed social activities of the young.

Perhaps the most important principle to come out of the experience of the Cultural Revolution was the re-establishment of the interdependence of women's solidarity and class solidarity. The functions of local solidarity groups among women are once again perceived to be two-fold in theory: to raise the consciousness of women both as members of a class and as women. The competing claims on the consciousness of women have once again been theoretically resolved by giving priority to the solidarity of women as members of a class. This is based on the view that without the establishment of socialist and proletarian interests there can be no substance to women's liberation (*Peking Review* 1973; *China Reconstructs* 1975). At the same time there is a renewed emphasis and evaluation of solidarity among women. The recent campaign to criticize Confucius and Lin Piao has gone some way to combine both women's special and class interests in one nation-wide study movement. From its outset this movement aimed at linking the experience of women's oppression to a study of women's history and their present position in China. The campaign drew attention to 'the social origins and class foundations' of the code of ethics that so discriminated against women. It was stressed that male supremacy was neither an immutable social principle ordained by heaven, nor one dating back to time immemorial, but developed by Confucius in a specific historical period at the time of the transition from slave to feudal society.

As a women's theory group pointed out at the beginning of the campaign, Confucius lived in a period that witnessed the gradual decline of the system of slavery and the ascendancy of the newly emerging forces. To bolster the authority of the declining slave owners he established the authority of the husband and the suppression of women as one of the foundations of their rule (*Guangming Daily* 1974). If the relationship between man and woman was likened to that of master and slave, not only would the ruling classes operate the exchange of women in their favour, but in turn the subjugation of women would, to some extent, compensate for the class position of the slave himself. In this belief Confucius is said to have established the maxims that 'women like slaves were hard to manage', 'the subordination of women to men was one of the supreme principles of government', and that 'the relations between husband and wife, like those between king and minister and between father and son were all, as those between master and servant, universal under heaven' (*Guangming Daily* 1974). It was on these foundations that ethical codes of conduct for women known as the 'three obediences', 'states of dependence', and 'four virtues' were developed. In criticizing Confucius women were encouraged to realize that the traditional division of labour and the evaluation of the sexes into inferior and superior categories rested on social rather than biological foundations. As one women's group concluded from its studies, 'the cruel oppression of women was not due to the biological distinction between men and women, but was rooted in the social system directed by a small handful of the exploiting classes' (*Guangming Daily* 1974). Male supremacy was found to be a common feature of societies under the rule of exploiting classes be it the slave-owners, the feudal lords or, nearer their own time, the capitalists. In the campaign Lin Piao has been singled out for criticism as representing a long line of statesmen who utilized the idea of male supremacy to bolster an outmoded social system (*People's Daily* January 27, 1974; *Red Flag* 1971). The campaign emphasized that only if women's groups are determined to identify the continuing influence of the traditional ruling ideology in their own lives and discredit its continuing use against their collective interests would they be able 'to emancipate their minds, do away with all fetishes and superstitions and support their interests despite the difficulties in their way' (*People's Daily* February 2, 1974).

How the dual and competing demands that have characterized the history of local solidarity groups can be resolved in practice when their interests conflict remains to be seen. However, their revival as an independent power base and their active role in the campaign criticizing Confucius and Lin Piao is recognition of the history of the role of female solidarity groups in redefining the role and status of women by women themselves. Although it appears to have required an exogenous force, the Communist Party, to effect initially the establishment of female solidarity groups in rural China, it was the direct experience of women themselves, which led them to argue for the revival of their solidarity groups in rural China, after their demise in the

Cultural Revolution of the mid-1960s. Their own experience confirmed the direct correlation between the presence of female solidarity groups devoted to their own socio-economic and political interests, and the furthering of those interests in society. The difficulties of combining the class interests of the revolutionary movement and the special interests of women in one struggle has produced a tension directly affecting women's ability to intervene on their own behalf. Despite this the periods of active intervention by the groups have proved invaluable over the years. In the last resort the struggle within individual villages and productive units could only be carried out and maintained by the vigilance of the women themselves, and in this respect their active solidarity in furthering their own interests has been instrumental in raising the self-confidence, consciousness, and common identity of individual women.

Notes

1 This paper is based on a documentary study of the history of the women's movement in China and on interviews conducted with local and municipal leaders of the Women's Federation in China in summer 1973. I am grateful to members of Luxing-she in Peking for arranging these interviews.

2 Since their establishment, these village women's groups have formed the local organizations of the women's movement. Each local group elects a delegate to represent them at the women's representative conferences and committees organized by the production brigade and the commune. This process of electing delegates is repeated at every administrative level. Committees and conferences of representatives play an important role at each administrative level, from local to national, in discussing or analysing past programmes and determining the future policies of the Women's Federation in the area represented.

3 It is an important principle in China that while the separate organization of women is encouraged on this basis, at the same time the Communist Party, the party of the proletariat class, has an overall leadership role. Article Seven of the Party Constitution adopted at the Party's Fourth National Congress in August 1973 reiterated this principle by stating that the Women's Federation, along with other popular organizations, must remain within the general guidelines set by the Party.

4 Of the six million new members admitted to the Communist Party between 1966 and 1973, 27 per cent were estimated to

be women (*People's Daily* 1973). In Henan province women accounted for 30 per cent of cadres of the agricultural production brigades (*People's Daily* 1972).

References

ALL-CHINA DEMOCRATIC WOMEN'S FEDERATION (1949) Present Woman Work in Rural Districts of the Liberated Areas. *Documents of the Women's Movement.* Peking: Foreign Languages Press..
—— (1950) *Women of New China.* Peking: Foreign Languages Press.
BELDEN, J. (1951) *China Shakes the World.* London: Victor Gollancz.
CHINA RECONSTRUCTS (1973) *Women's Liberation through Struggle.* Xu Guang. March.
—— (1975) *How We Women Won Equality.* Zui Yulan. March.
CONGER, S. P. (1909) *Letters from China.* Chicago: Hodder & Stoughton.
CROLL, E. (1978) *Feminism and Socialism in China.* London: Routledge & Kegan Paul.
CROOKS, I. and CROOKS, D. (1959) *Revolution in a Chinese Village.* London: Routledge & Kegan Paul.
—— —— (1966) *The First Years of Yangyi Commune.* London: Routledge & Kegan Paul.
CUSACK, D. (1958) *Chinese Women Speak.* Sydney: Angus & Robertson.
DAVIN, D. (1973) Women in the Liberated Areas. In M. Young (ed.), *Women in China.* Michigan Papers in Chinese Studies (15).
DIAMOND, N. (1975) Collectivisation and Kinship and the Status of Women in Rural China. *Bulletin of Concerned Asian Scholars,* January-March: 25–32.
EPSTEIN, I. (1939) *The People's War.* London: Victor Gollancz.
GUANGMING DAILY (*Guangming Ribao*) (1974) *Women can Prop Up Half of Heaven.* Red Detachment of Women Squad, People's Liberation Army. January 14.
HINTON, W. (1966) *Fanshen.* New York: Vintage Books.
MYRDAL, J. (1967) *Report from a Chinese Village.* Harmondsworth: Penguin.
MYRDAL, J. and KESSLE, G. (1973) *China: The Revolution Continued.* Harmondsworth: Penguin.
NEW CHINA NEWS ANALYSIS (1973) *Directive of the Government Administrative Council Concerning the Thorough Implementation of the Marriage Law. February 19, 1953.* March 19.
NEW YOUTH (*Xin Qingnian*) (1916) quotes from the Book of Rites (IX:24; X:51). In *The Way of Confucius and Modern Life.* Chen Duxiu.
PEKING REVIEW (1973) *Talking of Women's Liberation.* Wang Zi. March 8.

74

PEOPLE'S CHINA (1951) *Freed from Unhappiness.* Yang Yu. March 1.
—— (1953) *Child Care in China.* Gao Shang. July 16.
—— (1954) *The Story of Dong Yulan.* Yang Yu. December 16.
—— (1957) *Birth Control in China.* Zhou Nuofen. June 1.
PRUITT, I. (1967) *A Daughter of Han: An Autobiography of a Working Woman.* Stanford, California: Stanford University Press.
PEOPLE'S DAILY (*Renmin Ribao*) (1958) *Further Liberate Women's Labour Capacity.* Cao Gunchun. June 2.
—— (1962) *Conduct Work among Women in a More Patient, Thoroughgoing and Attentive Manner.* March 8.
—— (1969) *Cadres in Honan.* November 15.
—— (1972) *editorial.* March 6.
—— (1973) *editorial.* July 1.
—— (1974) *Smash Mental Shackles that Bind Women.* Yang Bolan and Zhan Beichen. February 2.
—— (1974) *China's Fisherwomen.* Zhen Ennu. March 30.
RED FLAG (*Hongqi*) (1964) *How the Problem of Women Should be Viewed.* Wan Mujun. October 28.
—— (1971 a) *Report of Revolutionary Committee.* Lochang Xian, Guangdong Province. February 1.
—— (1971 b) *Report of Writing Group of Communist Provincial Committee, Hunan.* February 1.
—— (1971 c) *Investigation Report of the Dongjin Brigade, Guangxi.*
—— (1974) *We Revolutionary Women Bitterly Hate the Doctrines of Confucius and Mencius.* Iron Girls Team of Dazhai Brigade. March 3.
SANDAY, P. R. (1973) Towards a Theory of the Status of Women. *American Anthropologist* 75(5):1682–1700.
SELDEN, M. (1971) *The Yenan Way in Revolutionary China.* Boston: Harvard University Press
SMEDLEY, A. (1944) *Battle Hymn of China.* London.
SMITH, A. H. (1900) *Village Life in China.* London and Edinburgh.
TENG YING-CHAO (1956) In *Report of the Eighth Party Congress.* Peking: Foreign Languages Press.
WENHUI NEWSPAPER (*Wenhui Bao*) (1968) *Role of Women on Revolutionary Committees,* June 14.
WOLF, M. (1974) Chinese Women: Old Skills in a New Context. In M. Rosaldo, and L. Lamphere, (eds.), *Women, Culture and Society.* Stanford, California: Stanford University Press.
WOMEN OF CHINA (*Zhongguo Funu*) (1961a) *Further Improve the Labour Protection of Members of Rural Committees.* August 1.
—— (1961b) *Respect the Opinions of Women Members on the Question of Payment.* November 1.
—— (1962) *Reference Materials for Training Basic-level Cadres.* February 1.
—— (1963a) *In What Respects Should we be Self-conscious?* October 1.

WOMEN OF CHINA (*Zhongguo Funu*) (1963b) *Treat the Relationship between Work, Children and Household Chores in a Revolutionary Spirit.* November 1.

—— (1966) *Letter from Branch of Women's Federation.* Shaanxi (Shansi). July 10.

WORKERS' DAILY (*Gongren Ribao*) (1959) *Strengthen Political and Ideological Work among Women Workers.* July 8.

YANG, C. K. (1959) *A Chinese Village in Early Communist Transition.* Boston: Massachusetts University Press.

YANG, M. (1945) *A Chinese Village, Taitou, Shantung Province.* New York: Columbia University Press.

YANG YU (1952) *Women of Wu Village.* Peking: All-China Democratic Women's Federation.

1978

THREE

'Women must help each other': the operation of personal networks among Buzaa beer brewers in Mathare Valley, Kenya

NICI NELSON

In this paper I will examine the way in which women produce and sell a local form of maize beer called *buzaa* in a Nairobi squatter area called Mathare Valley. Individual entrepreneurs utilize their personal networks to survive by illegal petty commodity production in an uncertain market. This daily economic co-operation supports a wider solidarity among these women. Feeling themselves isolated from and stigmatized by the larger society, because of their deviant behaviour and economic independence, they express a need to stand together as women against common enemies. These enemies are perceived and articulated as either agents of authority, for example, the police, or men in general. However, Mathare women have had less success working together to further their common aims than they have had in the daily solving of individual problems through the operation of their ego-centred networks.

The setting

Kenya has a population of eleven million people. Though only 8 to 10 per cent of the people live in urban areas, these are growing at the phenomenal rate of 6 per cent per annum. The high differential in income to be found between the rural and urban areas, the rapid population growth (3½ per cent per annum, one of the highest in the world), combined with a shortage of arable land have made migration to the city an attractive option for many people. Until recently it was mainly men that migrated: in the last census (1969) men still outnumbered women in the urban area. However the gap in the discrepancy in the sex ratio has been narrowing in recent years, indicating that there has been an increase in the number of women migrants, many of these being single women.

Kenya is a relatively successful mixed capitalist economy. A number of major earners of foreign exchange, such as tea, coffee, pyrethreum, and tourism are completely or partially run by parastatal bodies. However, there is much private enterprise at all levels, including a great deal of investment by multinational companies. The government also has controlling interest in a number of strategic industries such as banks and oil companies. (Colin Leys (1975) has described the contradiction in the government's economic nationalism and its dependence on foreign capital.) Though there was a respectable growth in the gross national product during the period of my research, this did not result in a significant increase in jobs in the non-farm sector, and there is growing unemployment among school leavers and even among University graduates. It is, however, impossible to measure this unemployment with any exactitude due to inadequate data and widespread underemployment (ILO 1972). One result of the lack of jobs in the formal sector has been the growing number of urban migrants who support themselves in the urban areas by petty commodity production in self-built squatter areas.

Mathare is one of these squatter areas, which may house as many as one-fifth of Nairobi's population. It is a young community, whose present building stock was begun after the end of the Mau Mau Emergency in 1962. Between 60,000 and 70,000 people occupy mud and wattle houses with cardboard roofs, or wooden blocks with tin roofs built on the slopes

78

of the Mathare River Valley fifteen minutes drive from the Nairobi Hilton. Approximately one-third of the inhabitants are owners of housing units, and the rest are tenants. The inhabitants are largely Kikuyu (or Kikuyu-related groups such as Meru or Embu), poorly educated migrants to Nairobi; 75 per cent are without land, and 80 per cent support themselves in the petty commodity sector (Ross 1973).

There is some disagreement over how many women live in Mathare, and how many of them are independent heads of households. To summarize the various sources briefly, there are probably more women than men in Mathare, and anything from 60 per cent to 80 per cent of them are heads of households (Etherton 1973; my own sample survey; data obtained from the National Christian Council of Kenya Survey in Mathare). Less than 10 per cent of them are employed in the formal sector, as opposed to 20 per cent of men. Most of these independent heads of households support themselves by brewing and/or selling illegal maize-millet beer, called *buzaa*, and also by various types of commercial sexual unions.

In 1972 I began two years of research in Mathare with my assistant Veronica Nyambura Njoroge. It was necessary to limit the scope of my work, and so I concentrated on Villages I and II, the two oldest villages with a preponderance of Kikuyu inhabitants. Most of the formal interviews were carried out with female heads of households, though I numbered many married women and men (both married and unmarried) among my friends and informants.[1]

Network analysis

During the last fifteen years many anthropologists have utilized the concept of networks in analysis. Basically this refers to a 'configuration of cross-cutting interpersonal bonds in some unspecified way casually connected with the action of this person and the social institutions of their society' (Barnes 1972:3). Networks used in this way are partial rather than societal networks. They are personal, ego-centred networks, containing links that join ego to friends, kinsfolk, and workmates. All individuals in society are at the centre of such networks. In large-scale, fluid, heterogeneous urban situations, networks can be a useful analytical tool showing the ways in which individuals link up with formal institutions, and even how institutions themselves are generated (Boissevain 1974).

For the purpose of analysis I will distinguish between two parts of a Mathare woman's personal network, the effective and the extended part. *Effective* networks are ones in which the members interact frequently, and links connect all the members. They are often described as dense networks. The *extended* network is by contrast a relatively open network and the members do not necessarily know each other (Epstein 1969). The instrumental effective network of Mathare women differs from most effective networks described elsewhere (Boswell 1969). Their effective network has fewer multiplex links, and less effective content, durability, and intensity than is normally the case. This is a function of the high degree of residential mobility within Mathare.

The networks I shall describe are not the complete personal network of a Mathare woman. They are the part abstracted for examination which relates specifically to *buzaa* brewing and selling. For this reason they are what is termed 'instrumental'. We will concern ourselves here with the *buzaa* brewing instrumental content of these links and will only note in passing other instrumental content (such as kinship ties) or expressive content.

Buzaa brewing and selling

Ross found that 60 per cent of his female sample brewed and/or sold *buzaa* (Ross 1973).[2] In my sample survey of Village II 75 per cent of women claimed to do so. The difference in the figures may be accounted for by the fact that my research was carried out nearly seven years later than Ross's, when Mathare's role as an entertainment centre may have become increasingly known.[3]

Kenya is one of the few African countries that makes brewing of traditional style beers illegal in the urban area. This may be partly due to a strong lobby by bottled beer and distilled spirit companies, who perhaps wish to prevent legitimate production of cheaper alcoholic drinks. (Admittedly this is pure speculation on my part.) In smaller towns in Kenya it is possible to obtain a licence to brew traditional beers commercially, but in Nairobi this is impossible.

A woman who wishes to brew needs several four and a half gallon tins called *debes* (large flat metal pans each measuring six feet long and three feet wide), and a clean drum which holds sixteen gallons. If she wants to retail beer she will need a minimum of a dozen clean half-litre oil tins called *mukevi* and these serve as beer mugs. This equipment is costly and few women own all of it.

The basic ingredients of *buzaa* are maize flour and millet yeast. The flour is dampened and kneaded and left in a dark place for four to ten days to begin fermentation. The resultant glutinous flour is fried for half an hour over a hot wood fire in the large frying pan. This step is hot and smoky, and easily spotted by police patrols; for both reasons, it is usually carried out at dawn. The flour is browned and then added to sixteen gallons of water in the drum. Yeast is added twelve hours later, and in another twelve hours the muddy-brown, thick mixture is ready to strain through a burlap sack. The sourish tasting beer is only drinkable for twenty-four hours, since the fermentation process cannot be arrested.

Although *buzaa* brewing is difficult and illegal, most women in Mathare support themselves by making it and it is mainly a female occupation there. Though Ross mentions that men may provide capital and do a portion of the heavy labour, I did not find this to be so common. Why this is so is not easy to say, especially since in the rural areas of the central highlands the brewing of beer was traditionally a male task. However, it is not within the scope of this paper to speculate on the reasons why *buzaa* brewing in Mathare is largely a female activity.

The reasons why so many women brew beer are clear when the alternatives open to them are examined. Women with no education, or a little education, can only find wage employment as houseservants or bar girls. The monthly wage for these types of work averaged sh. 50–100 for a sixty hour week. (For comparison, in 1974 the legal minimum wage was sh. 200.) A woman in wage employment would also have to find someone to look after her children, and a maid could cost as much as sh. thirty a month.

Buzaa brewing, on the other hand, can with minimum effort provide a basic subsistence, and with careful work can be quite lucrative. The monthly income of a brewer and seller (most women do both) ranged in 1974 from sh. 100 to 500. Women can do this work in their rooms, combining domestic and commercial functions in the same space. This creates its own stresses, but it does allow a woman with children to care for them while she works.

The difficulties in marketing buzaa However the brewing of *buzaa* is not an unmixed blessing and it is difficult and sometimes dangerous. The beer spoils quickly and must be consumed within twenty-four hours. This, combined with the peculiarities of the Nairobi market, means that women must buy and sell beer to each other wholesale, and there is great competition for customers. Constant police raids means the possible loss of equipment, interruption of work, the payment of bribes or bail money or fines, and even periods spent in jail.

Although most women in Mathare brew and sell beer, some women never brew, and only retail other women's beer, but few brew just for wholesaling. No woman can retail a sixteen gallon drum of *buzaa* in one day, and so she is forced to sell part of each brew wholesale to other women. For reasons to do with lack of capital, amount of physical labour, and difficulties of storage no woman brews every day, though some of the bigger brewers will brew as often as three times a week. Yet women prefer to have beer available for retail each day, in order to keep regular customers and to ensure that enough money comes in throughout the month. This means that finding a *debe* of *buzaa* is a vital part of each Mathare woman's morning.

Because Kenyans are paid monthly or bimonthly, their spending pattern is one of 'splurge and scrimp'. At the beginning of the pay period men drink and treat their friends lavishly, but by the middle of the month they are hoarding their pennies. Beer sellers must risk giving credit to selected customers in order to total sufficient sales over the monthly period. Recovery of debts, should the man choose to default, is impossible since they have no sanctions to force customers to pay. Customers come from outside Mathare and can easily disappear into the anonymity of the city.

Since women give retail customers credit they must themselves seek credit from those women from whom they buy beer wholesale. Certain women who brew more frequently collect a group of regular clients and permit them large amounts of credit. It is easier for a wholesaler to collect her debt from a customer since the latter is a resident of the Valley. However, women have been known to decamp in the night and move to another part of the Valley in order to avoid repaying such a debt.

Because women are often forced by economic circumstances to share rooms, competition over customers may occur: if two women try to retail in the same room there are quarrels over whose beer the men should drink. Rooms are small and this limits the number of customers that can drink at any one time. To avoid this kind of contest women often adopt a pattern of alternate brewing.

Daily official police raids and unofficial raids by off-duty policemen looking for bribes make it necessary for Mathare as a community to have a warning and protection system. Warning is the first consideration: the moment the police vans leave the main road to enter the village the news of their arrival spreads like wildfire. Anyone, man, woman, or child, who hears the news of police raids will inform as many people as possible.[4] Upon hearing such a warning each householder with *buzaa*, fermenting flour, or brewing equipment, will lock her door and run to stand along the road. That way she is not arrested if the police enter her house and find incriminating items.

Police occupy an ambiguous status in Mathare. Off-duty policemen form a large proportion of the customers. At other times these policemen come either in uniform on official raids accompanied by an officer, or in groups of two or three out of uniform 'hunting for money' as local people put it. Policemen often form liaisons with Mathare women, but woe betide the woman who quarrels with a policeman lover, or rejects his advances. She will then be the target of a campaign of harassment by the policeman and his friends on and off duty. Changing rooms, moving in temporarily with a friend, or even going home for an extended visit to rural relatives are the only ways in which a woman can protect herself from this type of persecution.[5]

Operation of Mathare buzaa brewers' networks Brewing *buzaa* is a difficult, uncertain form of economic activity and women

83

do not brew co-operatively, but function as individual entre-preneurs. However, that is not to say that they operate in these difficult and uncertain conditions alone. On the contrary each woman is at the centre of an effective and extended *buzaa* brewing network and she activates the links of these two net-works to cope with the special social and economic circum-stances of her life as a *buzaa* brewer.

The effective part of a Mathare woman's network, the dense part in which members interact daily, is synonymous with the residential cluster: the houses grouped around a court-yard or houses facing a common alleyway. Such a cluster is not formed in the first instance by people who are friends, and the only stable members will be those who live in the houses that they own. These house owners rent additional rooms to the first comers, seeming to disregard ethnicity, home area, age, sex, or relative status when choosing the next occu-pant. Though most tenants stay in that village of Mathare in which they initially arrived, they shift rooms frequently within the village.[6] Both men and women live in these clusters, both as owners and tenants, but few men are involved in beer brewing. The latter tend to work in the formal sector, or in other types of informal sector activities such as running butcher shops, making shoes or charcoal stoves. Those who own houses, or those who live with women as 'town husbands', will more likely be integrated into the effective network, but even here they usually only help in warning and protection against police raids (Nelson 1977).

One result of residential mobility within Mathare is that proximity is not a product or a cause of friendship. Few women claimed as best friend a roommate or neighbour and indeed sharing a room is often a business arrangement made necessary by the need to divide the cost of the rent. Yet each woman every day activates the links in her effective network to cope with a variety of problems related to *buzaa* brewing.

The content of this effective part of a woman's network can include friendship or kinship only if by chance neighbours are friends or kin, but for our purposes here we will con-centrate on the instrumental content related to *buzaa* brewing. Women borrow equipment from members of their effective network and they warn each other of police raids, hide each other's equipment, and lock each other's doors. It is members of the effective network who inform a woman's relatives or close friends when she is arrested. They also care for her children until members of the arrested woman's extended network can be notified. Members of her effective network are also those who rally to a woman when she cannot raise the money for a bribe or when she calls for help with an unruly customer, a thief, or a violent lover. Women in their gossip sessions circulate information among members of their network about the credit worthiness of various male customers, or the tendency for some men to become drunk and disorderly.

As stated earlier, keen competition for a limited number of customers makes it functional for members of an effective network to co-operate by brewing alternately. A woman who is in the process of preparing a brew will notify members of her network (both effective and extended) that her batch will be ready on such and such a day.

Finally women utilize links in their effective networks to meet the numerous, inevitable, small daily crises: running out of salt at a crucial moment, a baby crying when several customers are clamouring for attention, needing someone to run an errand, or a cup of tea when one's *jiko* (charcoal stove) is not lit. These daily reciprocal exchanges are part and parcel of 'neighbourly' behaviour and also include gossiping, joking, mutual hair braiding, and sharing food. Neighbourliness is an ideal for all residents of a cluster, and any woman openly flouting it is sanctioned by gossip, quarrels, and (if the offence is serious enough) by deliberate withholding of warning during a police raid. It can also lead to eviction by a landlady eager to rid herself of a trouble-making tenant.

Usually links between members of an effective network last only as long as women are co-resident. Once a woman moves she rarely sees the members of her effective network deliberately, though she may reactivate the links at times when she cannot find beer to buy. In addition, a woman moving into a new housing cluster may discover that one of her new neighbours is an ex-neighbour from years before. Knowing someone already resident in the area provides a quick introduction and orientation to one's new neighbours.

The extended part of a woman's instrumental *buzaa* brewing network includes friends and relatives living in or near Mathare who can and will co-operate with her in matters related to *buzaa* brewing. Most members of this network are friends, but a number of women have mothers, grown daughters, sisters, or other female relatives who are included in their extended networks. Recruitment of members of this network is on the same basis as the recruitment of friends in general. There is no time here to dwell at length on the criteria for friendship selection among Kikuyu women in Mathare, but the most important are ethnic background, home area, age, and relative status.

The links between a woman and members of her extended network are multiplex. Relatives share mutual rights and responsibilities relating to their respective statuses. Friends enjoy each other's company, share activities, and exchange secrets or advice in personal matters. Patron and client links are also part of these extended networks, but these relationships are obviously more formal and respectful.

The instrumental content of these links relates to the following aspect of *buzza* brewing: the buying and selling of *buzaa* wholesale and obtaining extended credit, exchanging information concerning credit worthiness of customers (male and female), putting up bail and collecting money for fines, and extended help in serious emergencies. The difficulties inherent in wholesaling *buzaa* and the credit relationships involved have been stated in the previous section. Women utilize the members of their extended network to obtain *buzaa* wholesale, to sell their own brews, and to ask friends to either give them *buzaa* on credit, or to give them a good credit rating to a third party. This pattern of *buzaa* wholesaling is the one most commonly found in Mathare, especially among more established or more successful brewer/sellers. As always, though, the actual situation is more complicated than the model. It *is* possible for a woman to walk into a strange woman's house and obtain a *debe* of *buzaa* on credit. Women who brew bad *buzaa*, or who are newcomers, or notoriously feckless will sell to anyone who comes in order to get rid of it. Those concerned with quality and minimizing credit risks utilize their extended network links to accomplish these ends.

Helping someone find money for bail bond and fines and assisting her in the various stages of her arrest and trial entails a great investment in time, energy, and money. There is much work involved in raising large sums of money, and many

86

hours must be spent waiting at police stations and court houses. This obviously has serious repercussions for the helper's family and business life, and for this reason women depend on their extended network for such help. Women never seem to begrudge the effort it requires, partly because they know that tomorrow they may be in trouble themselves, and partly because the greater intensity and commitment of links formed by kinship or friendship gives both parties greater scope in what they can ask for each other. To put it another way, such links have more latent credit. Similarly, women use their extended networks when serious domestic emergencies disrupt their lives. When a woman is seriously ill and someone must help her with the heavy work of brewing for several months, or when she must take her child to a clinic every day for weeks and cannot fry her flour, or when she must attend the funeral of a relative in the rural area, or the christening of a sister's child and must leave her children for a day – it is then that she turns to the friends or relatives in her extended network.[7]

Links in this part of a woman's personal network are of greater durability than those of the effective part of her network. Members are not residentially contiguous, and she must make an effort to keep in contact. She continues to do so even after they have left Mathare and she can no longer utilize them instrumentally; they will then remain part of her broader friendship network.

The frequency of interaction between members of an extended network is less than between the members of an effective network. Distance can limit visiting to once every two or three days, or less. Reciprocity, though important, is much more generalized when links are multiplex. There is greater leeway for give and take without strictly accounting for every minute, penny, or cup of tea.

To summarize, women manipulate their ego-centred networks, both effective and extended, to assist them in brewing and selling *buzaa* in an insecure urban environment. Living on the fringes of the formal urban economy, they are also cut off from kin and affinal networks in the rural area. Each type of network is utilized for different purposes. The dense effective network, synonymous with the resident cluster, is manipulated to cope with short term, daily problems. It is maintained by the ethic of neighbourliness and friendliness, which is an ideal for all women who are neighbours.

The open effective network is characterized by being friends who also co-operate in the more demanding situations arising out of the beer selling and brewing process. Friendship creates a tie of greater latent credit for a woman to call upon.

In both these networks mutual aid, reciprocity, and co-operation are stressed in relations between women, whether they be between casual neighbours or friends. This is one way of saying that Mathare women feel and display solidarity in social action. The two types of networks vary in their analytical significance for solidarity among women *per se*. The effective network, made up as it often is by relative strangers or casual acquaintances, hints at the possibility of a solidarity manifested by Mathare women as a status group. It is, after all, usual to find that friends help each other, practicing reciprocity and co-operation. It is less common to find these same values stressed for random collections of relatively temporary neighbours.

The stress on co-operation among neighbours reveals that women in Mathare feel that they must stand together or fall separately. That they do so at the present time by manipulating ego-centred, overlapping networks of friends and neighbours does not mean that they do not feel this solidarity. How successful this *ad hoc*, daily solution of problems is in the long run is another question: this type of solidarity can at best be a defensive strategy. Networks solve individual problems and their manipulation cannot bring long term institutional changes in larger social systems for the benefit of status groups.

Segregation and solidarity: some observations on Mathare

It is difficult to describe the segregation that separates independent Mathare women from the larger society as it is somewhat abstract. As migrants who have left their parents (because of pregnancies out of wedlock which are considered shameful by rural people), or their marriages (because of barrenness, neglect, mistreatment, quarrels with in-laws, or boredom) they are, to a certain degree, cut off from their rural 'respectable' backgrounds.

This is not to say that most independent Mathare women do not maintain contact with their parents and kin in the rural area. More than 30 per cent of them send one or more of their children to be fostered by their rural mothers and many make monetary contributions to their families. It is also true, however, that the families of these women much prefer to have their unmarried daughters living in the city where their activities will not give rise to gossip and censure from neighbours. It is, therefore, possible to view these women as outcasts from village societies.

As outcasts from 'respectable' society they are labelled in such a way as to set them apart, and all residents of Mathare are stigmatized by the Kenyan establishment at some time or other. It is not uncommon to hear Mathare referred to as 'that place of thieves and murderers'. Opposition and isolation affect both men and women there, but men, as a status group, are not labelled in quite the same way as women. Because of their economic independence, their free sexual mores, and their rejection of the normative role for Kikuyu women Mathare women are stigmatized by others as bad women: parasites leading men astray with drink and sex.

Wachtel has shown in detail the way in which the media and novelists in Kenya have portrayed the 'city woman' (for city woman, read *independent* city woman, or Mathare woman) as without virtue, as a temptress responsible for men's drunkenness, lack of judgement, violence, and disaster (Wachtel 1972). Indeed, Mathare is known as 'the place of *malayas*' (prostitutes). If a Mathare woman goes to a clinic or hospital and gives her correct address, she will find herself being lectured about living in dirt, filth, and drunkenness, or even being ignored by self-righteous nurses and doctors. The women of Mathare are affected deeply by this negative image, but their awareness of it helps to heighten a sense of sisterhood, mutual responsibility, and solidarity. This was frequently verbalized: 'Women must help each other' was a phrase often on the lips of women; 'the *harambee* [pulling together] of Mathare women must be strong' was another.

As Ross has shown, Mathare in the past has displayed much social and political cohesion as a community owing to the opposition it has had to face (Ross 1973). This point does not lessen the importance of the solidarity shown by women there; it merely clarifies the connection between isolation, opposition, and solidarity.

I have gone into great detail above concerning the operation of individual women's networks as clear cut manifestations of solidarity arising out of a common economic activity, *buzaa* brewing. What further extensions of this particular economic-based female solidarity did I observe? One of the most immediately striking is the invariable kindness and helpfulness women show to new arrivals. Women who have just arrived from the rural area and who do not have friends or relatives, often come to Mathare and wander around aimlessly looking for a room to rent. Residents have nothing but sympathy for such a wanderer, asking her into their rooms, giving her a cup of tea, a sympathetic ear to her troubles, and advice on where to find a room. Sometimes women will take a strange woman into their already crowded rooms for a night or a week until such time as she can locate a place for herself. These new arrivals have often experienced marital breakdowns and have come to Mathare because they have heard that it is a 'place of women' (an interesting stereotype). When a new arrival finds a place to live, her neighbours immediately begin to initiate her into the mysteries of *buzaa* brewing. This is necessary if they come from the highlands of Kenya because *buzaa* is not traditionally drunk in these areas, and women do not know how to prepare it. Although the market for *buzaa* is already a crowded one, women generously initiate these new arrivals with no thought that they might provide competition in the future.

Ross has pointed out that one of the important features of the Kanu (Kanu is Kenya's political party) committees, which organize Mathare Valley, is the presence of women members. The Committee of Elders, which like its traditional rural Kikuyu counterpart settles local disputes, also has women members. It was my observation that women members of Kanu and the Committee of Elders operated to some extent to protect the interests of their female constituents. One of these leaders had instituted a procedure for determining whether or not a couple were in fact married (either legally or customarily). This was done by sending a delegation to contact the woman's parents and verify the man's claim to the immunity of marriage. The Committee will not interfere in the affairs of a

90

married couple, but if the two are only living together it has powers to give the man a warning or to separate the couple forcibly. In addition, it was the Kanu Committee women members who claimed to have been instrumental in ensuring that women householders in Old Mathare were assigned their fair share of units in the Mathare Redevelopment Project designed to relocate Mathare residents.[8]

In the short history of Mathare a number of self-help groups have been formed for varying periods with goals important to women. Some of these groups raised money and contributed labour to build nursery schools throughout the Valley. Other women campaigned to persuade the City Council to put water pipes into the Valley. Women also claim to have formed delegations at certain critical periods in Mathare's history, which went and sought favours or patronage from national politicians. One such story that was repeated to me frequently, concerned a group of women who went to Tom Mboya, the MP for the area, soon after the Emergency was lifted. People had begun moving into the Valley again and the District Officer was busily bulldozing the new houses as fast as they were constructed. The women asked Mboya to persuade the District Officer not to destroy their homes and they say that he agreed to their request and Mathare was allowed to grow thereafter.

In 1968 when Mathare faced imminent danger of being destroyed by the City Council, a group of important local women joined a similar group of men to petition President Kenyatta to protect Mathare. Both men and women claimed their loyalty as ex-Mau Mau as a reason for mercy. Again the respondents felt that they had been successful, and that their delegation has resulted in the City Council's subsequent change of policy towards Mathare. Whether these events took place as described or not, it is revealing that women in Mathare feel that they have had an important role in shaping local history.

To avoid over-romanticizing the social cohesion to be found among women in Mathare, I feel it is important to add that there are also a number of factors that could militate against solidarity. First, there is the attitude and behaviour of some married women living in Mathare. These women often resent having to live among those defined by the larger society as 'malayas' (prostitutes) and often manifest an unco-operative and quarrelsome manner described as 'proud' and 'unneighbourly' by independent women. Few wives brew or sell beer, since their husbands feel that this activity puts them in contact with many strange men in a situation fraught with sexual connotations. However, not all wives are unco-operative and many respond to the police raids and the daily emergencies of life in the same manner as their unmarried counterparts. Those wives who are quarrelsome and unco-operative behave as such in order to set themselves apart from women labelled by society as immoral. They attempt to adhere to the acceptable normative role for Kikuyu women, and therefore they must avoid intimate contact with those who deviate from that role.

Another factor that could prevent further solidarity among Mathare women in the future is the emerging economic hierarchy. It is not yet a class distinction, though eventually it may become so. A few women, as well as men, have become relatively successful in petty commodity production. They have accumulated capital and bought land and houses in urban and rural Kenya, and have also become the leaders of the Valley. Up to now the interest of these richer women have coincided with those of their poorer sisters. In the future this may be less and less the case. For example, if the City Council should relax its restrictions against the commercial production of buzaa beer, it is possible that those women with the capital to do so would begin brewing and selling co-operatively in large, bar-like premises, similar to those that exist in the smaller municipalities of Kenya. I feel that eventually they would muscle out the smaller brewers and those who buy beer wholesale to sell. Admittedly this is hypothetical but it illustrates the type of change that could result in a divergence of interests between different categories of women in Mathare.

These factors aside, there is still a remarkable degree of solidarity manifested by Mathare women. It is a solidarity without a property base, though one might well ask: what female solidarity does have a property base? It is a solidarity with an occupational base, perhaps the closest comparison being the market women of Ghana. Most women in Mathare brew or sell buzaa, except married women or women with well-paid jobs in the formal sector. It is this common involvement with a means of subsistence that knits many women of Mathare together. It is in the common interest of all beer

brewers and sellers in Mathare to co-operate together: to fix
their prices, brew consecutively, reduce destructive competition, to help each other during and after police raids, give each
other credit, maintain an informal credit rating system for customers, and assist each other in the daily dilemmas of food
preparation and child-care. It could be said, therefore, that
this common interest provides a strong basis for solidarity
among women in Mathare.

However, women's solidarity in Mathare is not just a function of a common interest in a particular form of petty
commodity production. It is also a result of the active opposition these women face from the outside society. In the past the
active hostility of the City Council gave the whole Valley a
great deal of social and political cohesion. Ross has described
in detail the political solidarity that united the Valley against
outside opposition in the mid- to late-'sixties. There is, of course,
a striking degree of solidarity between Mathare residents regardless of sex. However, it is my contention that Mathare
women as a group display a solidarity which is manifested
more often and in different ways from that which Ross has
described.

In general, women are singled out for special criticism by
the mass media and by the general public as threatening the
whole domestic social order in Kenya. Though police action
in Mathare is sometimes directed towards locating particular
male criminals, it is usually concentrated on rounding up the
more easily identifiable and helpless female brewers. Thus
women with some justification feel themselves to be more
actively oppressed than men, both by the agents of the larger
society (the police) and by outside public opinion.

Women also experience a peculiarly ambiguous situation
which perhaps helps to heighten their sense of being oppressed.
The very people who are the agents of their 'oppression' also
use them for their own purposes at other times. The police
who raid and extort bribes from them are also their customers
and lovers. Employed men with respectable wives at home
(the very types that vilify and condemn Mathare women
as 'evil' in letters to the editor of the local newspapers) drink
and live with the women they disapprove of. Women perceive this ambiguity, and distrust, if not despise, men as a
category. They articulate strong feelings of anger towards

men and a need for women to stand united against a common enemy.

Conclusion

One could describe the operation of women beer brewer's networks in daily life as an active defence, which is largely successful in providing help in situations of insecurity, illness, police raids, beatings by customers and lovers, shortages of money, and all the other difficulties involved in surviving in an urban shanty town. As a defence it has been relatively successful within the limits of defensive action. It is easy to see that without their solidarity as expressed in their effective and extended networks, women would have much more difficulty surviving in the uncertain milieu of Mathare.

However, it is a truism that the best defence is a good offence. Women of Mathare rarely operate effectively on the offensive. Some of the examples given above of manifestations of a wider solidarity in Mathare have been offensive actions: the self-help groups formed to build nursery schools, the groups formed to agitate for piped water, and the delegations of women approaching politicians. Twice in the two years I was there, the women came to the aid of a woman being mistreated by policemen during a raid. On both these occasions the offensive against the police was subsequently joined by the men but the initiative was taken by the women in a spontaneous rallying to one of their sisters. Women do combine at times to express their solidarity on the offensive, and not without success.

Nevertheless, it is also true that women in Mathare have not learned to operate effectively as a group in the political arena, and they do not hold the top positions in the Kanu Committees. They also have an incomplete consciousness of the social, economic, and political factors that contribute to their present economically depressed and socially demeaned position in society. The very women who have become pregnant out of wedlock because they had no access to methods of birth control deny birth control to their daughters, who in turn become pregnant before they finish their education. Women who are unable to find jobs because they have no education, sometimes educate their sons in preference to their daughters because they continue to think of their sons as their future security.

Women who are forced to live a hand to mouth existence on the fringes of a capitalist system greatly influenced by the policies of multinational companies, which provides insufficient jobs for the population, do not criticize the system. They merely hope to be able to enter the system in the future either by amassing capital to buy land or buildings, or by educating a child well enough to have him or her employed in the wage sector. They may express anger at corrupt or unfeeling officials, politicians, or policemen but they do not express this anger in terms of a need for social change. They protest at the label they have received from a hostile society, but they have no clear idea of how to set about altering the situation. Indeed, Mathare women have not yet articulated a clear set of goals as a group, nor have they organized to campaign or fight for them. They have only succeeded individually on an *ad hoc* basis (for example, through personal networks) to meet, as they arise, the daily problems besetting them as women alone in the city.

Until women can begin to organize with common goals they will merely continue to fight a holding action that allows them to survive from day to day. Solidarity expressed in an ethic of co-operation and strategizing through manipulating networks may solve individual problems, but only organized solidarity – a group – can bring about significant changes in any system.

Notes

1 The method used in the research was participant observation and informal interviews. This was carried out in two of Mathare's ten villages, but I visited the other villages as frenquently as possible in order to ascertain whether what I observed in Villages I and II was similar to what seemed to be happening elsewhere.

These data were supplemented by a number of long, structured, but open-ended interviews with eighty-nine selected respondents. Due to the tense situation in Mathare *vis-à-vis* city and national authorities, it was difficult to interview anyone intensively who did not trust me to some extent. Therefore the sample is not a random one. I tried to stratify the sample on the basis of age, education, and status as owner or tenant. In the end I conducted a random sample survey in one of the villages, collecting basic demographic data.

I used the results of this survey to compare my interview sample with the total universe of Mathare women of that village. My sample was younger and better educated than the norm, possibly because such women were better able to understand and sympathize with what I wanted to do. In addition, there was a larger number of house owners in my sample than the norm in Village II. It is possible that more affluent women had more time to devote to this curious stranger with her interminable questions.

2 Maize and millet beer is a traditional form of beer throughout east Africa, and in addition some groups make a fermented honey beer. In recent years a form of gin distilled from sugar cane juice has also been introduced, called *changaa* in Kenya. In Mathare few people made honey beer and women rarely made gin, though many sellers retailed it along with *buzaa* (maize and millet beer). In the particular village in which I spent most of my time the distilling and selling of gin was relatively rarer than it was in the other areas of the Valley.

3 Mathare is ideally located to provide such an entertainment industry. It is surrounded by the staff quarters for Mathare Mental Hospital, the Police Lines, the Gsu Army Base, the Air Force Base, and Eastleigh which has a large population of single men whose families live in the rural area. These men flood into the Valley at night and on weekends in search of cheap beer, companionship, and sex. Bottled beer sold in bars in other parts of town cost sh. 1·50 in 1974 while a half-litre of *buzaa* cost only fify cents. Men also expressed a preference for their traditional styles of beer, and the informal, home-like circumstances in which it is sold. Women sell their beer in their individual rooms.

4 Children form small groups and run through the area singing riddle songs which warn the inhabitants. One of these songs runs: 'Bad things [police]; Hard sticks [police batons]; You'll be burned [arrested] and finished [fined or arrested]! Heads like tin bowls [police helmets].' Adults run through the alleys murmuring *'Tikwega'* [not good] or *'Miriamu'* [the police van] into every open doorway.

5 For example, when Wanjiru finished with her policeman lover, in a single week she was visited four times by off-duty policemen, friends of her ex-lover. Her room was broken into twice during raids and she lost a *debe* of flour, a tank of *buzaa* and paid sh. 70 in bribes. She finally gave her furniture into the keeping of her friend, gave up her room, and moved in with a friend at the far end of the village. When she felt that her ex-lover had lost interest in the affair, she returned to the section of the village she had lived in previously and found another room.

6 In my survey it was revealed that 33½ per cent of women had lived in Mathare two to five years, 35 per cent for six to ten years and 10 per cent for more than ten. At the same time, only 16 per cent had lived in more than one village of Mathare. Within the village they chose to stay in, women shifted more than once a year.

7 For example, Theresa was jailed for three months. She was not popular, and had no friends or relatives willing to lend her money or care for her four children. However, neighbours cared for her children during the three months, and as one woman explained each woman hoped that God would have mercy on her children if some similar disaster should befall her.

8 In the early 1970s City Council and the National Christian Council of Churches co-operated to build approximately 400 owner-occupier units and the same number of site and service sites in an area called New Mathare by locals. Certain Mathare owners were to be allocated these houses and plots with the proviso that all the recipients would tear down his or her units in Old Mathare. No provision was made for any tenants and naturally only a small proportion of the owners received new houses or plots.

References

BARNES, C. (1976) *Women in Kenya's Rural Economy*. Paper for Conference on Assembling and Collecting Data on Women's Participation in Kenyan Society, Nairobi.

BARNES, J. A. (1972) *Social Networks*. Addison Wesley Modules in Anthropology. Reading, Mass: Addison Wesley.

BOISSEVAIN, J. (1974) *Friends of Friends: Networks, Manipulators and Coalitions*. Oxford: Blackwell.

BOSWELL, D. (1969) Personal Crises and the Mobilization of the Social Network. In J. C. Mitchell (ed.), *Social Networks in Urban Situations*. Manchester: Manchester University Press.

EPSTEIN, A. (1969) Gossip, Norms and Social Networks. In J. C. Mitchell (ed.), *Social Networks in Urban Situations*. Manchester: Manchester University Press.

ETHERTON, D. (1973) *Mathare Valley*. Housing Research and Development Unit. Nairobi: University of Nairobi.

ILO (1972) *Employment, Incomes and Equality: A Strategy for Increasing Productive Employment in Kenya*. Geneva.

JACOBSON, D. (1968) Friendship and Mobility in the Development of the Urban African Elite Social Systems. *Southwestern Journal of Anthropology* 24: 123–38.

LEIBOW, E. (1967) *Tally's Corner: a Study of Negro Streetcorner Men*. Boston: Little Brown and Co.

LEYS, C. (1975) *Underdevelopment in Kenya*. London: Heinemann.

MIDDLETON, J. (1965) *The Kikuyu and Mamba of Kenya.*
London: International African Institute.
MITCHELL, J. (1966) Theoretical Orientations in African Urban
Studies. In M. Banton (ed.), *Social Anthropology of Complex
Societies.* London: Tavistock.
NELSON, N. (1977) *Dependence and Independence; Female House-
holds Heads in Mathare Valley, a Squatter Community in Nairobi,
Kenya.* Unpublished Ph.D. dissertation, University of London.
ROSS, M. (1973) *The Political Integration of Urban Squatters.*
Evanston, Illinois: Northwestern University Press.
—— (1974) Conflict Resolution Among Urban Squatters. *Urban
Anthropology* 3(1):110–35.
WACHTEL, E. (1972) *The Mother and the Whore: Image and
Stereotype of African Women.* Unpublished MS.
WOLF, E. (1966) Kinship, Friendship and Patron-Client Relations
in Complex Societies. In M. Banton (ed.), *Social Anthropology
of Complex Societies.* London: Tavistock.

FOUR

Women's organizations in Madras City, India

PATRICIA CAPLAN

Although men's voluntary associations have been studied in some detail by social scientists, women's organizations have received much less attention, with the possible exception of those in west Africa (Hoffer 1975; Little 1973). Is this because, as Tiger (1971) asserts, not only are there likely to be far fewer women's than men's organizations in all societies, but also 'where they do exist, the relative obscurity of the female organizations and their apparent unimportance for the macro-life of the community is both striking and provocative' (Tiger 1971:72)? As this article will show, women's organizations in India are neither few, nor obscure, and they impinge quite considerably upon the macro-life of the community. However, the question to which this paper addresses itself concerns the consequences for women of the existence of such organizations.

Women's voluntary organizations in India are extremely numerous, and a large number of urban women are members. Indeed, they provide the main field of activity outside the home for middle- and upper-class women, for the numbers who are employed are very small indeed (Baig 1976; Nath 1965; Hate 1948). In Madras city, which has a population of over 2½ millions (1971 census) there exist around forty major women's organizations, several of which are 'umbrella' organizations for smaller groups with a membership running into thousands.[1]

These organizations by their very existence constitute a form of sexual segregation, and might be expected to provide a suitable arena in which women could manifest some kind of solidarity. There certainly appears to be a need in Indian society for women to work together to improve their own lot. There is ample evidence, for example, that in certain crucial areas (diet, health care and so forth) women are much worse off than men (Baig 1976; Indian Council for Social Science Research 1975). This would appear to account for the extremely unusual ratio of females to males (930 per thousand). Women also have less access to education than men – 40 per cent of Indian males are literate, compared to less than 20 per cent of females (Bose 1975). In addition, far fewer women are in productive employment – only 13 per cent in the rural areas, and 7 per cent in the urban – and this proportion has been declining steadily over the past several decades (Nath 1965).

However, as I shall show, women's organizations do not provide examples of active female solidarity, mainly because the members lack any consciousness of their own oppression. They do not perceive their common predicament of dependence upon men, nor the relatively restricted range of options open to them. Furthermore, since many of the members use the organizations as a means of maintaining or gaining status, women are placed in a situation of competition with each other. Problems such as the high mortality rate of women, illiteracy, and lack of job opportunities are perceived by the middle- and upper-class members of women's organizations as being confined to lower-class women, and accordingly, members direct their efforts towards 'uplifting' these women.

The establishment of women's organizations in India

It is frequently asserted that women's organizations and the 'emancipation' of Indian women were by-products of the nationalist movement. To some extent this is true, although even the earlier nineteenth-century reformists such as Ram Mohan Roy and Swami Vivekananda considered the position of women as one of the major 'social evils' in Indian society at the time, and tried to prevent such customs as *sati* (widow self-immolation) and child marriage. Early in the twentieth century, two Irish ex-suffragettes and Theosophists, Annie Besant and Margaret Cousins, also pressed for women's rights, particularly the right to vote. In 1917, together with an Indian woman named Dorothy Jinarajadasa (wife of the then President of the Theosophical Society) they founded the Women's India Association at Adyar, just outside Madras, where the headquarters of the Theosophical Society are located. The officers of the Women's India Association and those from one or two other organizations, founded around the same time in other parts of India, were in that same year (1917) members of a women's deputation to the Montagu Commission, which had come to India to investigate possible reforms in the franchise system. The women presented a memorandum asking that, when the franchise was widened, 'women be recognized as people' and be given the right to vote under the same conditions as men (All-India Women's Congress 1970:17).

Shortly afterwards, Annie Besant was interned by the British, and the members of the Women's India Association were active in petitioning for her release. She was not only released by the British — but also elected President of the Indian National Congress, the first woman to receive such an honour.

The Women's India Association, like the handful of other organizations in existence elsewhere, continued to press for 'a woman's right to vote', but the British, who had not yet conceded this principle at home, were reluctant to set such a precedent. When the Montagu-Chelmsford reforms were published (1918), it was found that women's suffrage was deemed a 'domestic matter' (that is, to be decided separately by each state). Although this appeared initially to be a blow for women's suffrage, in fact, the Women's India Association, which was rapidly growing, was able to put pressure on Legislative Councils in the regions to sponsor resolutions on women's behalf. In 1920, Cochin and Travancore were the first states to grant qualified voting rights to women and then, a year later,

Madras Presidency followed suit. Thereafter many of the leaders of the women's movement were elected to prominent political posts.

By the mid-twenties, a few women began to be aware that in the course of these political struggles, other issues connected with women's welfare were being neglected, particularly education. Accordingly, in 1927, Margaret Cousins organized the first All-India Women's Conference. This became a standing body, and the umbrella organization for all the women's associations in India. (For some time it co-existed with the Women's India Association, but in the 1930s the latter became simply the Madras branch of the All-India Women's Conference.) Although initially working for the education of girls, it later turned its attention to improvement in women's legal status and working conditions. In 1931, the All-India Women's Conference, like the Women's India Association before it, became politicized when it met together with the Women's India Association and the National Council of Women (founded in 1921) to plan strategy following the second Round Table conference between the British rulers and the Indian national-ists. The women's organizations protested strongly against the proposed 'wifehood' qualification in the widened franchise because they said that it would tend to perpetuate the idea of the dependency of the woman on the man (Reddy 1956). This illustrates the early radicalism of much of the Indian women's movement – many of the women working in it seeing clearly that the root of the oppression of Indian women was their total dependence upon and subjection to men (Kaur 1968). As the law-giver Manu had stipulated so long ago concerning the subordination of the female: 'in childhood to her father, in adulthood to her husband, and in old age to her son'.

The spread of women's organizations and the participation of women in public life was supported by Gandhi. There is little doubt that, had it not been for his championing of this cause, it would have been much more difficult for women to leave their homes and participate in the nationalist struggle. Even so, his philosophy with regard to women is full of the ambivalence that persists in Indian society today. Gandhi wanted women to join his struggle: 'I would love to find that my future army contained a vast preponderance of women over men. If the fight came, I should then approach it with much greater confidence than if men predominated. I would dread the latter's violence. Women would be my guarantee against such an outbreak' (Gandhi 1942 : 167).

In other words, Gandhi thought that women, because they are 'by nature' self-sacrificing, would be more useful to his kind of non-violent campaigns than men. Gandhi drew upon certain aspects of Hindu ideology concerning women – woman as mother, or woman as faithful and chaste wife (like the heroine of the Ramayana, Sita), but never woman as an active or independent person, even though there were such women in Hindu mythology and history. Although Gandhi thought that women could play a useful role in public life, and that their 'nobler' natures would purify it, he did not consider that this should be at the expense of their domestic roles : 'Equality of the sexes does not mean equality of occupations.... Nature has created sexes as complements of each other. Their functions are defined as are their forms' (Gandhi 1942 : 167).

Indian women are fond of asserting that they did not have to fight for their emancipation, in the way that women in the west did. 'Our men handed it to us on a platter' is a favourite saying. It is indeed rather surprising that in a country where the ideology of female submissiveness is so developed, women achieved so many legal and political rights without a struggle. Some writers have attributed this to the influence that western radicalism had upon Indians during the fight for independence. Others have explained it in terms of the dominance of the mother-figure in the Indian family, and also in the cosmology. Of course, there is nothing unique about co-opting the energies of women to a struggle against imperialism, and then allowing the situation to return to one of *status quo ante* as soon as independence is achieved (Rowbotham 1972). In the aftermath of independence, many new laws were passed regarding women, enabling them to inherit property, to divorce, and so on.[2] These were the very legal reforms for which the women's organizations had pressed, but in fact they have had very little effect on the position of Indian women (Mazumdar 1976). Furthermore, since India now has very liberal laws in many areas concerning women, there are perceived to be few issues left for women to organize around.

Not only are the laws in most cases ignored or flouted, but the ideology concerning women in society as a whole has

103

actually changed very little. Their domestic role is still deemed to be paramount, and the ideal of the *patrivrata* (husband-worshipping wife) is still instilled into girls from their earliest years. This ideal is totally unchallenged by the women's organizations; indeed, they themselves have done much in the decades since independence to propagate such values. Furthermore, from being mainly reformist groups caught up in the nationalist struggle, they have nearly all turned themselves into social welfare organizations.[3]

The Central Social Welfare Board

In 1953, the Government of India set up the Central Social Welfare Board, a semi-autonomous body, to co-ordinate the role of statutory and voluntary agencies, and to give financial and other assistance to the latter. Welfare boards were also set up in each state to vet applications for grants and supervise agencies receiving them. Each state board sends a member, usually the 'chairman' (as these women are referred to), as representative to the Central Social Welfare Board in Delhi. The Central Board also sends members to the Central Planning Commission. The vast majority of the board members, at both the state and central level, are members of the women's organizations concerned with social welfare. At the state level, the members are chosen partly by the state government, and partly by the central government, but the chairman is, in effect, a central appointee, that is to say, more or less the personal choice of the Prime Minister (Kulkarni 1961).

Through the state and central boards, the women's organizations have acquired not only a new source of funding, but also a channel for their opinions to be heard at the highest level. In the years following the foundation of the Central Social Welfare Board, there was a proliferation of new women's organizations, all hoping to take advantage of the funds, and perhaps of the political channels too. However, the older-established women's organizations, like the Women's India Association, managed to hold their own, both in the amount of grants their institutions receive, and the numbers of their members who hold office in the state and central boards.

The Central Board recognizes several categories of welfare services for which it provides grants, and assigns priorities within these categories. Welfare services for children and for women are considered the most important; it is with the provision of these two types of service that most of the women's organizations are now concerned.

Women's organizations in Madras City

Women's organizations can be classified in a number of different ways. One that has already been mentioned is whether the organization draws its membership from a single neighbourhood, or from the whole city. Another important difference between organizations is language. Predominantly either English or Tamil is used, the latter being associated with neighbourhood associations, while most of the city-wide organizations use English. A handful of organizations meant expressly for north Indian women resident in the city use Hindi or some other north Indian language.

Organizations can also be classified by their activities. Some hold classes in singing *bhajans* (hymns), music, cookery, and handicrafts; these are meant primarily for the benefit of the members, and are usually organized on a neighbourhood basis. In addition, they usually run a small social welfare scheme, such as a part-time dispensary, or a nursery class for the benefit of poor children in the area.

Second, there are city-wide organizations, which see themselves as existing primarily to provide social welfare services for the poor. This they attempt to do either by running schemes or institutions themselves, or else raising funds to assist other social welfare organizations. Favourite projects are orphanages, 'rescue homes' (for girls or women considered to be in 'moral danger'), vocational and industrial training centres, employment units, nurseries, schools, and so forth.

Third, there are a small number of organizations for professional and/or highly educated women, several of which are affiliated to international organizations. These run seminars and discussion groups; most of them also engage in social welfare work for non-members. The one which I studied, for example, had set up a creche for the children of the lowest grades of hospital workers, and also started a day-nursery for the children of white-collar women workers. None of these organizations, however, with the possible exception of one for women lawyers, saw their role as that of a pressure group working to improve pay, opportunities, or working conditions for themselves.

The fourth kind of organization consists of associations set up to complement men's 'service' clubs, like Rotary; women are admitted to membership as the wives of male members.

The membership of many of these organizations was overlapping, and most of the women prominent in them were not only known to each other, but also linked through ties of caste, or husband's occupation. It was, therefore, impossible to isolate the organizations and study them as separate entities. The factor that most of these organizations had in common, and which also sometimes led to disputes and factionalism, was that all of them (whatever else they did) saw themselves primarily as social welfare organizations. I shall return to this question of social welfare later, but meanwhile I will consider the kinds of women who join the organizations.

Class and caste

The chief characteristic of the members of the women's organizations is that they are drawn from the higher social strata. Those studies carried out in India which have taken any account of class have used, in the main, the criteria of occupation, income, and to some extent education. Relatively little mention has been made of the way in which class manifests itself through life-style, which enables narrower status groupings to be distinguished within a particular class.

I have found it useful to distinguish an upper class and a middle class, based partly on economic and partly on occupational criteria. The upper classes consist of people who have an income in excess of Rs. 2,000 per month, and who are large property owners (for example, landlords), owners or directors of medium to large companies, senior government servants (for example, Indian Administrative Service officers), and successful doctors, lawyers, and judges. Within the middle class, I would also distinguish two sub-categories. First, those belonging to the upper-middle class: government servants, bank officials, managers and executives in industry with an income of Rs. 1,000-2,000 per month. Second, those in the lower-middle class: clerks and other white-collar workers, whose income does not exceed

Rs. 1,000 per month. This article is concerned mainly with the upper and upper-middle classes, from which the women's organizations recruit their members. There is a heavy bias in the occupations of their husbands towards industry, rather than the professions, or government service.

It is difficult to isolate a totally different life-style between the upper-middle and upper classes. Both invariably send their children to private, often English-medium schools. All hope to send their children to university, and the upper classes usually try to send their sons for post-graduate studies, preferably abroad. Members of both classes will have servants, although most upper-middle-class households can afford only one or two servants, while an upper-class family may have five or six (maidservant(s), cook, gardener, driver, watchman, and messenger). Not all people in the upper-middle classes have a car, unless they are provided with one by virtue of the occupation of one of the family members. Most, however, manage to run some sort of transport, even if only a scooter or motor-bike. Members of the upper classes, however, not only invariably run one car, but sometimes two.

The latter also tend to have large houses or flats of six or more rooms, while those of the upper-middle classes tend to be smaller with between two and six rooms. Middle-class families are also somewhat more likely to rent, whereas upper-class families generally buy their living accommodation. Members of the upper classes tend to own property such as land in the country, an extra house in town which can be let out, and stocks and shares. Some of them have inherited property, others obtain it because they earn enough to save and invest their surplus income in this way.

The upper classes are somewhat more westernized and cosmopolitan than the middle classes. The former are more likely to make inter-caste marriages (even so, this is a relatively rare phenomenon), to have travelled abroad, and also to belong to the more expensive recreational clubs in the city.

If class and status have been little discussed in relation to India, class in relation to women has received even less attention. In the last few years, the tradition of lumping women together with their fathers or husbands for the purpose of assigning them a class or status position has been questioned by feminist sociologists (Acker 1973; Hutton 1974; Oakley 1974).

While agreeing with such criticism, it has to be pointed out that it is more difficult to make a case for a woman having an independent class status in Indian society than it might be in the west. This is due to several reasons: first, very few women work outside the home; second, marriage is almost universal, and divorce and separation very rare; and third, arranged marriages ensure that class endogamy is the norm. In other words, women in India usually belong to family units, and there is a certain validity in treating the family as a class unit.

From the point of view of caste, the largest single category of joiners are the Brahmins. Many of the organizations are almost entirely Brahmin-dominated, and this is particularly true of the associations founded before or just after Indian independence. The leaders of these organizations were often involved in the freedom struggle, and the most prestigious are those who can claim to have been 'freedom fighters', that is, imprisoned by the British, and/or to have had direct contact with Gandhi. Such people are still associated with the Congress party, which formed the central (although not the state) government at the time of fieldwork. Another reason for the prominence of Brahmins in the field of women's organizations is that they are relatively well-educated in comparison with women from other castes.

North Indian women from business communities resident in Madras city also have a tendency to join organizations in relatively large numbers, particularly the all-Indian welfare organizations. In addition they also run their own community associations, which do not, in fact, restrict their philanthropic activities to members of their own communuity. Another category of members is provided by women from other parts of southern India, particularly from Kerala. Nevertheless, high-caste non-Brahmin Tamil women, with a few notable exceptions, are very poorly represented. Until very recently, such women received very little education, and even now they marry earlier than Brahmin women, and their participation in matters other than household and religious affairs, such as temple attendance, is not encouraged.

The women who join the women's organizations in large numbers are, then, from the upper-middle and upper classes, and are mostly Brahmins. Such women have a relatively good education – matriculation or a degree – a reasonable amount of leisure, and usually access to a car. Women of the upper-middle classes rarely join more than one organization, and most frequently this is their neighbourhood 'ladies club'. If they join one of the city-wide organizations they are unlikely to achieve office. However, women of the upper classes are 'multiple joiners', and it is they who dominate the committees of the most prestigious women's organizations in the city.

Women's domestic roles

The oft-stated norm regarding a woman in Indian society stipulates that the home is the most important part of her life, and certainly a great deal of her time is spent there. As an unmarried girl, her liberty to go out, other than to school or college, is much more restricted than that of her brothers. This attitude is prevalent because parents worry about their daughters' reputations, not because they are expected to contribute much to household chores, at least not at the class level of the members of women's associations.

Marriage is almost universal in Indian society, and the small minority who remain unmarried, like many members of the professional women's association, are considered aberrations. Marriages among the middle and upper classes are almost invariably arranged and, certainly in Madras, there is little attempt to challenge this norm among young people. For a girl, the process of finding a husband is often traumatic – her parents initiate contacts, and finally a suitable boy comes with his family to 'view' her. If she does not happen to be fair-skinned (the main criterion of beauty in India) she may be viewed and rejected by many prospective grooms. In any case, the problem of finding a boy with a suitable job and income may be great – the better the boy's occupation and background, the higher the dowry his family can command. Dowry among the urban middle and upper classes is quite a different phenomenon from the traditional *stridhanam* given by her parents to a woman on marriage. A girl still receives a large amount of gold jewellery from her parents, but in addition, the boy's family also receives a large cash payment. The frequently expressed rationale for this is that it helps to pay off the debts incurred by the marriage of the boy's sister(s).

Middle- and upper-class Indian women, then, have little say

in the choice of their mate. Since schools and colleges are rarely co-educational, and youth clubs non-existent, there are hardly any opportunities for young people of the opposite sex to get to know each other, so that 'love marriages' are extremely rare.

The fact of almost universally arranged marriage does, however, in some respects relieve women of the tremendous burden, which they have in the west, of finding, 'catching', and keeping a husband. Young women are free to devote themselves to their studies, and indeed, frequently do extremely well. Another aspect of this situation is that women are not placed in competition with each other, as western women are, and do not see other women as potential threats to their becoming and remaining wives. This contrast between the situation of Indian and western women has been remarked on by several perceptive Indian writers (Das 1976; Roy 1975).

It may be asked why middle- and upper-class parents send their daughters to college, given that husbands are invariably sought for them while they are completing their degrees, and that few of them work outside the home after marriage. The frequent answer to this question is that grooms want educated brides, who can speak good English, and not disgrace them on public occasions. Another reason given is that 'educate a girl, and you educate a whole family'. In India this is more literally true than elsewhere, for a major part of women's leisure time in the evenings is taken up with 'coaching' their children. School-children, even at the best and most expensive schools to which the members of the women's organizations send them, are placed in very large classes (forty to fifty children is common). There they are put through an educational system which demands a great deal of memorization and rote learning. From the age of five, when children enter school, their lives are punctuated by a regular series of examinations, and enormous pressure is exerted to ensure that they do well. Wealthy families can, of course, employ private tutors (who are often underpaid teachers making a little extra money) but even in such cases mothers usually sit with their children while they work.

If a groom is living with his parents, then a bride is likely to join their household. However, at this class level, most couples find it necessary to be mobile because of the husband's job, and usually do not remain in a joint family for very long.

Another factor in the establishment of a nuclear household is that many companies provide housing for their senior executives. Although a significant minority of the women studied are living in joint households, a new pattern seems to be emerging in the urban areas. After an initial period of joint living, the couple set up a nuclear household, although visits by the husband's parents will be frequent. When they become too old to live alone, or when one of them dies, they may then rejoin one of the son's families. It it thus much more likely to be the husband's parents who are living together with the young couple, in the traditional style, than those of the wife. Even so, I did discover several cases of the wife's parents living with a married couple, but this is only likely when there are no sons.[4] In some cases, where parents do not or cannot live with a married daughter, they may still receive considerable help in both cash and kind from her and her husband.

Only a minority of women were living in households that ' strictly speaking could be called 'joint', that is, where more than one married couple are co-residential (Kolenda 1968). The highest figure was 25 per cent in one organization where the majority of members were in their late forties and early fifties, and thus likely to have recently married sons and daughters-in-law living with them in the early stages of their married life.

However, for all these women, the significant factor was whether or not they had a mother-in-law or daughter-in-law residing with them. Such households might technically fall under the rubric of 'supplemented nuclear', according to the anthropologist's definition (Kolenda 1968). However, the women themselves would refer to it as a joint family, because the all-important factor was not the presence of two married couples, but rather the co-residence of a mother-in-law and daughter-in-law. Between a third and a half of the women in all but one organization studied were living in this kind of household.

Women have the major responsibility for the running of a household, and where two adult women are co-resident, a number of methods of division of labour were observed. In some, the mother-in-law organized everything, leaving her daughter-in-law free from domestic duties. In other cases, the daughter-in-law carried a heavy burden of chores, although the mother-in-law remained in overall control. In yet other households, mothers-in-law and daughters-in-law divided the chores, or else took it in turns to do them. However, when a mother-in-law became really old, she generally retired from the kitchen and spent more time in the *puja* (prayer) room and temple.

It is almost a *sine qua non* of middle- and upper-class households that they employ at least a part-time servant. Thus the heavy work of cleaning the house, washing clothes and dishes is rarely done by the housewife. Nevertheless, except in wealthy upper-middle or upper-class households, the wife has the major responsibility for cooking. South Indian food is extremely complicated and time-consuming to prepare, and most of the women who do not employ cooks rise between 5·0 a.m. and 5·30 a.m. to begin preparing meals for the family. Few such women are able to spend less than four hours a day in the kitchen, and some spend five or six hours there. However, for women of these classes, their burden is somewhat lightened by such labour-saving devices as a gas cooker, pressure cooker, and perhaps even a fridge, or electric mixer. All of these items cost a great deal more in India than they do in Britain and, in relation to Indian salaries, are extremely expensive. Women of the upper class have relatively light domestic duties, and these are generally supervisory. Most importantly, they can generally afford to pay a cook (who is usually a male Brahmin, and therefore relatively highly paid).

Few husbands will help in the kitchen, although some husbands do go shopping, and many will help with child-care. However, the frequently discussed issues of women's emancipation in India generally centre around women's right to work outside the home, rather than on men's participation in domestic duties. Partly, this is because servants are so freely available.

The extent to which men can participate domestically is also partially determined by the demands of their employment. Wives whose husbands spend long hours or days away from the house find themselves carrying most of the responsibilities, not only for the day to day running of the household, but also for most of the budgeting, and for making decisions concerning the children's education.

One important recent change for middle- and upper-middle-class Indian women has been the dramatic drop in the average number of children. Two children, preferably one of each sex, seems to be the almost universally desired norm; and in fact, very few couples, apart from those over fifty years old, exceed this. Even in cases where the first two children are both girls, there is a reluctance in most cases to try again for a boy; people said frankly that to marry two girls off properly, with decent dowries, would use all their resources.

This change, then, coupled with an increase in labour saving devices in the kitchen, and the relaxation of the most rigid rules of pollution and purity, would seem to indicate that women's domestic lot is becoming easier. However, as has happened in the west, in many ways, women's domestic burden remains great, for they too have internalized many of the western norms of the 'good wife and mother'. Indian women's magazines are full of advice on child-rearing, which emphasizes the child's need of the mother's attention during the early years. Later, as I have previously stated, women spend a great deal of time 'coaching' their children in school work.

The women's magazines and the mass media also help to foster a desire for a house that is nicely decorated, perhaps ornamented with the wife's handiwork. Cookery, complicated and time-consuming in its traditional form, now extends to baking western style cakes, making jams, juices, and so on. In short, then, fewer children and modern homes need more time and attention from women than that required a generation ago to cope with many children and old-fashioned kitchens. As the Report of the National Committee on the Status of Women in India notes: 'Among the well-to-do ... home-making is raised to a fine art, and trifling details assume exaggerated importance' (Indian Council for Social Science Research 1975).

This pressure to conform to the currently acceptable standards of a good wife and mother obviously precludes working outside the home. In fact only about 7 per cent of urban Indian women do so. Very few, even those with a college degree, have a marketable skill, since degrees in arts or domestic sciences are considered most suitable for middle- and upper-class girls. The generally accepted norm is that such girls should not work, either before or after marriage, and this is echoed by the women's associations. For example, articles in the annual reports or 'souvenir' booklets issued by the associations often condemn working women – whether they be unmarried or married, and whether they have children or not.

Conventional assumptions about the proper role of women, particularly in relation to families, are frequently and loudly voiced by the women's organizations. Devotion to duty in the form of service to husband, children, other relatives, as well as God and 'suffering humanity', is frequently extolled. For instance, one article on the role of the wife included the following passage: 'She is prepared to sacrifice her happiness if it is going to help her husband in any small way. She is always ready to give in to his wishes and values his well-being more than hers ...'[5] Even where more progressive views are espoused, the question is always related back to the family and its supreme importance: 'To a woman, the family is very important. Unless she has a happy family life she will not be able to emancipate herself. Emancipation, however, should not have any adverse effect on family life.' Similar kinds of ideas are also conveyed, perhaps slightly more subtlely, in short stories printed in souvenir booklets.

In this respect, then, the women's associations reiterate the prevailing ideology, which is expressed at all levels, from popular magazines to sociological studies. For example, a recent study points out that, 'The period since independence has been disappointingly inactive in terms of feminine progress' (Baig 1976:26). However, it still feels it necessary to stress that a 'militant movement to improve her [the Indian woman's] lot would be a loss of incalculable dimensions to the nation for it would rupture family solidarity, shatter the security children presently have in settled family life and remove the one element that holds the nation together' (Baig 1976:28).

Having looked at the ideology of Indian society regarding the proper roles of middle- and upper-class women, and their importance, both real and perceived, to the family, let us now consider why such women join the women's voluntary organizations.

Why do women join women's organizations?

Obviously the answer to this question varies in relation to the type of organization. However, three types of response were generally given to the above question – that they joined to 'learn new things'; to make friends; and to do social welfare work. I would also like to suggest several other reasons why women join organizations.

By 'learning new things' women meant that they joined an

association primarily for the sake of classes offered in such subjects as baking, *bhajan*-singing, and handicrafts of various kinds (doll-making, tatting, crocheting, embroidery, and so on). Some of these are 'traditional' activities, others are skills that women could not have learned at home, such as baking, which is not traditionally a part of Indian cuisine, but now considered very western and prestigious. Most of the members of women's organizations had attended classes of this kind, and the articles they made would be prominently displayed in their homes. Very few of the classes enabled women to learn skills which had any marketable, or even practical value. Nevertheless, they are considered 'suitable' activities for middle- and upper-class women, who are in any case the only ones who would have sufficient leisure and money to be able to attend them.

Making friends was also a very important attraction for women, particularly for those who joined the neighbourhood clubs. Where I lived in the south of the city, a whole complex of new suburbs had been built in the last decade or so, usually by government bodies, which then sold the properties to people on a long term repayment basis. People in these areas – mainly government officials and industrial managers – tended to be fairly mobile, because they were transferred frequently, and often people arrived as strangers to a particular suburb. Alternatively, even if they had lived in Madras for a long time, they left the crowded central areas, where their families might have been living for a generation or two, and tried to acquire their own houses. The women in these surburbs lived much the same kind of life as suburban women elsewhere: the men went to work in the morning, the children to school, and they were left alone. Naturally, then, they welcomed the chance of getting to know their neighbours through a women's club.

I found that it was much more likely to be women from nuclear family households who joined the women's clubs, and there are several reasons for this. Such women have more freedom in deciding how to allocate their time, whereas women with co-resident mothers-in-law usually have to consult them if they wish to undertake outside activities. Also some women who had elderly parents-in-law living with them had to spend a great deal of time looking after them, so that their leisure was much curtailed.

Interestingly enough, the friendship patterns of women in

the neighbourhood club often tended to cut across caste and even language differences, for the club included women from a variety of backgrounds. Two committee members who were close friends were an orthodox Brahmin woman and a Muslim woman; the non-Brahmin secretary had a close Brahmin friend, and so on. These types of relationship are of course great innovations, and it could be argued that these kinds of suburban women's clubs are 'institutions of urban adaptation' (Constatinides, Chapter 7).

However, it was noticeable that friendship between women did not appear to operate in those areas commonly found in other societies. At such crises as childbirth, illness, or death, it was relatives, however genealogically and geographically distant, who came to stay and help, not friends. Women did not exchange child-care services, because where such were needed, they were provided by servants and/or relatives. Women did not drop in and out of each other's kitchens while cooking, to gossip or to borrow a small item, mainly because caste and pollution rules preclude this.

So friendships made through the women's club generally manifested themselves in meeting at the club, and visiting each other's houses usually in the afternoon period, when household chores were finished, and children and husbands had not yet returned.

Friendship is also a very important consideration for the women who join the professional women's associations, particularly for those who have remained single, because this fact, together with their unusual degree of success in their careers, isolates them. For some of these women, the association was a veritable life-line, particularly for those whose families were not in Madras (Caplan 1977). Women in this association were much more likely to talk about their problems to each other than were those in other types of association. Furthermore, these women had some degree of consciousness of their own problems as 'deviants', particularly if they were unmarried. To this extent, the professional women's association acted very much as a support group. However, this was never seen as its manifest function: people always referred to it as a 'service' association, emphasizing that the social work aspect was its *raison d'être*.

For the women whose husbands belonged to men's associations which had women's counterparts, friendship was also extremely important, but here quite a different phenomenon emerges: friendship between *couples*. The men's association, and its wives' counterpart, demanded a great deal of commitment in time and money, and, in addition, members tended to spend most of their leisure time together. Furthermore, their children almost all attended the same school, they belonged to the same prestigious and expensive recreational club, and they frequently entertained each other at dinner parties.

There are a number of reasons for these differences. First, all the members in these clubs were north Indians – south Indians theoretically can join, but few did so. Consequently, the members saw themselves as part of a minority community in Madras, with very different life-styles from south Indians. Second, many of the male members were 'spiralists' and thus highly mobile. By joining this kind of association members could find equivalent groups wherever in India, or indeed the world, they travelled or moved to. Men found this extremely useful in business, and their wives welcomed a ready-made circle of friends when the family changed its residence or when they accompanied their husbands on business trips abroad.

In none of these associations, however, did the women's friendships really amount to an active form of solidarity. As I have said, they lacked any consciousness of the need to organize themselves in order to change their situation. Also most help and services required by these women was obtained from members of their own families, or from servants.

The third reason for joining a women's association, and one that was almost invariably given as the prime reason, was 'to do social work'. The subject of charity and social welfare in India is a vast one, and I do not propose here to do more than touch on some of the salient features, especially as they relate to women's organizations.

As already stated, voluntary social welfare work is the most acceptable occupation outside the home for middle- and upper-class women. However, they work in this field mainly in an administrative capacity, rarely engaging in work that brings them into direct contact with the agency's clients. Work of this latter kind is undertaken by women who are paid (albeit often meagrely) and whose background is lower-middle class.

There are often a number of factors influencing a woman becoming highly involved in voluntary welfare work. One, of course, is sufficient time and money, which means having sufficient servants. If she intends to become very involved and seek office, above all she must have a cook. A woman must also have access to transport, if she intends to join a city-wide organization. Social work is usually undertaken by women whose children are at least adolescent, if not adult. However, childless women also form a rather high proportion of women voluntary workers, since service to others is regarded as an acceptable substitute for having children. Some women come from families with a long tradition of voluntary work and have been encouraged by other female relatives, such as mothers and aunts, or else they may marry into a family with such traditions.

In spite of the fact that social work is considered acceptable, even fitting work for women, conflicts between domestic and extra-domestic roles can arise. Some women prominent in the voluntary organizations found it necessary to state emphatically that they 'always put their own families first'. The President of a newly formed organization emphasized constantly that the members must think of themselves as housewives, and that their participation in the organization must be confined to their leisure hours. Indeed, other studies, as well as some of the reports carried out by government bodies into the workings of the social welfare system, have pointed out the disadvantages of using voluntary workers, who are rarely able to give priority to this work (Maclay 1969; Planning Commission 1968; Planning Commission n.d.).

Husband's attitudes towards their wives' participation varied. On the whole it was middle-class husbands who tended to be more ambivalent, and to become angry if they felt that this threatened the domestic *status quo*. Partly, of course, this is because such families need the wife's domestic services, particularly in cooking, whereas upper-class families do not. In upper-class families, husbands perceived quite clearly the benefits of a wife who played a leading role in an important organization. As the secretary of one such organization reported to me: 'My husband is extremely proud of me – he tells all his business friends when he brings them home that I am the secretary of this social welfare organization.' Such husbands tend not only to approve of their wives' activities, but also to help them with contacts, and sometimes money.

How is social welfare carried out by the women's organizations? First, the attitudes of the members towards the clients must be considered. Terms such as 'uplift', 'weaker sections', and 'deserving cases' are frequently employed. Clients tend to be seen as members of a class that is virtually of a different species, whose needs and problems are quite different from those of the middle and upper classes.

An example may illustrate this attitude. During a committee meeting of one of the most prestigious social welfare organizations, it was reported that a women who had recently lost her husband had come to them for help, as she had no relatives and no means of support for herself and her young son. The members congratulated themselves on finding the boy a place in an orphanage (where she would be able to visit him once a month), and for the mother, a job as a maidservant. No mention was made in this case of the sanctity of the mother-child bond, a point that is raised so frequently when the question of educated women working outside the home is discussed. Another instance in the same organization occurred when it was suggested that this particular organization, which has relatively large premises, could provide a haven for wives turned out by their husbands. However, it was agreed by the committee that the setting up of such places could only contribute to social irresponsibility and encourage husbands to turn out their wives, or wives to leave their husbands on trivial pretexts.

There is, therefore, no sense of solidarity between the dispensers of charity and their economically less fortunate sisters, except in so far as it is thought to be more suitable for poor *women* to receive charity from rich *women*; otherwise the gulf between them is unbridgeable.

The second case quoted above was actually a rare instance of a problem *not* being viewed in terms of institutional solutions. On the whole, the women's organizations encourage the building of 'homes' – for orphans, for destitute women, for women in 'moral danger', or as training institutes. During 1975, it was suggested by the International Women's Year Committee that as many institutions as possible for women and children should be opened by both voluntary agencies and the government.

Indeed, this approach has been adopted by the state government, partially no doubt in response to pressure from the women's organizations (Oza 1974).[6] The erection of yet another institution is seen as tangible proof of effort being made on behalf of the poor, although it could equally well be argued that it acts as a means of *controlling* them.

The role of women's organizations in the wider society

I suggest that a major reason why women join the social welfare organizations is because they gain in status, or maintain the status they already have by virtue of their class position. There are a number of reasons for this assertion. First, to be able to engage in social work at all, women must have sufficient money to allow them access to cars, servants, and also to make substantial donations to the organization. In addition, they need to be successful fund-raisers, which means having contacts in industry who will place advertisements in souvenir booklets, wealthy friends who will give donations, or else buy the very expensive tickets for charity performances. Only women who can fulfill these criteria can hope to be elected to a committee, much less to hold office.

It is interesting to note that it is mainly the wives of businessmen who are active as committee members and officials of social welfare organizations.[7] As various writers on India have pointed out, industrialists and businessmen in India have not been accorded particularly high status – this is reserved for professionals and senior government servants (Rosen 1967; Singer 1971). This attitude may be partly due to the Indians' dislike of anything that smacks of manual labour, and partly because they have inherited British attitudes towards 'trade'. In any case, the wealthy class of industrialists is relatively new, whereas the more prestigious occupations have been in existence for longer. Of course, many industrialists and businessmen have a far higher income than even top civil servants, but this is not sufficient to earn them the prestige they desire. Rather this is gained through philanthropic activities, carried out by these men themselves, or else indirectly through their wives. It is particularly for this stratum, then, that the wives can play an important role in translating a family's wealth into social status – by enabling a family, which by virtue of occupation and income belongs in the upper class, to be accepted there by its life-style.

Money alone, however, is not enough, and a woman who wishes to participate successfully in the arena of the large city-wide women's organizations has to have certain skills. It is virtually impossible for her to participate unless she is fluent in English, although there are one or two exceptions to this. Good English is another reason why Brahmin women, who have a higher educational level than others, have been able to retain their dominance in so many organizations; why north Indian and Keralite women are likewise prominent, out of all proportion to their actual numbers; and why high-caste non-Brahmin Tamilian women participate very little. Brahmin women in particular have provided most of the State Welfare Board members.

This brings us to another aspect of the women's organizations: that is, their political role. Most of the organizations, as I have said, were founded by Congress supporters, and the members remain largely sympathetic to or else active members of one or other wings of the Congress party, although a minority are Jan Sangh or Swatantra (that is, right-wing) supporters. None, however, support either the DMK or ADMK (Dravidian nationalist) parties, or any of the left-wing parties.[8] Many prominent 'social workers' (as women active in voluntary social welfare work are termed) actively campaign for Congress at election time, lending their names and prestige to the cause. They also invite prominent Congress politicians to address their meetings. In addition, articles in the souvenir booklets and speeches on public occasions indirectly support Congress, particularly by referring to the great nationalist figures of the past, like Gandhi and Nehru, and by equating patriotism, social service and all the middle- and upper-class virtues with the Congress party.

Another way in which members of the women's organizations in Madras have traditionally shown their support for the central government and Congress party (for many years one and the same) is by the assiduous learning of Hindi, some to quite advanced levels. This, of course, runs directly counter to the anti-Hindi, pro-Tamil sentiments of the Dravidian nationalist parties which have held power in the state since 1967.

These parties have sought to lessen the power of the Brahmins, which was such a feature of the British period. During that time, they constituted approximately 7 per cent of the population in the Madras presidency, but they held 75 per cent of the civil service posts (Fürer-Haimendorf 1963). It is now much more difficult for Brahmins to obtain places in college or government jobs and, in the last generation, Brahmin males have begun to switch from their earlier occupations of government service and the professions, to go into industry.

When the D M K party came to power in 1967, many of the Brahmin pro-Congress members resigned from the State Social Welfare Board, and were replaced by non-Brahmin women, usually either from wealthy high-caste (although non-Brahmin) families, or else the wives of prominent D M K men. However, not many of these women remained board members for very long. Most lacked the essential skills : fluency in English, a wide range of contacts, and the necessary experience in administration and committee work. In addition, they lacked the backing of the Congress-dominated Central Board. In fact, several of the 'old hands' got their positions back on the state board in spite of the fact that they were Brahmins.

This is, of course, a classic situation in which a group, unable to organize itself by direct political means, chooses other less direct means (Cohen 1971). The Brahmins, partly because their numbers are few, and partly because the Congress vote has been split since the party divided into two, cannot command political power in Tamilnadu in the way that they once did. However, they have at least ensured that certain fields that they have long dominated do remain theirs. (Apart from the women's organizations, Brahmins also dominate the cultural life of Madras and the other major cities in Tamilnadu through the numerous musical associations or *sabhas*.) The central government can likewise use the channel of the women's organizations in order to mitigate to some extent the power of the state government.

Another political aspect of the women's organizations is that they not only enable women to achieve considerable power and influence through membership of the state and central boards, but also some 'social workers' have been invited to stand as members of legislative assemblies, or even as members of parliament. In other words, social welfare work can be a stepping stone to a wider political career (Chowdhry 1971;

Malkani 1968). For a woman, in particular, this is a vital step, although even a successful career in a prominent woman's organization is no guarantee of success as a politician. Many women in fact prefer not to enter the overtly political arena, and content themselves with social welfare, which enables them to play a public role and achieve a modicum of indirect political power.

To this extent, then, women's organizations enable their members to achieve a power and influence that is not otherwise possible. Even so, it must be realized that women 'social workers' are not contradicting the basic ideology concerning the paramountcy of women's domestic role – they are, in effect, acting as 'extended housekeepers'.

In this way, then, women's organizations for social welfare help to support the norms regarding the 'proper' role of women. Similarly, the organizations that teach their members baking or handicrafts actually do very little to challenge the conventional assumptions about middle- and upper-class women.

Of course, it could be argued, as indeed it has been, that by not challenging directly the norms of society regarding the role of women, Indian women have actually been able to accomplish much more than they might otherwise have done (Mies 1973). By *appearing* to conform, many women have actually been able to achieve a great deal, for example, political power. On an individual level, this argument might hold good, but on a wider scale, failure to analyse and challenge the conventional assumptions about women's roles actually means that change is very slow, and very sporadic.

If women's organizations tend to play an essentially conservative role *vis à vis* women, this is even more pronounced in regard to the working classes. Of course, there are members of the middle and upper classes who genuinely feel concerned about the state in which most of India's people are forced to live, and who try hard, as they put it, to 'do my little bit to help'. However, most of these people lack what Beatrice Webb once called 'the consciousness of collective sin' (Webb 1926:177). In other words they fail to see that the whole social system needs changing radically, not just reforming slightly, and they tend to think that the poor would be much better off if only they would drink less or have fewer children. There are others who do not even pretend an altruistic motive for their welfare work – they openly voice their fear of revolution, and hope that by patching and mending the social fabric here and there the necessity for real change, or the chance of violent change, can be fended off.

Conclusion

In concluding, then, we return to the question posed at the beginning of this article: to what extent do women's associations provide a context for women to manifest any kind of feminist solidarity? The answer is, of course, that on the whole they do not. Women's associations and the field of social welfare provide a means for women to achieve power and influence as *people* in the wider society; indeed, for most women, they provide the only means. For a small number of women, they provide a stepping stone to a political career in which they compete directly with men. The associations also provide a forum in which women can make symbolic statements about their relative class positions. In fostering a common life-style appropriate for the upper-class levels of the urban milieu, it might indeed be thought that such women are exhibiting a form of solidarity. However, the fight for power and prestige is seen as a zero-sum-game, and consequently women are in competition with each other, particularly for office.

Members of the associations are not aware of their oppression as women; indeed, they frequently assert that Indian women have no need of a 'western-style' women's liberation movement (Chitnis 1975; Thapar 1975). They certainly do not perceive that their problems are shared by women from the same background. Nor do they have any feeling of solidarity with the women of the working classes. On the contrary, the very vocabulary of social welfare is one of 'them' – the clients – and 'us' – the voluntary social workers. Given the enormous gulf between working-class and middle- and upper-class women in India this is hardly surprising.

It is, in fact, surely not insignificant that the major activity of the women's organizations is social welfare.[9] This field is one of the very few in which the middle and upper classes come into contact with the poor; in all probability the only other would be in the mistress-servant relationship. However, in relation to the needs of India's population, the voluntary organizations can actually achieve very little: as they them-selves admit, their resources in both money and personnel are insufficient. Even so their activities receive a great deal of publicity, and past achievements are frequently recalled. Hence the overall impression given is that things are in fact improving. In actual fact, life is getting more difficult for the poor in India, not less, and the gap between the classes is widening (Bettelheim 1968). Philanthropy provides a cross-cutting tie between the classes which masks the fact that their interests are opposed – the lot of the poor cannot be improved without a radical re-structuring of Indian society. Through their partici-pation in women's organizations, at least in their present form, women are acting primarily as members of a class, and seeking to preserve class interests.

Notes

1 Fieldwork was carried out in Madras between July 1974 and September 1975, and was financially supported by the Social Science Research Council.
2 The laws that have been passed since independence affecting women are: the Hindu Marriage and Divorce Act, 1955; the Hindu Succession Act, 1956; the Dowry Prohibition Act, 1961; and the Medical Termination of Pregnancy Act, 1971.
3 India is far from being a unique case in this respect – Wipper's study of the Kenya women's movement has many parallels (Wipper 1975).
4 Sylvia Vatuk found a similar situation among her middle-class sample in Meerut, a north Indian town, which may suggest that this is an increasingly widespread trend (Vatuk 1972).
5 I have not given precise references for literature produced by the Madras women's organizations as I wish to preserve their anonymity.
6 The Tamilnadu government decided in 1975 to open a large number of orphanages or 'homes of pity'. It was reported in the press that large numbers of children were virtually kid-napped and placed in these homes. The voices raised against this kind of approach are few and far between – the Director of the Madras School of Social Work wrote an indignant letter to the press, pointing out that institutionalization was not only out-dated, but wasteful of resources, and probably harm-ful. In reply, a letter from a prominent woman 'social worker' was published, which attacked schools of social work, and thereby, of course, a professional approach to social work (*Hindu*, May 19, 1976; May 26, 1976).

7 The single exception to this was the neighbourhood club which contained a large number of wives of government servants; this was because this particular suburb was designated as housing for government employees. Other occupations were, however, represented since many government servants who were posted away from Madras rented out their houses.

8 For more discussion of south Indian politics, and the anti-Brahmin Dravidian nationalist movement see Hardgrave 1965; Irschik 1969; Rudolph and Rudolph 1967; and Spratt 1970.

9 This is not of course peculiar to India. For an interesting account of the activities of Pakistani women's associations see Chipp 1970; for Bangladeshi women's associations see Jahan 1975.

References

A C K E R, J. (1973) Women and Social Stratification: a case of intellectual sexism. In J. Huber (ed.), *Changing Women in a Changing Society*. Chicago: University of Chicago Press.

A L L - I N D I A W O M E N ' S C O N F E R E N C E (1970) *Souvenir*. Delhi: All-India Women's Conference.

B A I G, T. A. (1976) *India's Woman Power*. New Delhi: Chand and Company.

B E T T E L H E I M, C. (1968) *India Independent*. London: MacGibbon and Kee.

B H A S I N, K. (ed.) (1971) *The Position of Women in India*. Bombay and Bonn: Leslie Sawhny Programme of Training for Democracy and Friedrich Naumann-Stiftung.

B O S E, A. (1975) A Demographic Profile. In D. Jain (ed.), *Indian Women*. New Delhi: Publications Division, Ministry of Information and Broadcasting.

C A P L A N, P. (1977) Professional Women in India. *Women Speaking* IV(15):12–14.

C H I P P, S. A. (1970) *The Role of Women Elites in a Modernizing Country: the All-Pakistan Women's Association*. Unpublished Ph. D. dissertation, Syracuse University.

C H I T N I S, I. (1975) Significance of International Women's Year for Women in India. In D. de Souza (ed.), *Women in Contemporary India*. New Delhi: Monohar.

C H O W D H R Y, D. P. (1971) *Voluntary Social Work in India*. New Delhi: Sterling Publications.

C O H E N, A. (1971) The Politics of Ritual Secrecy. *Man* (N.S.) VI(3):427–8.

D A S, V. (1976) Indian Women: Work, Power and Status. In B. R. Nanda (ed.), *Indian Women from Purdah to Modernity*. New Delhi: Vikas Publishing.

F Ü R E R - H A I M E N D O R F, C. V O N (1963) Caste and Politics in

South Asia. In C. H. Philips (ed.), *Politics and Society in India, Pakistan and Ceylon*. London: Allen and Unwin.

GANDHI, M. K. (1942) *Women and Social Injustice*. Ahmedabad: Navajivan Publishing House.

GOVERNMENT OF INDIA (1971) *Census of India*. New Delhi.

HARDGRAVE, R. L. (1965) *The Dravidian Movement*. Bombay: Popular Prakashan, New York: Humanities Press.

HATE, C. A. (1948) *Hindu Woman and her Future*. Bombay: New York Book Company.

HOFFER, C. P. (1975) Bundu: Political Implications of Female Solidarity in a Secret Society. In D. Raphael (ed.), *Being Female*. The Hague: Mouton.

HUTTON, C. (1974) Second Hand Status. Unpublished paper given at the British Sociological Conference on *Sexual Divisions and Society*, Aberdeen.

INDIAN COUNCIL FOR SOCIAL SCIENCE RESEARCH (1975) *Status of Women in India*. Synopsis of the report of the national commission on the status of women 1971–4. New Delhi: Indian Council for Social Science Research.

IRSCHIK, E. F. (1969) *Politics and Social Conflict in South India*. Berkeley and Los Angeles: University of California Press.

JAHAN, R. (1975) Women in Bangladesh. In R. Rohrlich-Leavitt (ed.), *Women Cross-culturally: Change and Challenge*. The Hague: Mouton.

KAUR, M. (1968) *Role of Women in the Freedom Movement 1857–1947*. Delhi: Sterling Publications.

KOLENDA, P. M. (1968) Region, Caste and Family Structure: a Comparative Study of the Indian 'Joint' Family. In M. Singer and B. S. Cohen (eds.), *Structure and Change in Indian Society*. Chicago: Aldine Publishing Company.

KULKARNI, P. D. (1961) *The Central Social Welfare Board: a New Experiment in Welfare Administration*. New Delhi: Indian Institute of Public Administration and Asia Publishing House.

LITTLE, K. (1973) *African Women in Towns*. Cambridge: Cambridge University Press.

MACLAY, S. (1969) *Women's Organisations in India: Voluntary Associations in a Developing Society*. Unpublished Ph.D. dissertation, University of Virginia.

MALKANI, N. R. (1968) Voluntary Agencies for Social Welfare. In Planning Commission, *Encyclopaedia of Social Work in India*. New Delhi: Government of India.

MAZUMDAR, V. (1976) The Social Reform Movement in India – from Ranade to Nehru. In B. R. Nanda (ed.), *Indian Women from Purdah to Modernity*. New Delhi: Vikas Publishing.

MIES, M. (1973) *Indische Frau zwischen Patriarchät und Chancelgleichkeit*. Meisenheim: Verlag Anton Hain.

NATH, K. (1965) Urban Women Workers. *Economic and Political Weekly of Bombay*, September: 1405–12.

OAKLEY, A. (1974) *The Sociology of Housework*. London: Martin Robertson.

OZA, D. K. (1974) Policies and Programmes of Social Welfare. *Social Welfare XX*:79–80.

PLANNING COMMISSION (1968) *Encylopaedia of Social Work in India*. New Delhi: Government of India.

—— (n.d.) *Study of Working of Voluntary Agencies in Social Welfare Programme*. Unpublished report (circa 1975).

REDDY, S. M. (1956) *Mrs. Margaret Cousins and her work in India*. Adyar: Women's India Association.

ROSEN, G. (1967) *Democracy and Economic Change in India*. Berkeley and Los Angeles: California University Press.

ROWBOTHAM, S. (1972) *Women, Resistance and Revolution*. Harmondsworth: Penguin.

ROY, M. (1975) The Concepts of 'Femininity' and 'Liberation' in the Context of Changing Sex Roles: Women in Modern India and America. In D. Raphael (ed.), *Being Female*. The Hague: Mouton.

RUDOLPH, L. I. and RUDOLPH, S. H. (1967) *The Modernity of Tradition: Political Development in India*. Chicago: University of Chicago Press.

SINGER, M. (1971) *When a Great Tradition Modernizes*. New York: Praeger.

SPRATT, P. (1970) *D.M.K. in Power*. Bombay: Nachiketa Publications.

THAPAR, R. (1975) Looking Back in History. In D. Jain (ed.), *Indian Women*. New Delhi: Publications Division, Ministry of Information and Broadcasting.

TIGER, L. (1971) *Men in Groups*. London: Panther Books.

VATUK, S. (1972) *Kinship and Urbanization*. Berkeley and Los Angeles: California University Press.

WEBB, B. (1926) *My Apprenticeship*. London: Longmans.

WIPPER, A. (1975) The Maedeleo ya Wanawake Movement: Some Paradoxes and Contradictions. *African Studies Review XVIII*:3.

FIVE

Women's solidarity and the preservation of privilege

GAYNOR COHEN

Solidarity is an elusive concept which refers to different patterns of collective action for different purposes under different circumstances. I will discuss in this paper the processes by which solidarity developed within two middle-class groups of women in two different societies, one in a London suburb and the other in Freetown, Sierra Leone. It is obvious that a development of this nature runs counter to the traditional ideology governing relationships within the middle-class family. Such an ideology emphasizes privacy, mutual companionship and support between the spouses, with men being the main economic providers and the main link between the family and the outside world.

Indeed, this ideology implies that solidarity is more likely to develop among the men who are in contact with each other and are thus 'more capable of forming bonds with other men to defend their families and social groups' (Rapoport and Rapoport 1977:349). Women, in contrast, are likely to perceive the care of the home and children as their first responsibility and, therefore, are 'naturally more concerned with their family than with forming links with other women to pursue extraneous goals' (Rapoport and Rapoport 1977:349).

This model of the middle-class family has not been challenged by the evidence of solidarity among women recorded in studies such as that of Young and Wilmott (1957) in Bethnal Green, or of black women in North American cities carried out by Ladner (1971). These studies concerned women from low income, socially oppressed groups, who could not rely on men for economic support. In the middle-class family model, it is axiomatic that women are guaranteed economic support by the male householder.

Neither of the two groups of women discussed here would see themselves as economically or socially oppressed. In both cases the principal role of women was child-bearing, child-rearing and socializing the child to conform to the values, norms, and beliefs typical of the middle classes. Such socialization aims at enabling the child to achieve the highest educational and professional success. It is because of their preoccupation wth these tasks, Frankenberg (1976) argues, that women remain isolated. However, the two cases discussed here, demonstrate the opposite – it was these very tasks that, far from isolating the women, prompted them to develop patterns of co-operation regulated by a special culture.

The British situation

The study in Britain was carried out on a housing estate in South London, and the estate consisted of 700 houses. A survey of the first 522 households moving into the estate showed that 30 per cent of the male householders were professionals and 43 per cent were executives or managers. The majority of both the professionals and executives were employed by national and international organizations. All the men were under forty-five – most of them in their early thirties – and felt strongly that they were at a crucial stage in their career development.

Mens' career pressures significantly affected their families' life-style. Career demands coincided with family demands. Most families had young children – under ten years of age – and it was precisely at this stage that wives most needed child-care assistance from their husbands.

The 'organization men' were prevented from giving such assistance because their jobs entailed considerable travel from home. Their daily commuting pattern to the London head office of their company meant that they left home early in the morning, before their children were awake, and returned late in the evening, when most children were likely to be asleep. In addition to this routine many had to stay away from home – sometimes one or two nights a week – in other parts of the country. In other cases travelling for the organization meant weeks spent overseas – often between two and ten weeks a year. Travel was built into their career spiral; the higher the job status the more frequent the absences from home. Willmott and Young (1973) reported a similar work pattern within their sample of professionals and managers.

Beneath the optimism that many men expressed about their career prospects lay a hint of uncertainty about the degree of security that their jobs offered. Not surprisingly this insecurity was felt most keenly by the older men and by those without a degree or professional qualification – only 30 per cent of 'organization men' had a first degree. Lack of academic qualifications did not appear to be reflected in salary levels but in mobility patterns. Those with qualifications had often moved between organizations, whereas those without had been reluctant to change employers. Older men, both the qualified and unqualified, were conscious of the fact that their careers offered relatively little job security.

The career achievements of most of these men were the result of their own efforts. None had inherited money, and for most of them their job status was higher than that of their own fathers. Nor did the older men appear to have saved money, for spending patterns were based on anticipated salary increases rather than on present salary levels. All were anxious to retain for their own children the advantages and status that they had achieved for themselves.

The wives were equally ambitious for the children even though their level of educational attainment was lower than that of their husbands. The majority had left school at sixteen, and only 20 per cent had professional or degree level qualifications. Their attention and energy were directed towards their children's future rather than upon their own career prospects. Family status depended upon husband's careers, and possibly for this reason women were prepared to accept the strain that husbands' career pressures imposed upon their family relationships. Most women on marriage had expected a partnership, with their husbands sharing the domestic tasks, the care of children, as well as leisure activities. Owing to their husbands' frequent absences from home this expectation could not be fulfilled.

Most women had resigned themselves to accepting what they regarded as their husbands' inevitable absences from home. Nevertheless the fact that the family status was insecure, resting purely on their husband's occupation with all its accompanying tensions, made women particularly anxious about their children's future. All wanted their children to achieve a high educational level, which would lead them eventually to secure professional positions. It is the way in which these women developed an environment and a culture conducive to success that I shall discuss. Before doing so, however, I will first summarize some of the research findings on the relationship between culture – that is, family background, attitudes, values, life-style and its symbols – and educational success.

Culture and education

The ties between family and school in Britain are very close: both have responsibility for socializing children. However, the impact of schools on the life chances of children is greatly affected by the children's family background. A Manchester Survey argued convincingly that, ' "home" variables have, *pro rata* nearly twice the weight of "neighbourhood" and "school" variables put together' (Wiseman 1967:369). This survey was undertaken for the Plowden Committee which concluded in its final report that, 'more of the variation in the children's school achievement is specifically accounted for by the variation in parental attitudes than by either the variation in the material circumstances of parents or by the variation in school' (Report of the Central Advisory Council for Education (England) 1967:84).

Yet parental attitudes are a dimension of class differences,

132

as critics of the Wiseman survey were quick to point out (Bernstein and Davies 1962). Sociological literature offers a number of studies providing evidence of the relationship between social class background and educational attainment or failure (Douglas 1964; Jackson and Marsden 1962; Kellmer-Pringle, Butler, and Davis 1966). The crucial significance of the child-rearing process through which values conducive to educational success or failure are transmitted, is also recognized (Klein 1965).

However, the evidence provided on the way in which this process takes place and on the relative weight of 'home' variables in determining academic success, is patchy and inconclusive. Those characteristics that appear to bear the closest relationship to educational attainment are : parents' attitudes and aspirations; language and the quality of verbal communication between parents and children (Bernstein 1961); the development of independence and confidence in children (Lavin 1965); and consistency and routine in children's time-tables (Newson and Newson 1968). All studies stress the significance of the mother–child relationship, but support from the fathers is also seen as influencing a child's success at school.

A report by the National Children's Bureau indicated that a child's attainment in school might be closely related to the interest shown by the fathers as well as mothers in the child's school progress (Lambert and Hart 1976). In middle-class families, where family status depends upon husband's occupation, it has been claimed that the incentive to achieve, particularly in boys, can be far more readily acquired through the father's participation in the socialization process than the mother's (McKinley 1964). The working-class boy, on the other hand, values his education less, as it tends not to be identified with his father's occupation (Bernstein and Davies 1969).

Factors affecting educational success will not only vary within but also between social classes. For social classes encompass a range of different occupations, incomes, and life-styles. A journalist claimed recently that 'achievement motivation', with its accompanying values and life-style, is a more significant index of 'middle-class' status than either occupation or income (Hutber 1976). Yet the struggle to achieve must be more intense within those middle-class families which might be classified as 'borderline', in that they lack such factors as job

133

security, educational qualifications, or substantial investments. For instance, a study of managers in industry and their wives revealed the anxiety of parents who came within this category in relation to their children's future education and occupation (Pahl and Pahl 1973).

There is little available evidence concerning differences within the middle class on the way in which aspirations, values, and norms are transmitted in the family. Bernstein, however, has distinguished two forms of cultural transmission. His main focus is upon the 'new middle class', which he sees as particularly vulnerable to any threat concerning their education. This is because knowledge and skills form a significant part of the 'property' of this group; for 'although property in the physical sense remains crucial, it has been partly psychologised and appears in the form of valued skills' (Bernstein 1975:103).

I have summarized this evidence in some detail, in order to emphasize the strength of the relationship between culture and education. Within the middle class the whole of the child-rearing process is significant in encouraging children to succeed, as is the participation of both parents within that process.

The threat to privilege

Families living on the housing estate belonged to a vulnerable section of the middle class in that they lacked substantial property assets, job security, and also many lacked educational qualifications. Women were entirely dependent upon their husbands for status and support. Both parents, therefore, felt it essential that their children should succeed in schools as the first step towards a secure career. Yet this ideal was threatened by the husbands' frequent absences from home. For it is not only social scientists who recognize the significance of both parents in encouraging educational success; the estate wives felt instinctively that their husbands' participation in child-rearing was necessary.

A further threat to the educational future of the children arose from the position of the housing estate itself. It was a middle-class enclave within a predominantly working-class district. The formal education system of the district, when the estate was first built, was poor. The area was served by a very inadequate secondary school, with only a limited number of

134

selected places available for children (on the basis of tests) in the grammar schools of a nearby town. In addition, families felt that interaction between their children and others from the surrounding district might jeopardize the advantages – of life-style, speech, behaviour, and attitude to school – which they were able to give their children. In relation to such problems a common culture developed among the estate women.

The response: co-operation between neighbours

Socialization in industrial societies involves privatized relationships between parents and children. The significant feature in this case was that the wives responded to 'the threat to privilege' collectively. The situation and design of the housing estate helped, for it meant that a number of women sharing a similar problem were living in close proximity. Their collective response contrasted with the popular conception of housing estates, portrayed in the literature as being populated by isolated women, 'unwilling to be identified with any group or to enter into relationships which might impose reciprocal obligations' (Frankenberg 1976:45).

Most women with young children on this housing estate (that is the majority of families) subordinated their own interests to those of their husbands and children. The demands of husbands' careers were accepted as a necessary evil and women turned to neighbours, who were in a similar situation, for help with domestic duties, which (given different circumstances) they might have expected their husbands to provide.

The first contacts between wives were on the practical basis of exchanging equipment and services. They helped each other with the initial 'settling in' problems and borrowed kitchen, gardening, and home decorating equipment. They exchanged expertise – from advice on sewing children's clothes, to first aid assistance from mothers previously employed as professional nurses. Most important of all, as families with young children, they exchanged services: mothers took turns in entertaining a group of children for a morning or afternoon, or in ferrying children to and from school. They installed baby-sitting alarms along a row of houses and alternated the evening's guard on neighbours' sleeping children. This degree of co-operation has previously only been noted in working-class districts among female kin (Young and Willmott 1957).

Solidarity and culture

The distinctive feature of these co-operating activities was that they generated support among the women. Through this solidarity a distinct culture developed which provided a resource for women lacking support from husbands. This did not usurp the husband's role within the family, or force wives to consider their own status separately from that of their husbands. In short, solidarity was seen as substituting for the husband's involvement with wife and children, given the fact that his career demands made it impossible – at least temporarily – for him to share such tasks.

Solidarity between women went beyond offering each other support with practical tasks, and led to the development of a specific 'estate style'. Not only did it give the estate a separate identity from the area surrounding it, but it also distinguished it from other middle-class communities.

The design of the estate was not very different from that of neighbouring council estates. Houses were built in terraced rows, density was high, and most of the open space available was communal. Most estate women were acutely aware of the narrow dividing line between their own and the adjoining estates and put considerable effort into maintaining 'standards' in their immediate area. Elaborate covenants were written into the leases of the houses, laying down certain standards of behaviour. Publicly, these covenants were often treated as jokes. The rule that stipulated that all washing should be taken down by mid-day Saturday for the weekend, was a standard target for jocular comments at many dinner parties. Yet in practice residents conformed to the standards set by the covenant and it was the women who kept vigil over them. When one non-conformist resident painted his house yellow instead of the standard white, the builder's agent received, within hours, six complaining telephone calls, all from women. It was also the responsibility of women to control their children so that the beauty of the foot-paths and communal gardens was not impaired. Women rationalized their attitudes in terms of the density of population: the rules were necessary, they claimed, in such a highly populated neighbourhood.

Certainly one consequence of these rules was that they emphasized the borders between this estate and the local authority estates. They also offered estate women an excuse for excluding non-estate children. For women, who were primarily responsible for the appearance of the estate, could only be expected to control their own children. Children from outside the estate presented a potential threat to estate property, and had to be excluded. In this way the women were able to protect not only their own property but also their own children, from outside contact.

Other aspects of the common culture of the estate – the women's dress, their behaviour, their attitudes and values – clearly set them apart from their neighbours. Many women said that their attitudes and even their behaviour had changed since moving to the estate. The change in fashion tastes, for instance, was particularly easy to identify. When the mini-skirt first received publicity many middle-class women greeted its arrival with some hostility. Later it was cautiously approved, by the standard womens' journals, as appropriate for teenage girls but not for women in their late twenties and early thirties. It was at this stage that the majority of women on the housing estate were wearing the new fashion with confidence. All women admitted receiving support in establishing both this and other fashion trends, from friends and neighbours on the estate. Many said that they would hesitate to wear similar clothes when visiting their own extended families. Similar norms were developed in other areas of domestic life. Even when walking past the uncurtained plate-glass windows, the common trends in furniture and interior design were evident. The development of such norms emphasized the distinctive identity of the housing estate.

My reason for describing some of the forms manifested by this estate culture is not that such a style is original or noteworthy in itself. It is only to illustrate the fact that these women developed and sustained particular cultural forms, which had the effect of clearly marking the boundaries between themselves and outsiders. In this way they were able to offer their children a protected middle-class environment. In addition these cultural forms were symbols of the solidarity between the women, which was to assist them with their fundamental problems of protecting the interests of their children.

Most women who participated in the estate culture had few contacts outside the estate. Many claimed that their network of contacts had narrowed since moving there, they had increasingly less time available for maintaining ties with friends or relatives from elsewhere. Daily routine involving shopping on the estate, collecting children from school, or attending the clinic meant that most wives were constantly meeting neighbours. Casual contacts were strengthened by the informal gatherings organized between the women themselves, such as coffee mornings, tea sessions, or sales parties of clothes, wigs, 'Tupperware', or make-up.

Dinner parties when husbands were home, lent further support to communication. At any such social gathering attended by both husband and wife, it was evident that husbands did not share or even fit into the estate culture. Communication between men was often spasmodic and superficial. Their attitudes were not based on shared experiences or interests, for men identified with the world of work – with their profession or their company. Their job consumed most of their time, and the estate culture was mediated to them by their wives.

Solidarity did not develop among all estate women, only among the majority who shared the common problem of raising children without support from husbands. Yet even among this group, there were differences – primarily of status, educational background, and attitudes – which had to be overcome. Despite the fact that the price range of the houses meant that the majority of house holders were likely to be middle class, the men's jobs varied considerably. Such differences were often accompanied by specific and conflicting family life-styles which, to some extent, were played down through an under-emphasis of the husband's actual job. One taxi-driver's wife reported that her husband had been convinced that when their professional neighbours discovered the nature of his work, they would be isolated. In fact it had been weeks before anyone had asked about her husband's job.

The wives' varied educational backgrounds did not hinder the development of solidarity. They all saw their domestic roles, particularly the upbringing of children, as their most important function. In addition, whatever the level of their own schooling, all the wives feverishly sought higher education for their children.

Culture and child-rearing

The formal schooling situation in the district changed mainly in response to pressure from estate families. A primary school was built on the estate itself and some time later a middle school was set up, recruiting mostly children from the estate school. The position in relation to secondary schooling, however, remained acute. Although the majority of children on the estate were under secondary school age, and although many of the families were likely to have moved before their children had reached that age, parents remained anxious. As they were very aware that the influence of the home is as important as that of the school, they tried to ensure that their life-style was one that would be conducive to academic success. The distinct estate life-style that developed was embedded in the culture that grew from the solidarity between the estate women. I shall now attempt to demonstrate the relationship between that culture and the grooming of children for success.

First, I would like to emphasize the importance of children on this housing estate, for the estate was clearly a child-centred community. Only 25 per cent of families were without children and they were hardly in evidence because their contacts and interests lay outside the estate. The very design of the estate was geared to the needs of children – central greens, traffic free roads, open spaces – where play could be observed by watchful mothers. Yet design in itself would not have been an adequate inducement for mothers to encourage interaction between children.

Children's play in most middle-class families is directly controlled and supervised by mothers, and takes place within the privacy of their own gardens (Newson and Newson 1968). This contrasts with the accepted mode of working-class mothers who allow their children to play, undisturbed by adults, in the street or other communal areas (Newson and Newson 1970:138). On the housing estate the solidarity and culture that women had developed meant that they did not mistrust the influence that other children in the neighbourhood might have upon their own. Children, therefore, played together in the protective environment of the estate and mothers were not driven to search outside for playmates for their children. This, in turn, had a reverberative effect upon the solidarity of women, for contacts between children increased the likelihood of contacts between mothers.

The common estate culture also included child-rearing patterns. The wisdom, which in other situations might be acquired from older kin or professionals, was gleaned from the collective knowledge and influence of the group. Its effect in standardizing attitudes to breast feeding, bedtimes, the establishment of routine, or the control of aggression was evident (Cohen 1977). When children were small, for instance, mothers tended to synchronize their rest periods. In this way arrangements could be made for children to play together at other times. At a later stage, similar adjustments were made over their bedtimes.

This need for assistance and support in child-rearing was felt just as keenly by those with children of school age as it was by mothers of younger children, for these mothers really faced the problem of encouraging their children to achieve in schools. Concern with children's educational standards did not manifest itself through the formation of any formal women's organization. However, it was very evident in any discussion between women on the estate and in the way they brought up their children. Mothers, for instance, encouraged high standards in children's task performances, and set a high evaluation on successful results. They were also demanding and encouraging in training children to be independent and self reliant. Even play at home was related to task performance and achievement. At a later stage mothers supplemented the formal training of the schools, by teaching children to read, or setting them exercises as a supplement to normal homework.

On the housing estate communication between women meant that these informal training techniques did not remain the property of individual mothers. The knowledge and experience of individuals was shared with the group. Property as well as knowledge was exchanged; for instance, educational toys frequently exchanged hands. The common pattern, whereby children spent time in households other than their own, also proved invaluable in diversifying the children's experiences

140

and in taking advantage of the different skills that mothers had to offer. Within some homes children would be allowed to indulge their creative instincts with clay or paint, whereas in others they might sew dolls' clothes, read or write, or get involved in more energetic outdoor activities. This estate training complemented the local nursery school education, which most children received for a few hours each day.

For older children, too, the estate culture provided an important supplement to their formal schooling. Its greatest significance lay in the opportunity it gave women to develop strategies conducive to their children's achievement. Through exchange of information women reached agreement on the respective value for their children of television programmes, books, cultural classes, and other outside school activities. This was then translated into a plan of action within the individual homes.

In any house, tea-time or coffee-time discussion between women could be relied upon to focus upon children, their achievements, talents, and the ways in which these might be fostered. Always discussed, too, were the teaching methods employed in the respective schools, the quality of the teachers, and the future possibilities for their children's education in that area. All this, despite the fact that many of the children involved were well under secondary school age. Most decisions in these areas – even in relation to the choice of school – were taken by the women, often acting on the advice of the group.

There were occasions, too, when schooling problems called for direct action by mothers against the school system. Again solidarity between women provided them with support for such action. For example, a letter from the Director of Education for the area stated that the estate school had the capacity to accept only the first child of families living on the north side of the estate. Subsequent children in these families would have to attend a school in a neighbouring area. Mothers of the first two children affected by this policy stood daily at the estate school doors for a whole month, demanding that the head teacher should accept the children. These mothers received support from other women who accompanied them to the school and finally the policy was reversed by the Director of Education.

As previously stated, the common norms developed between women were conveyed from wives to husbands. Most men, therefore, were made aware of activities on the estate and of the decisions reached jointly by their wives. However, it was essentially a women's culture and men were peripheral to it. Through bringing in their husbands in this nominal fashion, women were able to retain their ideal of shared role relationships. They were also able to put pressure on their husbands when they were home to participate in activities involving children.

The concern that women evidently felt about their children's educational future was given public expression through a campaign conducted by the husbands for better schooling on the estate. Through the Residents' Association pressure was put upon the local education authority to agree to set up a primary school on the estate itself. Later similar pressure led to the establishment of a middle school in the area. This secured a protected education for estate children and meant that they were not forced to mix within the schools with children from the neighbouring working-class district. It is interesting that the committee members of the Residents' Association were mainly men, although all claimed that the pressure for the drive for better schooling had come from their wives.[1]

Women on the estate used the culture created by their solidarity to bolster up their own notions of 'correct' family role relationships. In practice, it was obviously difficult to achieve any kind of real partnership. The culture created by women only supplemented the husband-wife domestic relationship and the father-mother child-care relationship. It certainly did not provide any substitute group, through which women might achieve status in their own right. It assisted them with their most crucial problem – that of achieving conditions conducive to educational success for their children. Through the estate culture, they minimized their own internal differences but accentuated the differences between themselves and women from other social classes outside the estate itself.

The second case concerns the way in which solidarity developed among Creole women in Freetown, Sierra Leone. A major problem for this group (as for women on the British housing estate) was how to attain for their children the privileges which they themselves enjoyed. Similar to the British situation, the only certain way of achieving this goal was through educational attainment. Again non-educational variables, which are embedded in the process of socialization, had as great an effect on attainment in Freetown as in Britain. With this group, too, the responsibility for socialization lay with the women.

The Creoles are the descendants of freed slaves who settled in the Freetown peninsula during the late eighteenth and early nineteenth centuries. The Freetown peninsula corresponds, roughly, to that part of Sierra Leone known until recently as the Colony, distinguishing it from the rest of the country called the Protectorate. The Colony came under the direct rule of the British Crown in 1807, whereas the Protectorate was not established until 1896. The Creole inhabitants of the colony prospered in trade and adopted the life-style of their European rulers to such an extent that they earned for themselves the now despised title of 'Black Englishmen'. They became Christians and eagerly took advantage of education as an important avenue to high status occupations.

The privileges enjoyed by the Creoles were severely threatened when the British, instead of handing over political power to them, introduced legislative reform, which eventually led to the transfer of State power into non-Creole hands. Yet political control derived not only from formal control of the legislature, but also from control of the senior positions in the Civil Service and the judicial system, where Creoles had considerable influence. Despite predictions to the contrary, Creoles remained the most influential ethnic group in the country. In the face of a popular anti-Creole campaign, reversal of the process of Creole assimilation of members from other ethnic groups, and an emphasis on detribalization particularly by Creoles themselves, they have nevertheless preserved their ethnicity (Banton 1957; Porter 1963).

Their status, however, was vulnerable, for it rested not on

143

the strength of numbers or hereditary privilege but upon academic merit. Just as the legislature had to open its doors to all ethnic groups in Sierra Leone, so did the schools. Creole children had to compete with children from sixteen other ethnic groups, all of whom appreciated the significance of education in the struggle for high social status. Despite this threat, Creoles maintained their leadership, for Creole culture itself provided resources that contributed to their academic careers.

Relations between the sexes

Creole culture, based on family, school, and church, distinguished the Creoles from the rest of the population. The Creole 'style' was unmistakable in their speech, their dress, their 'comportment', and their values. As Creole writers have pointed out, their culture was now an entity in itself (Jones 1968). However it is equally clear that this style was firmly based upon 'western' values, and these were instrumental in enabling the Creoles to maintain positions of privilege. Creole professional life-styles epitomized the 'western' family style to which most ambitious young Sierra Leonians aspired (Harrell-Bond 1975).

Yet in private, the Creole family did not correspond with the 'western' style of 'symmetrical' social and marital relationships. Marriage was not a partnership and wives could not rely on their husband's support. On the contrary, role relationships within the family were segregated and there was evidence of considerable mistrust between the sexes. Discontented young wives complained that their expectations of shared activities within marriage did not materialize.

Segregation between the sexes fostered and magnified the hostility between men and women. As far as wives were concerned this hostility was based on the discrepancy between expectations of 'western' standards within marriage and reality. For although Creoles were Christian and therefore monogamous, in practice most men had 'outside' families (Harrell-Bond 1975). Not only did this impose a great strain on the legal family, as resources had to be extended to cover the needs of all children, natural and legal, but it also threatened the inheritance rights of legitimate children. Distrust of men was

144

not confined to legal wives, and outside wives could rely even less on support from men.

This hostility between the sexes was an important factor in modifying the tension between legal and outside wives, for women responded to this lack of male support by developing co-operative relationships among themselves, and where possible, by reducing their own financial dependence on men. The majority of Creole women were employed in the labour market, and the money that they earned they kept for themselves. Although some spent this money on luxuries, the majority put most of it aside as security for themselves and their children. Women were even reluctant to invest their money in the 'family house', the most common form of property investment in Freetown and described by Fyfe as 'Freetown's gilt-edged security' (Fyfe 1962:471). There had been too many cases of wives losing all rights in the 'family house' on the death of the husband, despite any financial contribution they might have made towards it.

Creole women were faced with two contradictory problems. On the one hand they needed to maintain a Creole culture, because it offered advantages both for their children and for themselves (note, no other ethnic group in Sierra Leone had so effectively sponsored education for girls). The Creole culture was in turn based on a popular conception of 'western' values and practices. On the other hand, the insecurity experienced by women, both within and outside legal marriage meant that in practice they could not maintain this western notion of 'partnership' between the sexes. Women were forced into competition with men for money and status, which threatened the public image of harmony between husband and wife.

Solidarity between women helped them with both these problems. First, it helped them to preserve a Creole culture and so retain their 'western' image. Second, solidarity offered resources to Creole women in their struggle for occupational success. However, before demonstrating the process through which this was achieved, the relationship between Creole culture and educational success in Freetown must be examined.

Culture and educational success in Freetown

In Sierra Leone, most schools are concentrated in Freetown.

Thus Creole children, most of whom lived in Freetown, had an immediate advantage by virtue of residence. However, there were other more subtle ways through which Creole children gained advantage over others in schools. Hidden 'selectors' as Banks (1968) has called them, affect academic achievement, and were transmitted by both the family and church.

The church's history in Freetown was closely linked with that of the schools. Even non-mission schools were Christian and for Creole children the religious climate of the school presented no conflict with their home background.

One of the most important 'home' variables affecting academic success was language. In Freetown, children learnt through the medium of a foreign language: English. However, it was a language with which Creole children were familiar and nearly every Creole could communicate in English.

Other important variables were discipline and training for independence, both imposed by the school and by the Creole family. There was considerable emphasis upon control and routine in childrens' lives. Professionals as well as non-professionals encouraged their children to perform household tasks and the latter had regular meal times and bed-times.

The Creole kinship network also linked Creole families with the schools; and Creole children often had kinship ties with their teachers. Although this placed great pressure on Creole children, it also meant that there was no conflict of values between the home and the school. On the contrary, the Creole family supported and strengthened the schools in the task of grooming children for educational success.

Women and the development of Creole culture

Creole culture, therefore, is the variable that significantly affected the academic attainment of Creole children, for more Creole than non-Creole children gained access to 'status' schools. From a sample survey of children at six 'status' schools, two-thirds were Creole. University entrants were certainly most likely to be recruited from these 'status' schools. I shall now discuss the influence of solidarity between women on preserving a Creole culture. Family, school and church were inextricably linked with Creole culture, but for analytical purposes I shall discuss them separately.

Kinship The basis for co-operation between women in many societies, is kinship. Among Creole women, links with kin were maintained between both rich and poor. Busy professional women assiduously maintained ties with mothers, sisters, aunts, and cousins. The obligations that this imposed upon them were heavy; maintaining contacts took time, energy, and also money. For the wealthier Creoles had constantly to meet requests for financial help from poorer relatives for christenings, or weddings, or to foster their children during their school days.

Creole family life was punctuated by intensive rituals and ceremonials which achieved three major functions. First, they strengthened the links between all Creoles. In a country like Sierra Leone, such links are invaluable in developing a network of relationships through which support can be mobilized (Cohen 1974). Second, they emphasized the distinctiveness of Creole culture, and underlined the boundary between Creoles and others. Finally, they necessitated co-operation between women who organized and controlled them.

These rituals marked key family events such as births, deaths, or marriages. They were lavish and involved considerable organization, which depended upon the industry and co-operation of the women. A wedding, for instance, might be accompanied by ten or more parties. The greater the number of parties, the greater the prestige of the wedding. 'Big' women in Freetown were invited by many brides or grooms to act as sponsors and this usually entailed throwing a party. Such 'big' women mobilized the support of a number of their friends and relatives in organizing the party.

There were a number of tasks involved in this enterprise and for some weeks prior to the wedding many women gathered in the house of the sponsor and worked together, sewing clothes and so forth. The wedding dress itself was but a small part of the sewing enterprise which each wedding involved. Most of the work went into producing the *ashobi*. This is a term – Yoruba in origin – given to a uniform dress which will be worn by a number of women at the same time. Sometimes as many as forty women guests at the same party could be seen wearing a garment, identical in style and material. This was a visual expression of solidarity between a group of women.

147

Another essential task was the preparation of food. This was also a co-operative effort. On the day of the wedding the respective houses of the hostesses echoed with the noise and activity of a number of women engaged in this common task. In addition, female guests rarely arrived empty handed at the party. Each carried with her either a bottle of gin, whisky, or brandy, or a bowl of food. Without this army of female support a busy hostess, with many other demands on her time, could not have coped with the enormous task involved.

Not only was the organization of the wedding party female-dominated but a stranger arriving on time might be forgiven for assuming that the party itself was designed by females for females. For female guests arrived one or two hours in advance of men. They sat around the room drinking and talking in pairs or in groups. Some danced together, being joined occasionally by young boys or old men. Late in the evening the men would arrive together having come directly from 'the lodge'. The 'lodge' was one of a number of masonic lodges in Freetown, and nearly all members of these masonic lodges were Creoles (Cohen 1971). Their arrival was accompanied by much commotion and by loud and cheerful greetings from the women.

Yet even after the men had arrived, the sexes tended to remain separate. The women continued to gossip and dance downstairs, while the men sat upstairs. It was at a later stage in the party, after much alcohol had been consumed, that men and women got together to talk or dance. These wedding parties were only one example of the ceremonials surrounding the family. There were many others which involved close friends as well as kin. All these occasions had the common features of drinking, dancing, and eating together. All included both sexes although a degree of segregation was evident between them. However, it was always the women who designed, organized, and controlled the form and content of these ceremonials. They decided who to include and who to exclude and, in this way, determined the boundaries of the kinship and friendship network.

School Similar ceremonials were associated with church and school, and these too were controlled by women. Each of the status schools had a number of associations attached to it and each was likely to hold its own ceremonials, such as 'old girls' dances or meetings, some of which were the chief social events of the year in Freetown. There was also a considerable overlap in membership. Members of one association might be serving on another, or teaching in a different school or, again, serving on the Board of Governors of yet another school. The associations brought educated women together and through their co-operation educational assistance was often given, through scholarships, to girls from less wealthy homes.

The 'big' women involved in the drive to promote vocational training for less academic girls were all members of the associations attached to the main 'status' girls' school. While I was in Freetown their efforts reached fruition and a new, modern YWCA school for girls was opened. I must emphasize, however, that although these formal associations did further the opportunities of females from all social classes, it was mainly Creoles who were likely to benefit. This was due to the Christian basis of the schools and the lack of competition from non-Creole girls.

The significance of solidarity between women for women's education, could be seen at each educational level. Formal women's associations were waging a campaign for nursery schools. At the other end of the scale the influence of the female Creole network was evident at University level. Many of the female students at Fourah Bay College, for instance, were recruited from the main 'status' girls' school and it was no mere accident that the majority of members of the most exclusive sorority were also past students of this school. This sorority too had its own ceremonials. It set standards for its members and honoured well known past members, who were usually women who held important professional posts in Freetown. These often gave assistance to sorority members when their time came to search for jobs.

Church Like the schools, each church had a multiplicity of associations linked to it. Again, the most important of these were sustained by women. Each association had its own ceremonials and its own uniform and many were involved in fund-raising activities to support the church. Less formal church associations, such as the mothers' union or the Young Wives' Association, helped develop solidarity between Creoles of

149

different social classes, for these church associations had branches in town and village and attracted membership from the professions as well as from market gardeners or traders. Certainly it was the rich and eminent women who held office, similar to those ladies of Madras who were the leading lights in womens' organizations in India (Caplan Chapter 4). Unlike the Madras situation, however, the poor were not excluded from membership. Yet the Christian basis of these organizations ensured that it was mainly Creoles who were members – again marking a boundary between Creole and non-Creole women.

Shared membership of women's organizations enabled poorer Creoles to maintain kinship and friendship links across social class lines. These links were important for giving poorer Creoles a style of life which shared many of the features of the life-style of Creole professionals. They were also important for the education of children from poorer Creole families.

The practice of 'traditional fostering' – whereby children moved between households within the Creole 'big' family – was a common phenomenon. It provided the means whereby children could be fostered for educational reasons. Children from relatively poor families in the villages frequently spent the duration of their secondary schooling within the households of wealthier relatives in Freetown. This type of fostering served to break down the barriers of social class and to allow the less privileged Creoles to compete within the school system.

I began this section by pointing out the cost to women of their high level of participation in both the informal organizations of the family and the formal organizations attached to church and school. For these women were not the leisured middle-class women of India who joined clubs in order to gain friendship. Most Creole women were employed outside the home, and the fact that they put time and effort into participating in these organizations must inevitably raise the question: what was it all for?

First and foremost it helped women solve their major problem: assisting their children to attain educational advantages. Through women's co-operation around these three areas – family, school, and church – they helped to develop and sustain a Creole culture, which in turn supported Creole children in the struggle for academic success. Women's groups entailed continuous contact and exchange of services and nearly all Creole women were thereby enmeshed in a highly complex network of obligations which encompassed both rich and poor. It was on the basis of these obligations and through such continuous interaction that Creole culture was strengthened and sustained (Cohen 1974). Through the culture, a separate Creole identity with all its attendant privileges was maintained.

Solidarity and sex roles

Female solidarity helped Creole women cope with their second problem – that of competing with men for money and status, while at the same time retaining their Creole image based on accepted western values of family role relationships. Thus co-operation developed between women in sustaining the ceremonials and group organizations associated with family, school, and church, and also supported Creole women in their struggle for independence from Creole men.

For Creole women their ideal type of woman was a 'strong' woman, who could hold her own in competition with a man and who had achieved financial independence through her occupational role. Women's own educational qualifications offered them the opportunity of competing in the labour market denied to the British housewives on the housing estate. Furthermore, the demands made on them as mothers did not hinder them from taking up employment, again in contrast with their British counterparts. The Creole network itself offered a supply of related and non-related child minders. As security against the possibility of a diminishing supply of such caretakers in the future, womens' organizations were giving their full support to the drive for establishing formal day-care for children under five.

Again solidarity between women often provided them with contacts through which jobs might be obtained. Poorer Creoles used the links afforded them by kinship and religious organizations in their search for jobs. Even the highly educated university and school leavers were helped by influential members of womens' educational organizations. This solidarity between women developed despite the fact that some women were individually hostile to other women as 'outside' and

151

'legal' wives. All suffered from a sense of insecurity and this united them in their determination to achieve financial independence.

Despite this competition and hostility between women and men, the public Creole image was maintained. Women, as I have shown, were primarily responsible for maintaining this image and were clearly anxious to preserve it in any preliminary discussions with strangers. They were reluctant to confess to having anything other than companionable relations with their husbands. 'Outside' children were most often presented to the stranger as distant relatives. Formal public occasions were attended by husbands and legal wives together. The virtues of monogamy were loudly and publicly proclaimed from every pulpit and young men solemnly warned against adultery at every marriage ceremony.

Men were as anxious to comply with this public image as were the women. Obviously they also gained through the preservation of a Creole culture. Indeed segregated associations offered men too the opportunity for developing solidarity. Cohen (1971; 1974) has given a detailed account of the role played by Freemasonic groups in the development of male solidarity.

Yet on the whole women had far more to gain through maintaining the boundary between the Creoles and other groups. Their Creole culture offered them advantages in education and in the labour market, which affected the degree of authority they held within their own households. For Creole women, unlike their counterparts from other ethnic groups, the household was their own private domain which they were not forced to share with other wives or with their husband's kin. Creole women, therefore, were the pillars of Creole culture, for their own status and that of their children depended upon its maintenance.

Conclusion

In both the cases described, solidarity among groups of women was developed in the course of their struggle to socialize their children in accordance with the values and norms of their class. Such socialization formed an integral part of the educational process of the children in ensuring their academic success and eventually their recruitment to the professions. The women were in this way ultimately concerned with the social reproduction of class relationships.

The culture of the housing estate distinguished and protected if from neighbouring areas. Its main characteristics were conducive to the children's educational development and offered support for parents' aspirations for them. This culture grew from the solidarity between the women, which compensated for the particular vulnerability of individual families on the estate.

Creole culture was also sustained by women through their co-operation in intensive activities associated with family, school and church. It was a culture synonymous with western Christian 'civilized' values, which offered Creole children distinct advantages within the school system.

Solidarity developed among women in both groups despite the fact that it contradicted the ideology concerning the respective roles of men and women in middle-class families. Within both groups women on marriage had expectations of a partnership with their husbands and of a degree of conjugal solidarity which in practice was never realized. The careers of the British husbands kept them away from home, while traditional norms affecting sex-related activities separated Creole men from their wives. Yet at the same time, it was this segregation between the sexes that made it possible for solidarity to develop and flourish in both situations, although such segregation was incompatible with the accepted ideal of partnership between husbands and wives.

Both cases of female solidarity had varying consequences upon the status of the women themselves and upon the relationships between husbands and wives in the two situations. Solidarity among British women achieved its primary aim: to assist the women concerned in their task of social reproduction. It also provided women with companionship in the absence of their husbands. It did nothing, however, to raise the status of the women concerned. None of the women made use of this solidarity – as they might have done – to undertake paid employment, or further training, which would have led them to achieve an independent status for themselves. On the contrary solidarity actually supported the ideals of husband-wife role relationships within these families. It helped to support but not to supplant husbands' roles within the family. Among Creole women, however, solidarity did help them to achieve a status of their own in providing them – through child-care services – with the opportunity for access to an independent source of income. It was solidarity among the women which sustained a Creole culture, which in itself gave Creole women educational advantages in relation to women from other ethnic groups. An independent source of income was necessary for Creole women given that they could not rely on economic support from Creole men.

Solidarity in both these cases developed between a relatively small number of women and was a response to their social class position rather than to their position as women. It had little effect, therefore, on the wider power relations between the sexes in either society. Indeed the preservation of privilege in each case depended upon the women's ability to maintain clear boundaries between themselves and others. This effectively inhibited the development of a feminist consciousness.

Note

1 Although the pressure for better schooling initially came from the wives, men's public involvement in the struggle through the residential associations was in keeping with the traditional ideology governing relationships within the family, according to which men are seen as the main link between the family and the outside world. As stated on page 136, solidarity between women supports the ideal notions of husband–wife role relationships within middle-class families.

References

BANKS, O. (1968) The Sociology of Education. London: Batsford.
BANTON, M. (1957) West African City. London: Oxford University Press.
BERNSTEIN, B. (1961) Social Class and Linguistic Development: a theory of social learning. In A. H. Halsey, J. Floud, and C. A. Anderson (eds.), Education, Economy and Society. Glencoe, Ill.: Free Press.
—— (1965) A Socio-linguistic approach to social learning. In J. Gould (ed.), Penguin Survey of the Social Sciences. Harmondsworth: Penguin Books.
—— (1975) Class Codes and Control. (Vol. 3) London: Routledge & Kegan Paul.
BERNSTEIN, B. and DAVIES, B. (1969) Some Sociological Com-

ments on Plowden. In R. S. Peters (ed.), *Perspectives on Plowden*. London: Routledge & Kegan Paul.

COHEN, A. (1971) The Politics of Ritual Secrecy. *Man* 6(3):427–48.

—— (1974) *Two Dimensional Man*. London: Routledge & Kegan Paul.

COHEN, G. (1977) Absentee Husbands In Spiralist Families. *Journal of Marriage and the Family* 39:595–604.

DOUGLAS, J. W. B. (1964) *The Home and the School*. London: MacGibbon & Kee.

FRANKENBERG, R. (1966) *Communities in Britain*. Harmondsworth: Penguin Books.

—— (1976) In the Production of their Lives, Men (?) ... Sex and Gender in British Community Studies. In D. L. Barker and M. S. Allen (eds.), *Sexual Divisions and Society: Process and Change*. London: Tavistock.

FYFE, C. (1962) *The History of Sierra Leone*. London: Oxford University Press.

HARRELL-BOND, B. (1975) *Modern Marriage in Sierra Leone*. The Hague: Mouton.

HUTBER, P. (1976) *The Decline and Fall of the Middle Class and how it Can Fight Back*. Harmondsworth: Penguin Books.

JACKSON, B. and MARSDEN, D. (1962) *Education and the Working Class*. Harmondsworth: Penguin Books.

JONES, E. (1968) Freetown, the Contemporary Cultural Scene. In C. Fyfe and E. Jones (eds.), *Freetown: A Symposium*. London: Oxford University Press.

KELLMER-PRINGLE, M., BUTLER, N., and DAVIS, R. (1966) *11,000 Seven Year Olds*. London: Longman.

KLEIN, J. (1965) *Samples from English Cultures* vols I & 2. London: Routledge & Kegan Paul.

LADNER, J. (1971) *Tomorrow's Tomorrow: The Black Woman*. New York: Garden City.

LAMBERT, S. and HART, N. (1976) Who Needs a Father? *New Society* July 8.

LAVIN, D. E. (1965) *The Prediction of Academic Performance*. New York: Wiley.

MCKINLEY, D. G. (1964) *Social Class and Family Life*. Glencoe, Ill.: Free Press.

NEWSON, J. and NEWSON, E. (1968) *Patterns of Infant Care*. Harmondsworth: Penguin Books.

—— —— (1970) *Four Years Old in an Urban Community*. Harmondsworth: Penguin Books.

PAHL, R. and PAHL, J. (1973) *Managers and their Wives*. London: Allen Lane.

PORTER, A. (1963) *Creoledom: The Study of the Development of Freetown Society*. London: Oxford University Press.

RAPOPORT, R. and RAPOPORT, R. (1971) *Fathers, Mothers and Others*. London: Routledge & Kegan Paul.

REPORT OF THE CENTRAL ADVISORY COUNCIL FOR EDUCATION (ENGLAND) (1967) *Children and their Primary Schools (Plowden Report)*. London: HMSO.

WILLMOTT, P. and YOUNG, M. (1973) *The Symmetrical Family*. London: Routledge & Kegan Paul.

WISEMAN, S. M. (1967) The Manchester Survey. In *Children and their Primary Schools (Plowden Report)*. Report of the Central Advisory Council for Education (England). London: HMSO.

YOUNG, M. and WILLMOTT, P. (1957) *Family and Kinship in East London*. London: Routledge & Kegan Paul.

SIX

Women and their kin: kin, class, and solidarity in a middle-class suburb of Sydney, Australia

MAILA STIVENS

This article reports some of the main findings of a study focus-ing on kin relations in an Australian city. In general, I discuss some of the theoretical issues raised by the consideration of kin relations in capitalist societies like Australia. Specifically, I am concerned with the prevalence of kin structures in which women occupy a focal position and relate the theoretical problems to material collected among mainly middle-class households in a suburb of Sydney.[1] I argue that kin relations in Australia are the site of a number of contradictions. One of the most significant of these is that while they are implicated in many of the conditions of women's subordination, kin ties are also the locus of a solidarity among female kin that can transcend women's structural isolation.

The frequent tendency for bilaterial kinship structures in capitalist societies to be focused on women both as mothers (as in the so-called 'matrifocal' family) and more generally on women *qua* women, has been amply demonstrated in an ever-growing body of material.[2] Little work has been carried out in Australia in this field, but the findings of my study were in line with other research overseas. My informants viewed women as the focus of kin relations; women saw their kin more often than men, helped each other and expressed feelings of solidarity with other female kin more often. However, questions relating to the nature, basis, and scope of these frequently strong ties among female kin pose some fairly difficult problems. What is kinship in such a situation and why do such feelings of solidarity exist among women and their kin?

The first problem – the specification of the nature of kinship – has a long anthropological history (Needham 1971). The reification of kinship that tends to pervade even the most elegant and precise studies of kin relations in pre-capitalist societies is most marked in studies of kinship in capitalist societies. Kin relations in the latter are usually seen as somehow more 'pure' than in those situations where they are clearly embedded within economic and political structures.[3] This notion of 'purity', as well as reifying kin relations, implies a reduction to the affective content of kinship relations. These basically atheoretical expressive or interactionalist approaches are quite unhelpful.

To conceptualize kin relations in capitalist society it is necessary to distinguish several distinct aspects of such relations. The 'family' and 'kinship' are not undifferentiated concepts but must be broken down into the structures composing them. In the case of kin relations it is possible to pose the key structures: procreation; production; socialization; and sexuality. These separate structures in a concrete combination produce the 'complex unity', that is, kin relations (Mitchell 1971). These structures may be unevenly developed – their specific combination at one point in time marks the 'institution' at that period. I see the elementary family in Australia as an aspect of wider kin relations, in which the particular combination of the separate developments of the structures differentiates it from wider kin relations. For example, the elementary family is still (in spite of educational developments) the primary socializer. Yet some significant socialization also occurs in wider kin circles. The complex unity of structures constituting kin relations is involved both in economic reproduction within the elementary family and wider kin circles (that is, domestic labour), reproducing labour power, and class structures, and in the reproduction of ideology.[4]

It is clear that kin relations, at least within the extended family, retain some importance within Australian society.[5] The view that kin ties have very little importance in 'industrial' society arose from a lengthy flirtation with the Parsonian thesis concerning the increasing isolation of the elementary family in such societies. Much of the mainly empirical work designed to show the continuing importance of kin ties has been superficial and atheoretical, overtly pre-occupied with measures of frequency of contact, residential proximity, geographical mobility, and the positive function of kin relations, while ignoring the contradictions inherent in such structures.[6]

It was probably no accident that the atheoretical normative approach to kin studies in capitalist society was allied to a sanguine view of the 'family', to the ideology that the 'family' formed the building block of society, the fount of morality, and social solidarity. Although disputes were acknowledged, there was little recognition of the contradictions within the elementary family, of the possible tragic depths of conflict and violence mirrored in literature and the psychoanalytic tradition. While popular culture debated the 'death of the family' and kin ties, many sociologists refuted this, meticulously constructing kin networks and charts of kin exchanges. The possibility that kin relations in capitalist society could be theorized only in relation to women's situation was completely missed, even though the consistent finding about women-centred kin structures should have alerted some to that possibility. It is possible to argue, indeed, within a marxist framework, that kin relations form a separate 'mode of reproduction' that necessarily locates women in privatized domestic units performing domestic labour and socializing children (Harrison 1973).

Sociologists have tended to make much of supposed class differences between the female-centred kin relations of the working class (for example, Young and Willmott (1962) on Bethnal Green in London), and the supposedly more male-centred middle-class kin relations of the middle class (Bell 1968). These differences have been overdrawn. Middle-class and working-class women's situation as wives and mothers is structurally comparable. Both are located within kin relations, which structure their situation as domestic labourers. In the second part of this article I argue that women in Australia occupy a focal role in kin structures in the middle class as well as in the working class, and that this focal role is intrinsic to the construction of kin relations in present-day Australia.

To explore this it is necessary to look first at the articulation of women's situation in work and in family/kinship structures. In Australian ideology (and much social science in general) the two are consistently identified. The ideology supporting women's domesticity glosses over their extensive participation in the workforce – women's primary ideological location is within kinship structures as domestic labourers. The vociferously oppressive Australian version of 'a woman's place is in the home' structures women's work situation by relegating them to isolated housework and child-care. The housewife, producing no value and economically dependent on her husband, is seen as the securer of a privatized haven, while her husband mediates with the outside world.

Under advanced capitalism, the ideological elaboration of women's situation as biological reproducers within the domestic domain has intensified, with ever greater stress on the nurturant functions of motherhood (Mitchell 1971). This stress on the biological and social reproduction of children has been allied to the construction of a subjectivity in which the family is the privatized source of love and succour, a retreat from a harsh world and a repository of privacy (Zaretsky 1976).

The tendency of sociologists to see the family and wider kin circles as limited consumption units overlaid with rich symbolic structures neglects the vital point that kin structures are integrally implicated in the relations of procreation, and in the reproduction of both economic and ideological aspects of the social totality (Secombe 1974). These productions do not occur in the elementary family household alone, although that is the primary locus of the private domestic labour performed in isolation by the housewife. My study, and other studies in Europe and America have shown that a not inconsiderable amount of domestic labour is exchanged between households related by kin ties, some of it by men as well as women.

Extra-familial kin relations have been curiously absent from feminist analyses of capitalist society. Attention has focused on the elementary family and its relation to ideological reproduction and subjectivity, but other kin relations have been rather overlooked. The domestic labour debate, for example, has neglected the way that practical kin aid exchanged by women between households transcends the otherwise isolated housework situation.[7] This is only one of the contradictions within kin structures in Australia. Perhaps the most significant of these is that, while women's relegation to private domestic labour in the elementary family household isolates them, the devolution of elementary family ties through the life-cycle forms the ever widening kin circles within which women's feelings of solidarity with kin are realized. These relations, which help to structure women's subordination in both their economic and ideological aspects, carry within them the potential for women to act together in a limited way to improve their situation.

Like kin exchanges of labour, some parts of kin ideology transcend the isolation of the elementary family. This transcendence explicitly undermines the ideological primacy of the conjugal bond, that is, that one should love, honour, and oblige one's relatives, but this should not over-ride one's primary bond with the spouse. Any intervention by parents or others is deplored as threatening a necessary conjugal solidarity. Such action, however, does occur and can provide real strength for women, a strength both mocked and feared by men. Help, care, and 'moral support' for my female informants came from kin ties mediated by and through women, in spite of the prevailing ideological pressures against female solidarity. One instance of these pressures is the constant denigratory jokes about mothers-in-law, usually the wife's mother. Doctors, psychologists, and other 'professionals', too, promote the idea that women who retain strong ties with female kin like their mothers or sisters are dependent and infantile.

In the following section, I present some of the findings of my study of sixty-nine households in North Bay, a middle-class suburb of Sydney. The section contains an outline of the informants' work patterns and aspirations for themselves and their children; and material on their kin ties and kin ideology.

The class background

Most of the main breadwinners in the study are sellers of labour, the majority professional and white-collar workers.

They live in a class society not very different from that of other capitalist countries, although certain distinctive features differentiate the country's historical development, in particular, the high proportion of foreign ownership of capital, the concentration of ownership, and the important role historically of state intervention in the economy (Encel 1970). An overall predominance of service occupations and a high proportion of urban living have been consistent features of Australian society, produced mainly by the extensive bureaucracies and trading centred on the six state capitals.

While the media present Australia as a middle-class, suburban nation, there is little evidence that embourgeoisement has occurred within the working class. There are indications, though, that a long period of working-class affluence has left its ideological marks on that class in terms of their acceptance of ruling class hegemony (Connell 1977). Privatization, too, appears to be prevalent in varying degrees among middle class and working class alike.

Despite manifest inequality, the much vaunted Australian ideologies of egalitarianism have retained much force in the key arenas of the media. Nonetheless, most Australians are willing to describe themselves in class terms. Whatever the formulation of the notions of equality, though, Australian beliefs in the essential equality of *men* have rarely included *women*. Not surprisingly, overseas observers have tended to depict Australia as being more of a man's country than other capitalist countries.

A number of explanations have been proposed for this: in the nineteenth century men greatly outnumbered women in pioneer settlement in rural areas. Women's scarcity thus led to an internally contradictory ideology in which they were placed on pedestals and prized as possessions (McKenzie 1962). With the Depression conditions became extremely severe and male workers acted to protect their jobs by excluding marginal workers from the labour force, particularly women, who were less organized.

The Second World War promoted women's situation, but did little in the long run to change the sexual divisions within employment. Nonetheless, women's employment has risen steadily from 19 per cent in 1954 to over 30 per cent in 1969. Yet the 'woman's place' ideology has held sway, one of its principal agents being women's non-consciousness of their situation. Their own auto-oppression has compounded the controls placed on them by trade unions, schools, and the media.

The men's employment

Most of the men in the North Bay study had middle-class jobs – only 19 per cent were skilled or semi-skilled workers – the majority of whom had middle-class parents.[8] Few of the middle class appeared to be the status-aspiring, geographically mobile spiralists of the popular middle-class stereotype. More than half the men had been geographically mobile, some as immigrants from overseas, some from country towns in New South Wales and other parts of Australia, but few intended to move again. For the 21 per cent of the middle-class 'breadwinners' who had been upwardly occupationally mobile, there had been two separate channels of mobility – one involving part-time education, often some years after entering the work force, the other involving local on-the-job promotion.

Most of the informants, male and female, rejecting the idea that Australian society is egalitarian, were adamant that Australia did have a class structure. They pictured this generally as a many-layered, complex system, based on varying combinations of such factors as money, occupation, and education. The professional and other non-manual families expected advancement in career and income to occur within this class structure and in the case of a sizeable proportion were confident that success would reward effort. However, some had marked doubts about the costs of 'getting on' and seemed more concerned to gain a *reasonably* high level of material comfort and security, though not necessarily an enhanced social position. A quote from an industrial chemist illustrates this attitude :

'Something is coming up next year. But after that I've gone as far as I can in the laboratory. I can only go into technical sales. I'm not sure if I want to push my way up this ladder. My last boss ended up in the grave. I don't know if I want to take up all my time with work, if I'm going to retire in twenty years to the grave.'

More research would be needed before one could say that these informants' reservations about promotion were typical of other non-manual workers in Sydney.

The women's employment

Seventy per cent of the North Bay women had worked outside the home at some time in their lives. Over a third were working at the time of the study. They held the familiar female jobs: shop assistants, clerks, and the like.[9] For most of them their work lives had been discontinuous: paid work after leaving school, withdrawal to the home for marriage, housework, childbearing, and child-care. Sometimes they returned to paid employment while continuing to put in long hours as housewives. Practically none of the husbands did a substantial share of the housework.

Few of the older women had been employed after marriage. Although two had defied their husbands and sought employment, most older women accepted in varying degrees the masculine prerogative of the husbands' control over his wife's employment. Of course, some did not wish to work. A forty-two-year-old lab technician's wife maintained:

> 'I like housework. My husband would collapse if he was asked to do something ... I'm an odd person ... very ordinary ... I'm an old biddy who would like to potter in the garden. I'm old fashioned enough to think he's boss. I can put up with anything my husband does more easily than he can me, for the sake of peace.'

Women gave two main reasons for going to work: to gain extra comforts – 'Mum's the extras girl!'; and to alleviate the feelings of boredom and isolation associated with being captive wives – 'I'm sick to the back teeth at home!' Few worked for the intellectual and emotional stimulation alone, although they valued the companionship work provided. Because most of the bored younger women had few qualifications, there were few satisfying jobs open to them. The demands of childbearing also severely limited work opportunities.

These jobs were not seen as a source of prestige by the women or their husbands. It was implicit in most of their perspectives that a woman would rely on vicarious satisfaction from her husband's position. Independent action on her part, like getting a better job than her husbands', was seen as very threatening: 'I've got a friend. Although she loves him and he loves her, she's outgrown him. She's a buyer. They send her everywhere ... If she's not careful she may spoil something more valuable.'

Women's involvement in husbands' and children's social achievements

Professional husbands' career successes were related with quiet pride and wives seemed highly involved in future aspirations. Only one woman expressed well-developed doubts about her position as a woman and a need for more than vicarious rewards. Her husband was a professional engineer:

> 'My feelings are very mixed ... I don't want to be his camellia. He used to stand and watch me grow. I've grown thorns ... This uni[versity] course has a lot to answer for. It's been good for me but extraordinarily bad for our marriage. Suddenly I realized I was a person. I now assert myself.'

Some of the wives of other non-manual men were highly involved in their husbands' social aspirations, but the opportunities for derived status were less. These women tended to comment on the frustrations of their husbands' jobs or to express worries about the effects on their husbands' health. Wives of the skilled workers mostly stressed what 'good' and 'keen' workers their husbands were.

Women's dissatisfaction with their marriages tended to focus on their husbands' inadequacies as husband/father/breadwinner. It rarely seemed to centre on overt ambivalence about their own situation. Indeed, middle-class women have a substantial degree of investment in the *status quo*, despite the central duality of their work situation. Their husband's occupational prestige and rewards, except for dual-career families, are nearly always greater than those they can command for themselves in employment and such work always involves a series of compromises. It can add to problems in the husband-wife relationship apart from domestic management difficulties. Several husbands saw their wives' work associates as sexually threatening: 'If the manager rang me, he said it was a boyfriend!' Working-class women had less to lose by acting independently, but their access to resources was less by virtue of their class situation. Women's economic dependence was perceived as the crucial problem by those in unhappy marriages: 'It's a toss up if you have a roof over your head and schooling for the children or no emotional tension', as one woman said.

Both women and their husbands had high aspirations for their children. This was tempered in some cases by the realization that their ability to provide what they saw as the main avenue for the realization of these goals – education – was restricted by their means. Such aspirations focused more on sons than daughters and many of the men expressed doubts about higher education for girls. However, a sizable proportion of the women disagreed with their husbands, stressing that a girl never knew what might happen. Professional households were ambitious for both sons and daughters, wanting them to go to university. The managerial and semi-professional households favoured sons' education more than daughters': 'I think people know too much. They're much happier without psychology. There are shops and offices, positions for girls where they can meet nice people.'

The routine white collar households had great faith in education:

'When you have an only son, you picture him in an important job.'

'I was the nagger who screamed and ranted. My younger son is an architect. He mostly practises on girls! I wanted them both to be professionals ... I never wanted them to be older and pushed around.'

'If I say it myself, he's done wonderfully well. My sons didn't do the Leaving [New South Wales Leaving Certificate at the end of High School]. I was very disappointed, but [the youngest's] got a wife and five kids, two motor cars and a great big two storey house at Upper Northside!'

Most informants disclaimed such status considerations in relation to their children, although professional men and their wives tended to attribute this to their neighbours:

166

'One thing about North Bay, it doesn't put an inordinate amount into houses and cars. If you get kudos in North Bay, it's an intellectual one. I see among the parents in school the number one kudos is IQ. I find it obnoxious. Parents use children as pawns.'

Status clearly played a part in non-manual parents' educational ambitions for children, particularly those who wanted their children to be professionals. None wanted their children to become entrepreneurs and a large number mentioned the rewards of security and self-realization that they associated with the careers secured with education. Twenty-eight per cent of their sons had gone to university, 18 per cent of their daughters. If the occupations of the male informants, their fathers and their sons are compared they show a steady shift to non-manual – 72½ per cent of the fathers had non-manual occupations compared to 81 per cent of the informants, and 87 per cent of their sons.[10]

Kinship ideology

There was a certain amount of variation in the expression of ideas about kin relations and family life, but fairly universal agreement about the basic 'rules'. Informants felt a sense of obligation for kin, ranging from a minimal obligation to 'keep in touch' to a strong sense of moral responsibility, particularly to those closely related genealogically. Calling a person a 'relative' was placing them in a category of people whom one ought to regard with some affection, and a sense of obligation and responsibility – 'blood is thicker than water'. Most of my informants stressed the rather selective way this actually worked. A few professional and semi-professional households introduced a dissenting note by quoting the old saying: 'You can choose your friends, but not your relatives!' However, such ambivalence was comparatively rare. Many expressed the view that the ideal pattern of family and kin relationships was an important pattern for the greater good of society at large and troubles in society were often attributed to faulty family life.

Informants' ideas about women's focal role in kin relations were well-devoloped and many people were very explicit about the strength of ties between female kin. Kin relations were

167

symbolically associated with women – 'women's business'. As one small businessman joked: 'It's a woman's job, talking!' Informants thought that women, rather than men, felt the obligations to keep in touch with kin. It was usually the woman, they said, who said to the husband, 'Have you rung your mother?' One woman (married to a commercial traveller) told me that she and her brother were 'more for closeness': 'Yet we don't see so much of him. It's probably because Mary [his wife] has so large a family. It's the wife's contact with relations that determines it. A wife has more duties to her family.'

Three-quarters of the informants thought that the mother-daughter tie was the closest parent-child tie. A number of women mentioned that they had a horror of becoming 'unnaturally' or 'unhealthily' close to their sons. This closeness to daughters was seen as an instance of a more general sense of solidarity between female kin and expressed as such:

'Sons are not as loyal as daughters. They don't have the same conscience to their mothers.'   (Sales manager's wife)

'I think a daughter comes home. A son doesn't.' [Why] 'Because their wives won't let them!'
(Manager and his wife)

'The mother-daughter tie is closer. The tie is stronger with females. I feel closer to my sister than my brother.'
(Economist's wife)

Many women expressed a need for having female kin – particularly sisters. One woman (from a middle-class background, married to a skilled worker), underlined this when she referred to a friend with 'husband trouble', to whom she was giving 'moral support': 'She has a problem. Her hubby's not the best. She hasn't a mother and she has a sister who married well. She [the sister] doesn't understand.'

Many of the informants had very strong ties with their sisters and relied on them for much moral support and practical help, as well as for a large amount of sociability. Several women said their sisters were their closest friends and others who had none felt the lack strongly: 'We [she and her sisters] were tremendously close. As they passed away, I was thankful I have children!' (Postal clerk's wife).

168

'I have no sisters!' exclaimed a seventy-year-old postal worker's wife, telling me about visiting some 'cousins' she saw (HFZDs – her husband's father's sister's daughters). 'I'd be lost if I didn't have someone. There's quite a bit going on in that family ... If you've got ones close, you don't go so far!' (Genealogically, that is).

These notions about solidarity with female kin existed alongside a set of beliefs about the importance of conjugality. Relationships between the partners in a marriage and their respective parents and other in-laws were seen as potentially threatening to the unity of the married couple. Several informants quoted cases of broken marriages among kin and friends, which they attributed to in-law problems.

'You asked me about in-laws. They can break up a marriage. [My son and his wife] they were living in the house with the mother-in-law's brother.'
(Skilled worker's wife, middle-class background)

'I feel a mother can lose her son when he gets married. It turns into a mother-in-law/daughter-in-law relationship. My husband's mother thought he wouldn't get married.'
(Compositor's wife, middle-class background)

'I think there's an inbuilt thing about mothers and daughters. You must be prepared to lose a son entirely. A daughter-in-law is never like your own.'   (Sales representative's widow)

'Not too many mothers-in-law like sons-in-law. You're trying to please your husband and she's trying to please hers.'
(Small businessman)

Difficulties with in-laws were quoted to me frequently, especially problems of interference and criticism. It was easy to get on with in-laws, said one woman, if they didn't get 'sticky beaky' and personal. 'My son's in-laws are marvellous. They treat him as their own.' One woman spent 'twenty-seven years trying', finally waking up to the fact that 'they'd never like me'. 'Through children you become friends,' an engineer's wife suggested, adding self-consciously, 'I sound like the blessed Woman's Day!' Informants were naturally anxious about their own roles as parents-in-law: 'I was more concerned when

Michelle was engaged that I would be a good mother-in-law, rather than whether they'd be happy!'

The theme of virtue in independence recurred throughout the interviews. Great emphasis was placed on the need for a couple to be independent from their parents, financially, emotionally, practically, and residentially. It was thought 'suicidal' for adult children to live with parents after marriage. If it became necessary for an elderly parent to move in it was thought better that he or she should live with a daughter.

Of course, women did not have a complete monopoly of feelings concerning solidarity with kin. Although few men expressed such notions their involvement was by no means marginal. The obligation to kin, particularly 'immediate relatives' – parents, siblings, and children – was felt by both men and women, and entered into with varying degrees of willingness. This ranged from extreme solicitude and enthusiasm to a more grudging: 'He was a nice old fella, but it's not the same with someone in the house.'

While there was a minimal obligation to keep in touch, most people felt the onus was on them to do more than this. Although some felt variable degrees of obligation to attend family gatherings, the majority of both men and women stated that they felt a strong sense of moral responsibility to help out in any way possible if kin were in need. The closer the tie genealogically, the greater the obligation. Not unexpectedly, feelings for children were the strongest. Some informants identified so closely with their adult children that they did not see their obligations to them as comparable to their feelings towards other kin. As one elderly man put it: 'All our lives we've been doing things for our children, and that ... rearing them up. They've been good. They come and see us. That's our life.'

The extended family and other kin

In this section I outline the relationships between my informants and their kin and examine some of the interrelationships between kin relations, class structures, and the structures of Australian women's situation. I conclude with a discussion of women's consciousness of solidarity with kin. My primary interest is extended family relations.

Geographical distance, distribution, and contact

The idea that geographical distance necessarily decreases the intensity of kin relations was not borne out by my study. A number of the geographically mobile informants had arranged for kin, especially parents, to follow them in their travels, both within Australia and from overseas. In spite of considerable geographical mobility, most informants were in contact with almost all their immediate kin apart from some siblings, mainly men's brothers. Contact with more distant kin was more variable although the frequency with which they were seen was in a more or less inverse relationship with distance. Great use was made of the telephone (including trunk calls) and letters in maintaining contact. Also as most of the households had at least one car, they were well able to travel some distance to see kin. It is an obvious point that there is little reason why distance should result in any lessening of emotional commitment to kin. Eight informants had moved to North Bay to be near kin and others lived in kin clusters in North Bay and other suburbs. All of these involved clusters of matrilaterally related kin.

(a) *Parents* Under half of the men in the study, and even fewer of the women had lived away from home before marriage. In spite of the ideological stress on residential independence, 35 per cent of the households had formed composite households with parents at some point after leaving the parental home. The great majority of these shared a home with the women's parents. Also, more women than men lived within three miles of their parents. Overall the women's contact with their parents was greater than the men's. For example, of the 60 parents in Sydney, 22 per cent of the men's fathers, 33 per cent of the men's mothers, 58 per cent of the women's fathers, and 76 per cent of women's mothers were seen weekly or more often. Informants maintained contact over quite considerable distances. Most rang parents in Sydney at least once a week and trunk calls to other parts of Australia on a regular basis were common; almost all distant parents were written to at least once a week. It was often the women who activated their husbands' contact with their own parents, and husbands were drawn frequently into their wives' extended family. Upward and downward occupational mobility were difficult to document meaningfully with such a small sample, but did not appear to have affected contact to any significant extent, apart from some lessening of contact between fathers and sons. The close bonds between women tended to mute elements of competition.

(b) *Children*   Just under half of my informants had at least one child over school leaving age. Only a very few of the unmarried children who were working or studying were living away from their parents, and some unmarried sons in their thirties and forties had stayed on in the parental home. The children's extended economic dependence on their parents during a period of higher education was the major factor in these residence patterns. Approximately three-quarters of the informants' adult children were living in Sydney. Again visits were exchanged generally at the weekend, about a quarter 'popping in' during the week as well.

(c) *Siblings*   Forty-two per cent of the men's brothers, 68 per cent of the men's sisters, 52 per cent of the women's brothers, and 61 per cent of the women's sisters were living in Sydney. Sharing a home with a sibling was rare but sizable proportions lived within close reach of their siblings. Only a few had moved to North Bay specifically to be close to a sibling – in all three cases a woman moved to be near a sister.
   Contact showed an important bond between same-sex siblings and rates between cross-sex siblings were much lower. Significant proportions of siblings were seen quite infrequently. This underlines a lesser obligation to keep in contact with siblings, compared to the strong stress on maintaining intergenerational lineal ties between parents and children, even where affection is lacking. The frequency of contact with siblings appeared to be more directly related to the degree of affectional closeness than the contact between parents and children. The greatest contact by far was between women and their sisters, although men also saw a lot of their brothers in Sydney. Contact between cross-sex siblings was relatively infrequent: 'I see him rarely!' said one woman, 'Like brothers!' Women often mediated the relationship between the husband and his siblings – phoning and writing – and in the absence of siblings of their own,

the women also often became close to the spouse's siblings.

(d) *Other kin* Ties with kin beyond the extended family were rather limited among these households, but again there was a decided bias towards contact with kin on the wife's side. Ties with women's mothers' siblings and women's sisters' daughters were very important. For some elder women the latter tie was their closest kin tie outside the elementary family. Far more women were in contact with kin beyond the extended family. For example, 27 per cent of the geographically mobile women and 39 per cent of the Sydney women were in contact with first cousins, compared to 3 per cent of geographically mobile men and 18 per cent of the geographically immobile men.

Men appeared to be drawn into their wives' wider kin circles, particularly those who had married Sydney women. The shape of these kin circles, however, was highly variable depending on such factors as distance and intangible processes involving personal preference and selectivity.

Kin aid

I see the provision of kin aid, in Australia at least, as very much a constant process, reproducing both the structures of kin relations and class relations.[11] Among these North Bay families, kin aid was continuous, although often associated with key points in the life-cycle. Kin aid, both financial and practical, given to young couples in the early years of marriage was common, especially where the man had returned to full or part-time education. Owing to declining health and income, old age was also an area of special need, where aid from close kin acted as a welfare back-up.

Differences in class and geographical mobility have figured in discussions about the extent of such aid (Fletcher 1965; Litwak 1965; Osterreich 1965; Sussman 1965). However, I found such differences had relatively little effect on financial aid, although distance naturally affected practical aid dependent on proximity. There was little evidence that these mainly middle-class informants differed from the much smaller number of working-class informants in their wish to help and be involved with adult children and other close kin. They may have differed

173

in their actual ability to help, but that is another matter.

The main areas of aid exchanged among these families, other than financial, were care in illness, the provision of a home for elderly parents and newly married adult children, babysitting, help with do-it-yourself projects, general repairs, and very importantly, emotional support. Much of this was the province of the woman. Help provided for parents included taking an elderly mother shopping, help with housework, care during illness, particularly protracted final illness, and house repairs. Most of this aid was provided by daughters and their husbands – in line with most of the informants' ideas that it was a daughter's place rather than a son's to provide such services.

Informants were very frequently called upon to provide 'moral support' for their parents and other kin. It is difficult to separate relations of sociability and support, to characterize simply the quality of relationships. While mothers were turned to in crises, older women seemed more likely to turn to their daughters for emotional support than the other way around. The extent of moral support either way depended on the quality of the relationship, of course, and overt ambivalence was expressed in a number of cases. For example, a woman schoolteacher, married to a public servant, stated:

'My mother would like to see me every day. I phone her every two or three days, or she rings me, in the middle of dinner! We get some peace this side of the harbour!'

Even in such cases much time was spent helping parents out:

'My husband's mother is not well, and my mother suffers from depression, so I sit and talk things over with her.'
(A schoolteacher)

'I was very close to my mother in early life. It was the mother–daughter relationship, but I was the mother. She confided in me. We're quite close, but I wouldn't confide in her.' (Wife of a small business owner)

'Mum's the worrying kind ... we shield her from trouble.'
(Wife of a commercial traveller)

Practical help from parents mainly concerned babysitting, help at childbirth, knitting, and sewing – mostly the prerogative of mothers. More of the women's parents than the men's had provided this aid. Similar types of practical aid were exchanged between the informants and their children: the provision of a home, babysitting, child-care, knitting, sewing, car repairs, help with construction jobs, and again most importantly, emotional support. Such help was given more frequently to daughters and their husbands than to sons and their wives. Aid from adult children to elderly informants included help with housework, shopping, house repairs, and gardens. Again, daughters and their spouses were more likely to provide this than sons. Informants clearly derived a great deal of emotional support from adult children and women in particular relied on their daughters.

Much less aid was exchanged between siblings. This involved mainly child-care, and a great deal of manual labour on each other's houses and gardens – clearing land, building, decorating, and general repairs. Help appeared to be given more in response to a particular, sometimes unusual situation of need, than was the case between parents and children. The main emphasis in sibling relationships appeared to be on companionship and particularly in the case of women, on mutual support. In some cases the ties between same-sex siblings were very intense. Strong feelings of solidarity with a group of sisters were found among middle-class and working-class women equally. While some women expressed very ambivalent feelings about their mothers, it was noticeable that the most enthusiastic descriptions of relationships with kin were made by women about their sisters: 'We see a lot of them all,' said a fifty-two-year-old accountant's wife of her three sisters, all older than her. 'We go to a show, or to the beaches. – I'll bet you never get four so close!' [Did the husbands go too?] 'No! It's the girls! We don't want them!' [What about friends?] 'There's nobody much. My main interest is my sisters ... The closest friends I have are my sisters.'

'I moved here because of my sister. I see her every day ... I think sisters are very close. You might have your disagreements, but you don't alter. My sister and I are very close. In any troubles, etc., I go to her. She has a sympathetic way to her.'   (Seventy-year-old widow of a small businessman)

Some of the strongest sister bonds existed where women were

involved in marital difficulties, like this manager's wife : 'I see her regularly ... She's married and separated. He's [Z H=sister's husband] much the same as mine! She's the only outlet I have ... My sister is really my best friend!'

Captive wives also relied on their sisters to a great extent for sociability and support. Men who were close to their brothers were far less articulate about what these relationships meant to them.

Aid exchanged with kin outside the extended family was very limited. But some women were active in helping maternal aunts and nieces (Z Ds – sisters' daughters).

Financial aid

I have noted my reservations about the view that financial extended family aid in the middle class flows mainly through male links. Even if the husband is the financial 'manager', the women's influence in the disposition of such aid is not necessarily limited. In a situation where 'family business' is symbolically associated with women such a definition may well undermine the ideological association of men with money and allow women to initiate the proceedings. This clearly occurred in many cases among my informants. The women's role in independently providing kin aid depended on the degree of their economic autonomy, either as wage earners or as women with an independent income – mainly widows. Women's differential mortality means that inheriting widows can have extensive autonomy in the disposition of help to kin and of property, especially houses.

Financial aid to parents ranged from paying the rates on parents' houses, phone bills, and remittances abroad, to quite large scale financial support, particularly from upwardly occupationally mobile individuals.[12] One of the main areas of financial aid given to elderly parents – the provision of a home for a widowed parent – involved a sizable financial subsidy of the parent, usually the woman's. Fifteen per cent of the men and 20 per cent of the women had received large financial help from their parents, mainly as loans or gifts, such as the deposit on a house, or a redistribution of assets on retirement. Such aid as when a business failed or loans to help pay for a divorce also occurred.

I have noted above the informants' active involvement in promoting their children's educational and occupational achievements. Many of the children had grown up during a period of extensive expansion in educational opportunities which the informants had been concerned to exploit, especially for their sons. The processes of career mobility had been aided extensively by help with deposits on houses, loans for cars, guarantees on loans and mortgages, and expensive gifts, as well as help with hospital bills and university fees. Slightly more sons than daughters had received such help, but the outlay for the sometimes lavish weddings of some of the informants' daughters (some costing up to £1,000) tended to balance this. Children's financial aid to parents usually comprised only small amounts.

The main mechanism for reconciling independence and dependence was giving aid on socially recognized occasions like marriage. Generally husband and wife acted together in giving aid to their children and women played quite a significant role in its disposition. A number of women also disposed independently, to further their children's interests, sometimes in opposition to their husbands' wishes.

Siblings exchanged aid (small loans) only very rarely. This tended to flow through male links, but as women were commonly the mediators in these relationships it is hard to know the actual processes of decision-making concerning the disposition of such aid. Monetary help was mainly for houses and other occasions like wedding receptions.

These ties between kin, then, were important in providing sociability, mutual support, and help between kin, and maintaining and promoting the class situation of members of the extended family. Women were the main mediators of these relationships as well as drawing husbands into their kin circles. These ties were especially important for women and they expressed a need for female kin and relied on them for mutual support. Those with overt problems like unhappy marriages were particularly dependent on female kin for support. Interestingly, nearly all the husbands in these unhappy marriages had withdrawn from contact with kin, and were either members of a male friendship group or else somewhat socially isolated.

But, most informants saw kin 'socially' more than they saw friends. This fund of sociability was not limited. Although professional households had a much greater involvement with friends than white-collar and manual households, all groups showed comparable patterns of involvement with and reliance on kin. The enduring nature of kin ties, even within kin structures that allow a great degree of selection as in Australia, gives them a significance that friendship ties lack.

Conclusion

The matrilateral stress in kin relations that I found in this Sydney suburb parallels that reported for other western societies. This centrality of females has been a consistent feature of such diverse sociological constructs as the extended family of the British working class and the matrifocal family in the Caribbean, and has been explained in several differing ways: that the strong ties between female kin form a defensive women's trade union (Young and Willmott 1962); that the greater the degree of female domesticity, the greater the cohesion of the extended family, due to the increased mechanical solidarity of women (Rosser and Harris 1965); and that female solidarity devolves from the close ties between mothers and daughters and between sisters (Firth, Hubert, and Forge 1969). I consider these explanations inadequate. These patterns cannot be explained by reference to women's common domesticity alone, or the extension of sentiment, but only through a consideration of the complex unity of structures constituting kin relations.

In my view the essentially inductive constitution of such separate entities as the 'extended family' and the 'matrifocal family' has obscured key structural similarities in kin relations under advanced capitalism. Although many marxists hold that the state's educational arm is overhauling the 'family' as a reproducer of ideology, I think they underestimate the continuing significance of the family and other kin relations in the reproduction of ideology, as well as in economic reproduction. Kin relations may be 'hidden' by ideology, but that is another matter. These relations in their ideological aspect can be seen as structuring processes integral to social reproduction: the relegation of women to domestic units both as reproducers of the labourers, and as a reserve army, and the reproduction of class relations.

In their economic aspects, kin relations structure both a limited exchange of 'domestic' labour between households in the form of kin aid, and property transfers and other redistributions in the sphere of circulation. As the relations of procreation they structure biological reproduction. My account of kin aid shows how domestic labour in kin circles outside the elementary family contributes to the reproduction of labour power. Help with pregnancy, childbirth, child-care, housework, and home repairs contributes to physical maintenance, and the extensive 'moral support' contributes to 'psychological maintenance' (Secombe 1974).

It is, therefore, possible to argue (somewhat circularly) that kin relations play a (sometimes limited) role in the reproduction of both labour power and the relations of production. Consequently the subordination of women within kin structures as non-productive domestic labourers is required by the system. This, of course, involves women in a key contradiction for the demands of advanced capitalism also require women to emerge periodically from the 'reserve army' to work outside the home.

Many feminists see the privatized elementary family as oppressing women through an internalized subjectivity – the love ethic which glorifies the conjugal bond. This can be seen as an ideology structuring women's situation within the household to the demands of the system. Yet, as I stated above, it is the very devolution of elementary family ties through the life-cycle that forms the ever-widening kin circles within which women's kin solidarity is realized.

It is possible to interpret the expressions of solidarity among female kin as an elaborate defence against the undoubted male dominance of Australian society in general and the super-ordinate position of the husband in particular. But it is only overtly expressed as such when some degree of disengagement has occurred, either partial or whole. In the case of partial disengagement, a woman disenchanted with her marriage may have recourse to complaints to female kin and/or friends (and even, as happened with over 10 per cent of my female informants, to the female social researcher). Such complaints frequently appeal to the rich store of sex antagonism within Australian culture. Few of the women in my study expressed any consciousness of women as a separate entity or of their own situation as women – all complaints were directed at the husband. This disengagement may lead to divorce and most probably to remarriage and re-engagement.

But the nature of these overt expressions of female solidarity *contra* men is rather more complex. They are highly contradictory, for they may well be expressed in the absence of disengagement. Women will express satisfaction at having kin for sociability, and for the exchange of financial and practical help, and moral support. This solidarity is certainly not perceived as defensive and neither are the effects of its realization. In my study, women as kin aid dispensers played an important part in helping their husbands, children, and others to maintain or improve their class situation.

Kin solidarity helps structure these processes and the role of kin ties in welfare back-up, redistributing resources around kin circles, and maintaining and promoting the class situation of members of the extended family. As suggested above, domestic labour, embedded in these kin relations, reproduces both economic and ideological aspects of the social totality (Secombe 1974).

It is clear, then, that women's consciousness of solidarity with female kin is not a simple product of the domesticity embedded in kin ties, nor a defensive measure, but a complex consciousness arising within complex structures. To explore this further, one has to look at conceptualizations of consciousness and ideology. Up till now I have skirted these issues, and this is not the place to explore these highly complex and as yet unworked-out problems. However, the extremely important idea of ideology's materiality should be noted (Althusser 1976).

Ideologies in Althusser's view are not mere representations or reflections (albeit 'distorted') of a concrete 'reality', but are lived in relations, structuring 'the real actions of concrete humans' (Adlam, Henriques, Rose, Salfield, Venn, and Walkerdine 1977:23). Ideology is a representation of the imaginary relationships of individuals to their real conditions of existence. It is not simply generated by the positions of subjects as economic agents.

There are numerous problems, here, which lie beyond the scope of this article, not the least an inherent reductionism and economism (Adlam, Henriques, Rose, Salfield, Venn, and Walkerdine 1977; Hirst 1976). The important point to be stressed is that the Australian women's consciousness of kin solidarity bears no simple relationship to their situation as domestic labourers. This consciousness of being akin is not merely a 'representation' or a 'reflection' of 'real' ties, the kin relations in which domestic labour is embedded and yet which transcend women's isolation in domestic units. The complex unity of structures forming kin relations cannot generate consciousness of kin solidarity in any simple way. Rather, this consciousness, in itself contradictory, arises within a social totality and has relative autonomy.

In this article I have suggested, first, that the female focus to, and the female mediation of, kin relations are at the heart of the constitution of the reproductive structures of kin relations in Australia. Second, that the ideological coherence of these structures is sustained by a complex consciousness that symbolically associates kin relations with women. Although this is implicated in many of the conditions of women's subordination, it provides some limited escape from its own restrictions.

Notes

1 The research reported in this article was carried out in 1968 and 1969 in the Department of Anthropology, University of Sydney and financed by a Commonwealth of Australia Postgraduate Scholarship. The study was undertaken as an exploratory project investigating kin relations and class in a local area of Sydney. The suburb I chose, which I have called 'North Bay', is a pleasant area of tree-lined streets, four miles north of the centre of Sydney, with a 'solidly middle-class' reputation. Initially five households, introduced through mutual acquaintances, were interviewed. Having decided against a stratified sample, I drew a 1 per cent random sample from the electoral roll. This produced a list of ninety names, of which seventeen had already moved, eleven refused and three were unable to co-operate. A further five interviews were conducted with people active in voluntary associations. The total of households interviewed was sixty-nine. Because of the proportion of widows in the sample, and because a number of husbands were less interested in being involved in the project a greater number of women than men were interviewed – sixty-six women, forty-four men. Thus a larger proportion of the material was obtained from women by a female interviewer. Interviews usually lasted two to three hours each, followed by a period of casual conversation, and most households were seen three times in all.

Following Firth, Hubert, and Forge (1969), the classification of household composition comprised: married couple only (twenty); elementary family (twenty-eight); married couple with widowed parent (one); married couple with married children (one); extended family (six); widowed person alone (seven); widowed person with adult children (unmarried) (three); siblings only (one); single person and widowed parent(s) (two); total: sixty-nine. Four per cent of the informants selected in the samples were single, 78 per cent married, 3 per cent separated and 15 per cent widowed.

2 For example, the work of Young and Willmott (1962), and Rosser and Harris (1965), in Britain; and Sussman (1965), Litwak (1965), and Adams (1975) in the United States. See also Smith's (1973) discussion of the 'matrifocal' literature.

3 'The metropolitan situation ... presents kinship operationally in a very different light from that in rural or indeed in many urban societies. This is the nearest thing to "pure" kinship we are likely to get ...' (Firth, Hubert, and Forge 1969:3).

4 The concept 'ideology' presents many difficuties. For Althusser, ideology is neither a 'representation' of a concrete 'reality' nor a distorted representation. Ideology is seen as a representation of the imaginary relationship of individuals to their real conditions of existence, as a lived in relationship between people and their world. This theorization refers to ideology in general only. The question of the distinctness of a number of ideologies within one social formation is unresolved. For Althusser, the social formation comprises a complex unity of different levels or instances, each of which is relatively autonomous. Ideology as a distinct social level in the social formation, he argues, intervenes directly in the reproduction of the conditions of production in class society. It is the ideological structures, of which the 'family' is one, that secure the reproduction of the relations of production (Althusser 1976).

5 I follow Rosser and Harris in their definition of the 'extended family'. 'An extended family is any persistent kin grouping of persons related by descent, marriage or adoption which is wider than the elementary family in that it characteristically spans three generations from grandparents to grandchildren' (Rosser and Harris 1965:84).

6 For discussion of kin relations' continuing importance in Britain see Anderson (1971); Fletcher (1965); Young and Willmott (1962). For a summary of American findings, see Reiss (1967).

7 There is not the space, here, to go into the 'domestic labour debate' in depth. See, Secombe (1974); Gardiner (1976); Harrison (1973); and Chapter 1 this volume.

8 The sixty-seven men's occupations (including the deceased husbands of nine widows in the samples) comprised: one

clergyman, seven professional engineers, four industrial chemists, five accountants/administrators in banking, one industrial advocate, two public servants in professional and administrative grades, one naval officer, six managers of medium-scale enterprises, one principal of a technical college, one non-graduate teacher, one musician, three inspectors in public services, one lab technician, three clerical grade public servants, five commercial travellers, four accounts clerks, three owners of small businesses, one foreman, and twelve skilled tradesmen.

9 Of the forty-eight women who had ever worked, twenty-five were working at the time of the study, thirteen had worked at some stage after marriage but were not working at the time of the study, and ten had worked before marriage only. Of those working, five were graduate teachers, four non-graduate teachers, one social worker, two nurses, three part owners/workers in a family business, sixteen secretaries and clerks, five shop assistants, a hairdresser, four skilled workers, three semi-skilled workers, four service workers, and one woman doing piece work at home.

10 It might be considered androcentric to take the male's occupation as the key one. However, in the present predominant constitution of domestic groups in Australia, the male is still generally the main breadwinner and status creator of the domestic unit in ideology, and his occupation the most reliable marker of the elementary family household's class situation.

11 For discussions as to whether the exchange of kin aid occurs at times of crisis and difficulty only, or is a constant process see Bell (1968); Sussman and Burchinal (1962).

12 For example, 17 per cent of the men's parents and 14 per cent of the women's parents had received substantial financial help. These percentages are calculated on the basis of parents alive at some stage during the informants' adult life.

References

ADAMS, B. N. (1975) *The Family: A Sociological Interpretation.* Skokie, Ill.: Rand McNally.

ADLAM, D., HENRIQUES, J., ROSE, N., SALFIELD, A., VENN, C., and WALKERDINE, V. (1977) Psychology, ideology and the the human subject. *Ideology and Consciousness* (1):5-56.

ALTHUSSER, L. (1976) *Lenin and Philosophy and others Essays.* New York and London: Monthly Review Press.

ANDERSON, M. (1971) *Family Structure in Nineteenth-Century Lancashire.* Cambridge: Cambridge University Press.

BELL, C. R. (1968) *Middle-Class Families.* London: Routledge & Kegan Paul.

CONNELL, R. W. (1977) *Ruling Class, Ruling Culture*. Cambridge: Cambridge University Press.

ENCEL, S. (1970) *Equality and Authority*. Melbourne: Cheshire.

FIRTH, R., HUBERT, J., and FORGE. A. (1969) *Families and Their Relatives*. London: Routledge & Kegan Paul.

FLETCHER, R. (1965) *The Family and Marriage in Britain*. Harmondsworth: Penguin.

GARDINER, J. (1976) Political economy of domestic labour in capitalist society. In D. L. Barker and S. Allen, *Dependence and Exploitation*. London: Longman.

HARRISON, J. (1973) The political economy of housework. *Bulletin of the Conference of Socialist Economists* Winter:35–52.

HIRST, P. Q. (1976) Althusser and the theory of ideology. *Economy and Society* 5(4):385–412

LITWAK, E. (1965) Extended kin relations in an industrial democratic society. In E. Shanas and G. Streib (eds.), *Social Structure and the Family: Generational Relations*. Englewood Cliffs: Prentice Hall.

MCKENZIE, N. (1962) *Women in Australia*. Melbourne: Cheshire.

MITCHELL, J. (1971) *Woman's Estate*. Harmondsworth: Penguin.

NEEDHAM, R. (ed.) (1971) *Rethinking Kinship and Marriage*. London: Tavistock.

OSTERREICH, H. (1965) Geographic Mobility and Kinship: A Canadian Example. *International Journal of Comparative Sociology* 6:131–44.

REISS, P. J. (1967) Extended Kinship relations in American Society. In H. Rodman (ed.), *Marriage, Family and Society*. New York: Random House.

ROSSER, C. and HARRIS, C. C. (1965) *The Family and Social Change*. London: Routledge & Kegan Paul.

SECOMBE, W. (1974) The Housewife and her Labour under Capitalism. *New Left Review* (83):3–26.

SHANAS, E. and STREIB, G. (eds.) (1965) *Social Structure and the Family: Generational Relations*. Englewood Cliffs: Prentice Hall.

SMITH, R. T. (1973) The Matrifocal Family. In J. Goody (ed.), *The Character of Kinship*. Cambridge: Cambridge University Press.

SUSSMAN, M. B. (1965) Relationships of Adult Children with their Parents in the United States. In E. Shanas and G. Streib (eds.), *Social Structure and the Family: Generational Relations*. Englewood Cliffs: Prentice Hall.

SUSSMAN, M. B. and BURCHINAL, L. (1962) Parental Aid to Married Children: Implications for Family Functioning. *Marriage and Family Living XXV*:320–32.

YOUNG, M. and WILLMOTT, P. (1962) *Family and Kinship in East London*. Harmondsworth: Penguin.

ZARETSKY, R. (1976) *Capitalism, the Family and Personal Life*. London: Pluto Press.

© *Maila Stivens 1978*

SEVEN

Women's spirit possession and urban adaptation in the Muslim northern Sudan

PAMELA CONSTANTINIDES

This article examines just one aspect of a many-faceted spirit possession cult of healing called *zaar bori* in the northern Sudan. Spirit possession cults called *zaar* exist throughout most of the Middle East and North East Africa. Among Muslims, the cult's following is predominantly female. This article examines the way in which the cult groups form a series of overlapping women's solidarities, and the implications this has for female solidarity in such a tribally heterogeneous and sexually segregated society. It is my hypothesis that the cult has provided one of the prime bases for such female solidarity as exists in the urban areas, and that it has played an important role in women's adaptation and integration into multi-ethnic urban society.

Zaar and the wider society

In the northern Sudan, as in other Middle Eastern countries, the *zaar* cult undergoes recurrent bouts of attack from the predominantly male religious and secular educated elite. During the last 100 years, Muslim teachers and theologians have described the *zaar* practices as 'un-Islamic innovations'. More recent approaches on Sudan radio and television have condemned the cult as typical of bad tradition versus good tradition, in other words as an example of the type of 'superstitious' and 'backward' custom inhibiting the course of true progress.

In an attempt to defend the *zaar* from its indigenous critics I think it should be pointed out that the cult is not all that traditional, having been introduced into the Sudan in the decades following the conquest of that country by Mohamed 'Ali in 1821. More important, it is my contention that in the past, as today, the *zaar* cult may well have provided its followers with a means for adapting to the very urban society now considered synonymous with progress and modernity in the Sudan.

Outside observers always seem to be surprised by the tenacity of the *zaar* cult in present day Sudan, where it remains extremely popular among women. Modernists (and even the occasional anthropologist) have predicted its inevitable end, and yet so far it appears to thrive. Although it has spread to the rural areas, it remains most widely practised in those towns, like Omdurman, where it first became popular. Harold Barclay, an American anthropologist who has studied a suburban village near Khartoum, describes the submersion of the village life in that of the capital (Barclay 1964). He predicts that secularization will be an inevitable result of participation in a national, more modern economic and political system. According to Barclay, it will be cults such as that of the *zaar* – which he calls after Redfield the 'little tradition' – which will be most severely affected in this process. Yet he admits that 'the *zaar* cult as an exclusively women's sodality appears to thrive today' (Barclay 1964:272).

Modernity is relative, and the Sudan has been moving towards a nationwide political and economic system ever since the establishment of the Turko-Egyptian administration in the 1800s. Part of this process has been ever-increasing urbanization, with a considerable movement of the rural population to the towns. In my opinion it is less interesting to speculate whether the *zaar* cult will eventually cease to be active, than it is to examine the reasons for its sustained activity over the past 150 years.

Ritual and social change

Until Ioan Lewis's 1966 Malinowski Memorial Lecture, spirit possession cults often tended to get rather peripheral treatment from people in this country interested in the study of ritual. Spirit possession cult movements, like various millennial and revivalist movements all over the world, did not usually fit in with the variously modified status-quo-maintenance theories of ritual, which have such a long and respectable history in anthropology. The introduction and spread of such cults seemed to be related uncomfortably closely to periods of rapid social change in the societies in which they arose or into which they were assimilated.

In a paper published a few years ago, Alice Dewey set herself the task of explaining how and why a particular Javanese ritual not only survives, but even thrives, in a completely changed social context (Dewey 1970). Basically, as I understand it, her point is that rituals that are ego-centred are capable of considerable adaptation. They are used to aggregate supportive groups around an individual at a life-crisis point, but the basis on which such groups are recruited can change, sometimes quite flexibly, as the social context changes. To put it in more extreme terms, the same ritual which, in a small, traditional, homogeneous society might be carried out by a structurally pre-defined group, may, in a large, heterogeneous society, itself define the group.

Zaar is a healing cult and its ritual is primarily ego-centred. As far as the urban centres of the northern Sudan are concerned, it would also be true to say that the ritual makes the group – in a sense that will become apparent during the course of this paper. Historically speaking, it is different from the sort of ritual Dewey refers to, since it is relatively new. Moreover, it is apparently a product of the urban environment.

In an attempt to support the basic contention of this paper, I would now like to turn to an outline of the post-conquest history of urbanization in the northern Sudan, together with a sketch of the social organization. This will be followed by

187

a brief description of how the *zaar* cult works, and of the organization of cult groups.

Social organization and the growth of urban areas

The first and most fundamental point to be made is that we are discussing a Muslim society. The northern Sudan is in fact distinguished principally in terms of the widespread use of the Arabic language and the practice of Islam. Most of the sedentary riverain tribes also lay claim to Arab descent, and it is these who form the dominant groups numerically, politically, economically, and socially. Most of the data in this paper refer to these sedentary Nileside people.

Apart from some ancient Red Sea ports, large-scale urbanization in the Sudan really began with its conquest by Mohamed 'Ali of Egypt in 1821 and the establishment of the Egyptian colonial capital at Khartoum. The opening up of the White Nile route to the south and the subsequent trade in slaves and ivory led to the rapid development of Khartoum and the establishment of a growing European trading community.

When the rebellious forces of the Muslim purist, the Mahdi, succeeded in overthrowing the colonial establishment in Khartoum in 1885, Omdurman became the Sudanese capital. Within a few years the then village of Omdurman expanded enormously to become the major city that it is today. In 1896 the Anglo-Egyptian reconquest of the Sudan began. Omdurman was taken in 1898, and 1899 the Anglo-Egyptian Condominium was established, to last virtually until Sudanese independence in 1956.

The primary need to extend administration and communications led to general development within the Sudan in the post-reconquest years. The process of urbanization, begun in the Turko-Egyptian period, increased at a more rapid rate. Kitchener's military railway was adapted for civilian purposes and extended to a railhead opposite Khartoum at the end of 1899. Around it developed the new town of Khartoum North, where much of the Sudan's light industry is now concentrated. A railway to the Red Sea was completed in 1905, which led to the creation of the new towns of Atbara and Port Sudan in the east. In 1911 a railway line was taken southwest to El Obeid, leading to the great expansion of this old trade centre, and the creation of a new town, Kosti. The railway system brought some of the first industry, and the first labour unions, to the Sudan. Then came the harbour system of Port Sudan. The Gezira cotton scheme opened vast labour opportunities and made a large town out of its administrative centre.

The new economic demands and opportunities meant an expansion of the labour migration from the rural areas into the towns, and many settled there permanently. According to the pre-Independence Census of 1955–6 one person in twenty in the total population, including the southern provinces, lived in only the ten *largest* towns in the north.[1] Also, more of the migrants to these towns came from the northern province (the home of most of the northern riverain tribes) than from any other area. A 1964–5 sample population survey of the ten largest towns showed that, in most cases, the majority of migrants living there were relatively long term residents, having migrated in before Independence in 1956. The sex ratio of persons moving into the large towns has remained fairly constant: in the period up to 1956, 60 per cent were males, 40 per cent females; in 1956 to 1960, 61 per cent were males; in 1961 to 1964, 63 per cent were males.

Roughly speaking there have been two categories of male migrant to the towns. The first comprises those coming in to seek long term employment and who have brought their wives and families with them. The second category consists of those seeking temporary or seasonal employment in order to obtain cash over a short term, who have mostly been single or who have left their wives and families in the home village. Overall, though, it can be seen that quite a high proportion of women have moved with their menfolk to the towns and long term immigrants have tended to settle permanently there. Between the 1955–6 Census and the 1964–5 survey, the proportion of urban residents who admitted to being immigrants, as versus permanent urban dwellers, had decreased considerably.

During the Anglo-Egyptian period the *zaar* cult rituals, until this time apparently practised principally in the older urban centres of Suakin, Khartoum, and Omdurman also began to be taken up in the new provincial towns, and from there spread out to the rural villages. The Sudan Government Archives record the protests of the religious and secular elders at the growth of the cult. Witness, for example, a letter from a Nazir in Gedaref town, written in 1933 and addressed to the British District Commissioner. He begins: 'I beg to inform you that there is in this town a sort of untrue disease called Zar, supported by old women who pretend that they can give the necessary treatment. This disease has spread to a great extent ...' He goes on to complain about 'poor husbands' who suffer financial ruin trying to provide for their wives' and daughters' treatment in the cult, and the moral dangers to which the women are exposed, since they meet together with unrelated persons from all walks of life. He concludes hopefully, 'your approval is requested to prohibit this untrue disease'.

I would now like to turn to a brief and highly generalized description of the 'traditional' social organization of the northern riverain groups and look at the position of women within that framework. I would then like to examine what happens when a woman moves into a large town like Khartoum or Omdurman, and what happens when she joins a *zaar* cult group. My ultimate intention is to demonstrate that, in the towns, the *zaar* cult provides women with a basis for association additional to, and sometimes to a large extent replacing in importance, relationships based on more traditional means of social alignment.

Women in villages

If we take as our starting point the period prior to the Turko-Egyptian conquest, then the picture that we have is of a series of tribes strung along the Nile from Wadi Halfa on the Egyptian border to Sennar on the Blue Nile. The tribes have a recognized territorial base and are composed of individuals claiming ultimate kinship ties. As Barclay says:

> 'The history of the northern Sudan in the past century and a half has been mainly characterised by the breakdown of the tribes as political and territorial entities. The Mahdist rulers in particular sought to crush their power. And although there has always been some intermixture among the Arab tribes, it became noticeable under the Turko-Egyptian rule and most pronounced from Mahdia times onwards.'
>
> (Barclay 1964:97)

As a tendency this is undoubtedly true, and is reflected in the high degree of cultural homogeneity that characterizes the northern Sudanese today. An ultimate product of the trend is the sort of suburban village studied by Barclay which, like the capital city it adjoins, is founded on the principle of tribal heterogeneity.

However, there are vast areas of the rural northern Sudan that are still relatively 'traditional' in this sense. I would like to take the example of the Northern Province, with which I am familiar, and which has provided the most substantial proportion of migrants to the towns. Here there is a marked association of tribe and territorial area. Within the territory of each tribal grouping are villages based on patrilineal lineages of the tribe. The village economy rests principally upon cultivation of gardens and date palms by the Nile, together with a little animal husbandry, mainly sheep and goats. In both cultivation and domestic tasks, considerable reliance is placed upon the labour of wives and daughters and, for the wealthier households, upon male and female servants. Before the abolition of slavery in the Sudan these latter were household slaves, most often of southern origin. Former slave families often maintain close ties with the lineages who owned them and continue to act as servants in the modern idiom.

Women have no formal role in political or economic decision-making, though their informal influence is often considerable. They may own and inherit property, as is laid down in Islam, but such property is almost inevitably controlled on their behalf by kinsmen. Women remain members of their lineages throughout their lives and are always known by their fathers' name, never their husbands'. Divorce is fairly common, though some of the social pressures against it will be outlined later in this paper. Men may legally have up to four wives at any one time, though again both social and economic pressures make one wife at a time the norm.

Marriage patterns are characterized on the whole by lineage and village endogamy, though this tends to be counteracted to some extent by politically or economically astute matches with other lineages, and by the practice of lengthy, sometimes permanent, uxorilocal residence. The preferred forms of marriage (at least for a first marriage) tend to be in order of preference, with a Fa bro child; Fa sis child; Mo bro child; Mo sis child.

In practice this means that a village, or a group of villages within easy reach of each other, tends to be made up of several lineages which are heavily intermarried, so that any individual can trace some form of relationship with most other members of the village.

This has particular implications regarding the social activity of the women, who are confined not only by the economic division of labour to domestic activity, but also by the Muslim system of moral behaviour to stay within the company of kinsmen and women. In the village, social and kinship ties are largely co-terminous, giving shape to the women's total social lives. The system of sexual segregation and the seclusion of women which characterizes the towns, is much less marked in the rural villages. This is because its main purpose – to seclude women from unrelated males who do not have the honour of her lineage at heart – is to some extent negated by the context. Women are able to pursue extra-household activities, such as vegetable gardening, tending domestic animals, and drawing water, with relatively little constraint. For any specialized services they can call upon neighbours who are also kinsmen and women, and upon their own domestic servants. In the towns all life-cycle ceremonies are attended by sexually segregated congregations – one in the men's and one in the women's quarters. In the rural villages, because people are much more closely interrelated, it is common to see sexually mixed public gatherings on such occasions. This extends also to the religious activities of Islam, where, for example, related women play a public supportive role in the ritual activities of the Muslim brotherhoods or *tariqaat*, a phenomenon not seen in the towns.

It is probably in the in-marrying villages that we see the greatest examples of female solidarity in action. However, even here, though mutual support may give women considerable leverage *vis-à-vis* men, it is basically solidarity of the type described as passive in this volume. Notionally such villages, or at least parts of them, consist of related men and women marrying each other, controlling lineage property, and producing children for the lineage. However, men hold the dominant roles and take the major initiative in political and economic decisions. Women, though, aim at both the physical and ritual control of their greatest asset, their reproductive capacity. It is specialist women who circumcise young girls, perform any necessary incision on circumcised brides, and deliver babies.[2] It is women who take the leading part in the ritual accompanying female circumcision, marriage, and childbirth. It is noteworthy for what follows, that perhaps the only 'traditional' profession open to women apart from midwife is *zaar* cult group leader, and that much of the symbolism surrounding female *rites de passage* is reflected in the *zaar* ritual.[3]

Undoubtedly women are aware of the benefits they gain by being members of a solidary group based on kinship and affinity. Indeed, they strive quite consciously to maintain the nature of that solidarity by exterting joint pressure on decisions affecting the arrangement of marriage and divorce. Women can call upon the ideals and norms of kinship behaviour when applying moral pressure on men to absorb the 'spare' women of the lineage and thereby marry women congenial to the existing group. The same sort of moral pressure is applied when the question of divorce or the subsequent marriage of a husband threatens the position of one of the women in the group. Instead of one woman acting alone in protest, as may be the case where the marriage partners live in town, a united group of 'bedroom advisers' affects the decisions of the men of the lineage.

Although women are equally desirous of the improved living standards associated with a move to the towns, they have good reason also to be anxious about its value in terms of their security. Marriages to women of other tribal affiliation is quite commonplace in the towns where individual men have greater freedom of action in arranging unions for themselves. Though he should consult, or at least inform her, it is possible for an urban man to arrange a divorce, or an additional marriage, without his wife's foreknowledge. Wives and mothers left behind in the rural areas fear that their husbands or sons will marry 'strangers' without consulting them. Some of the informal village-help associations formed by men in the towns receive quite specific directives from the elders and womenfolk left behind in the village – namely to ensure that young men from the village are kept under a close degree of moral control and are strongly persuaded to look towards their village and lineage of origin when seeking a wife.

What happens, then, when a woman from such a village accompanies her husband or kin to an urban centre? Immediately, her range of social activity is likely to be restricted. The over-riding presence of the market economy removes certain subsistence tasks from her; while the absence of domestic slaves and probable lack of close kinswomen means that she has somehow to obtain specialized services from 'strangers'. At the same time the moral system to which she adheres requires that she should seclude herself from unrelated males, and the cash economy allows her father or husband to support her in seclusion.

Of course she will seek out women of her own village, or at least, if these are not available, members of her own tribe. This is easy if the family stay with already established kin, and particularly where certain wards of a town are densely settled by members of a particular tribal group. However, this is not often the case: lack of space in crowded towns, house and land allocation rules, and town-planning restrictions, may not allow it. Her position may, in fact, be very similar to that of the Mirpuri immigrant women in Bradford, where pride in newly acquired status and modern amenities is offset by the isolation engendered by the different nature and implications of *purdah* in urban Britain from *purdah* in rural Pakistan (Saifullah Khan 1976).

Of course I am not suggesting that men do not also experience the initial shrinking of their sphere of social activity when they first move to the towns, but merely that the women's confinement to the domestic sphere makes it relatively more severe. Historically, the male migrants' involvement in the extra-domestic economy led them to develop new forms of association based on work. For example, an early and very strong trade-union movement grew up within the industrial workshop of Sudan railways. Out of work associations developed sports clubs and existing forms of associations broadened taking on new roles. After the Turko-Egyptian conquest there was a marked upsurge in the membership of Muslim brotherhoods, and in the towns these took a decided multiethnic character. The first national political parties were ultimately to develop out of these. It is interesting to note that brotherhoods practising ecstatic forms of *zikr* (chant) became very popular in the towns, and came under criticism from more orthodox Muslims only a little less severe than that bestowed on the *zaar* cult. Indeed, in many aspects of ritual and approach, *zaar* cult groups can be viewed as functional counterparts to Muslim brotherhoods; a fact noted by Barclay (Barclay 1964).[4]

The woman coming into the town is in a new social situation and what she needs to find is some basis for association with her fellow women, an association that could provide the same possibilities for urban adaptation that the religious brotherhoods, and work and sports clubs, do for men. Membership of the same tribal group could be one basis for association, taking the place of closer kinship connections where these were absent. However, a more common factor is needed if some basis for association across ethnic boundaries is to be found. One such common factor could be illness – however defined.

The traditional Sudanese healer, the Islamic *feki*, only offers private treatment in a one-to-one relationship. The healing cult of the *zaar* is recognized as specializing in 'women's ailments'. Furthermore it offers both the promise of cure and ongoing membership of a common interest, multi-ethnic group, and a widely ramifying network of *zaar*-based contacts.

The zaar cult

A woman suffering from almost any form of physical or emotional malaise will normally seek out the whole spectrum of available forms of diagnosis and treatment. Among these will be diagnosis in terms of possession by *zaar* spirits. A *zaar* cult leader will be consulted either because she lives nearby, or she is famous, or she is a kinswoman. Nowadays, some cult leaders are of free-born descent, though many are of slave descent (which makes them to some extent ethnically neutral), and a few are male homosexuals (which makes them sexually neutral in their society's terms).[5] The great majority of cult leaders are women, and are addressed as *shaikha* (the feminine form of *shaikh*) a term used to address secular and religious leaders, especially the heads of Muslim brotherhoods. This does not imply that the cult leaders have necessarily been to Mecca (though some have done so with their income from the cult) nor that they have any Koranic knowledge. The majority of cult leaders are, like most Sudanese women of their age and background, illiterate and without formal instruction in Islam. The title *shaikha* merely indicates respect for their leadership and knowledge of cult ritual.

A *shaikha* becomes a cult leader by first suffering spirit-caused illness herself, usually said to be particularly severe, and subsequently acting as assistant to the cult leader who treated her. Often she takes over the whole or part of her own cult leader's activities following the latter's death or retirement. The *shaikha* is an intimate of the spirits by virtue of her own possession and acquired lore. She is not a shaman in the sense of 'mistress of the spirits' but a fellow sufferer with her patients. A free-born *shaikha* may have as the nucleus of her following her own kinswomen, but cult leaders see themselves, *qua* healers, as rising above divisions along kinship and ethnic lines. They deliberately seek a wide and multi-ethnic following and go out of their way to declare their ethnic impartiality – a claim more readily believed of those of slave or non-Sudanese descent, who can genuinely stand in an interstitial relationship between the different tribal groups.

The diagnostic procedure can take several forms. The cult leader may invite the new patient to attend a ritual she is giving for another patient, either in the latter's or the *shaikha*'s home. There the newcomer may respond to the drumming in a manner indicating which spirit or spirits are causing her illness. Or she may stay with the *shaikha* for a period of time, when special incense appropriate to each group of spirits will be administered to her. She will be encouraged to enter into a state of trance, speak with spirit voices, or mime to indicate which spirits are possessing her. If the patient does not respond in this way the *shaikha* herself may prepare for a dream revelation, placing a piece of clothing of the patient together with some so-called 'key of dreams' – incense, perfumes, sweets, and so forth – under her pillow at night. She will then tell the patient whether or not she believes her to be possessed by *zaar*, the names of the spirits possessing her, and what they require to stop making her ill. The demands of the spirits always include that a ritual, with spirit costumes and sacrifice, be held by the patient.

Meanwhile, if the patient accepts the diagnosis, the *shaikha* will perform a small ritual called 'the opening of the box'. This is a box of special incenses for the spirits, and the ritual is one of initiation: it commits the person to that *shaikha* and to attending the five or so rituals that the *shaikha* gives annually for all her followers. The cult leader may try and time this initiation to coincide with one of these annual 'public' rituals. In this case the patient will have an opportunity to meet most of the other followers of the cult leader at one time. Depending on the reputation of the *shaikha* as a cult leader, her following may range from about fifty to several hundred women. In any event the leader will encourage a new patient by taking her along to 'private' *zaar* rituals, which she gives for other followers. Strictly speaking, though women may attend and dance at the rituals of any cult leader, they remain the followers of the cult leader who 'opened the box' for them. If, however, they move to another district or town they may join the following of another *shaikha* who will diagnose a new set of symptoms as being caused by yet another group of spirits.

As we have seen, there are two types of *zaar* ritual: 'public' ones given by the cult leader for her followers; and 'private' ones sponsored by individual followers. Both types involve a group of people, but in each case the group is recruited on a different principle. The focal point of the 'public' ritual is the cult leader, and the group consists of all her initiated followers (called her daughters) who are bound to attend every such ritual she gives. The focal point of the 'private' *zaar* is the patient, and the group comprises those who have some form of actual or potential social interest in the former. The group may change its composition for the same individual, and will be different for each individual follower of a particular cult leader, though there is always some degree of overlap. This is because two people have the right to invite guests to a private ritual, whether it is held in the sponsor's or the cult leader's home. They are the *shaikha*, who always invites a core of her individual followers and would-be followers along, while the individual for whom the ritual is being held invites all those socially important to her. These may be kinswomen, affines, neighbours, and, of course, fellow members of her cult group. Some of the former may not be *zaar* followers, others may be followers of a different *shaikha*. Thus women who are not *zaar* cult members, and members of different cult groups, are constantly meeting and coming into contact with each other in the context of rituals which may last from one to seven days. This provides them with a town or city-wide network of actual and potential social relationships which are *zaar* activated and extend well beyond the individual cult group based on one particular leader. The network includes other women of all socio-economic categories, from the wife of the President of the Republic (as has been the case in the past) to former slave women and prostitutes.

There is ample evidence that women actively use this network to form friendship and patron-client relationships, to promote economic transactions, and to offer and gain services.[6] Moreover, once established, the network tends to extend well beyond the actual activities of the cult itself. The reciprocity principle is quite strongly institutionalized in the northern Sudan. Those who attend and support any ritual occasion expect the host or hostess to do the same for them. Guests always contribute to the expenses of the host, or hostess, with gifts of cash or food. The amount given is remembered with great accuracy – sometimes it is written down and read out at the time – and when host or hostess becomes guest, he or she is expected to give at least an equivalent amount. Almost any ritual occasion is seen as an opportunity to discharge such obligations. Thus membership of a *zaar* cult group leads to invitations not only to the cult rituals of others, but also to various life-cycle rituals such as circumcisions, childnamings, and weddings.

The *zaar* is a complex social phenomenon and obviously it fulfills many purposes. As a healing cult it offers the promise of cure from illness (however defined) in a sympathetic association of fellow-sufferers. It also, of course, provides an *explanation* for the illness, and its terms of diagnosis – possession by foreign, morally neutral spirits – might be viewed as bypassing more socially-charged alternative diagnoses, among which are punishment by God, possession by devils (*shaitaan* or *jinn*), or the evil-eye or sorcery of one's fellows (Lewis 1971).

Its ritual also provides otherwise rare opportunities for drama and entertainment. During days and nights of drumming and singing, those possessed by their spirits don elaborate spirit costumes and dance, entering into states of trance. Although both the categories of spirit and the individual spirits are fairly stereotyped, they represent a wide range of experiences and allow for different degrees of controlled and uncontrolled emotions and violence. By displaying the different possession behaviour appropriate to different series of spirits, a spirit possessed woman can express most of the things that affect her, including desire for increased wealth or status, fear of death, fear of childbirth, or dismay at barrenness or low fertility. Elements of cross-sexual hostility, tension and competition concerning members of her own sex, and anxieties about adequate fulfilment of a woman's designated social role, all play a part. There is certainly little doubt that the participating individuals find tremendous emotional release in these sessions, as well as a chance for personal and often competitive display before other women.

Furthermore, in a very real sense the *zaar* cult is a key which opens out the social life of women in the towns. Through the cult 'strangers' enter into relationships of reciprocity in ritual contexts, and hence, by definition, are no longer 'strangers'.

On all these ritual occasions, both *zaar* and otherwise, the women gathered together have a chance to promote the reputation of their family or lineage, and to raise the topic of marriageable daughters or employable husbands and sons. Although marriages are formally arranged by men, the forum for exchange of information provided by the *zaar* cult can be very useful. It is also useful in the informal politics of gossip, with which the women complement and feed the formal political sphere controlled by men, because of the social range of cult followers.

There are also opportunities for a wider range of economic activities to occur. Personal services that in the village women would have obtained from their kinswomen or family slaves, such as hairdressing, body massage, and depilation, can be obtained from former slavewomen who are cult followers. Women with particular specializations such as making certain drinks, foods, sweetmeats, or clothes, can use a *zaar*-based network for distribution and exchange. Some women become highly successful entrepreneurs in this way. I knew one woman of Egyptian descent who made frequent trips to Egypt for medical treatment or to visit relatives. On each occasion she brought back in her rather massive personal baggage desirable consumer items scarce in the Sudan. These she distributed through her zaar-based network, collecting payment in instalments when she attended the rituals given by her cult leader.

I do not want to overstress this aspect, because the cash economy is after all almost totally dominated by men. Nevertheless, though the expenses of a zaar ritual are usually paid by the patient's father, brother, son, or husband, I was surprised at the number of women who footed their own bills out of money they had gained in this domesticated economic system.

It, therefore, can be seen that the cult provides a means for voluntary association on a basis of some flexibility. There are really two sides to the zaar cult. On the one hand the initiated member joins a group, consisting of all the followers of one particular shaikha. This group is obliged to come together several times a year at the cult group rituals given for them by their leader. Apart from this, individual members of the group are constantly visiting the cult group leader, staying with her a while, seeking advice, minor treatment, and supplies of zaar incense. There is, therefore, considerable interaction between the group members and the cult group leader, and between the cult group members themselves. Though the emphasis is on the religious and healing aspect of the cult, women are sometimes explicit about its club-like functions. When I asked women if they belonged to any of the modern women's associations they would often laugh and say 'not unless you count the Naadii az-zaar' – literally the zaar club.[7]

On the other hand, there is a zaar cult network which goes far beyond the groups based on individual leaders; and it includes both actual members of cult groups and non-members. This is the network brought about by invitation and counter-invitation to the 'private' zaar rituals of individuals.

It appears that the flexibility of the cult, and the possibilities that it provides for adaptation into urban society, rest to a large extent on this ego-centred aspect. By far the greater number of zaar rituals held are those for individuals. While each cult leader gives up to five annual rituals associated with Muslim festivals, it is possible for each to give from ten to forty or more 'private' rituals. There are numerous cult leaders in the towns (in one ward of Omdurman where I worked there were five known to me) and a *zaar* enthusiast with enough time, energy, and money could attend a *zaar* ritual in some capacity virtually every week.

Conclusion

In this paper I have attempted to show how membership of a *zaar* spirit possession cult group helps to counteract the initial shrinkage of the women's sphere of social activity when they move to the towns. I have attempted to demonstrate some of the ways in which the cult provides urban women with a basis for association additional to relationships based on more traditional means of social alignment. It will be readily apparent that the new relationships formed do not in any substantial way threaten the basic premises and mores of Sudanese Muslim society. These are the dominance by men of the formal political, economic, and religious spheres of social organization, the segregation of the sexes, and the seclusion of women.

Women gain principally from cult group membership what they would automatically have received in their villages of origin – the companionship and support of a group of women with a common interest. What the cult also offers them is an introduction to a widely ramifying network of women comprising all ethnic and socio-economic categories; links well suited to the needs and requirements of urban life. Instead of suffering relative social isolation in the towns, *zaar* cult group members have a peer group among whom they can seek support in personal crises *and* compete for goods, services, and status.

I have left open until now the question of the attitude of men to *zaar* cult groups. If I hypothesize that the cult provides one of the few bases that exist for female solidarity in the towns then the questions remain: what sort of solidarity is it, and whom does it serve?

The attitude of men towards the cult is frankly ambivalent. On the one hand they are either outraged by, or ridicule, it. On the other they pay the often substantial bills for their womenfolks' cure by the cult. The relative secrecy of it inspires both deep suspicion and intense interest among men. They fear that immodest and even heretical acts take place and that

201

their honour may be impugned before 'strangers' by their wives' spirit-possessed revelations and behaviour. However, they also fear that their honour will be impugned if they *fail* to seek a solution to their wives' illnesses or distress. Many men believe in the *zaar* spirits, and no man wishes to have his wife unwell since, at least for as long as she is his wife, his household and his descendants through her depend on her well-being.

It is not apparent that men as a category are substantially threatened by the nature of such female solidarity as is expressed by the cult, and I do not believe that its members seek to challenge the basic social order. The male politico-religious establishment has reacted sharply to the cult in the past, much as the secular male-dominated educated elite ridicule it today. However, the potential for active female solidarity that the establishment seems to fear has not come to fruition. *Zaar* cult groups have not, for example, like their counterpart the Muslim brotherhoods, developed their potential as political groupings. Heretical practices, such as drinking blood from the ritual sacrifice, which incurred much wrath among the religious hierarchy in the cult's early days, have now largely been dropped in conformity with their wishes. Behaviour considered immodest among women, such as smoking and drinking alcohol, certainly takes place in cult ritual. However, among the more 'socially respectable' groups such behaviour is controlled and confined to those parts of the ritual addressed to spirits, such as the European and Ethiopian spirits, who demand it.

Where the cult group provides most backing for women is *vis à vis* individual men – the husband or father upon whose interest and support a woman's status ultimately rests. While, in part, a woman's status is ascribed and derives from the standing of the lineage into which she is born, it is also partly achieved and depends very much upon the marriage arranged for her. The ideal for a woman is fully to exercise her reproductive powers in the context of a stable and economically comfortable marriage, with a man of at least equivalent lineage status. Fundamental, then, to a woman's aspirations, as indeed to a man's, are financial security, her own health and fertility, and the health, fertility, and potency of her spouse. Anything that threatens her goals, be it her own ill health, infertility, or some action or lack of action on her spouse's or kinsmen's part, needs to be counteracted either directly or ritually. A husband's or kinsman's acceptance of a spirit-possession diagnosis, and their willingness to bear the financial burdens of a *zaar* ritual, is public affirmation of a woman's importance to them. *Zaar* cult leaders both use their own relative status and freedom, and marshall the opinions of their followers, to put considerable moral pressure on men to meet their wives' and daughters' ritual needs.

The cult's confrontation with individual men rather than with the male establishment *per se* is reflected in the stories and legends cult leaders tell concerning the success of the *zaar* cult in the face of male disapproval. These always take the form of how some well-known government or religious leader attempted to repress *zaar* practices until his own wife/sister/daughter became seriously ill through possession. Consequently he was forced for her sake to agree to a ritual being held in his household. The most famous of these legends concerns one of the most important figures in Sudanese history, the Mahdi himself. According to *zaar* followers, he outlawed the cult and persecuted defiant practitioners until one of his own womenfolk became ill, whereupon he was forced secretly to approach a *zaar shaikha*.

My own findings regarding the cult are much in line with those of Grace Harris in her study of Wataita women's spirit possession in Kenya (Harris 1957). Harris compared the possession ritual as a women's ritual with equivalent men's rituals. She suggested that in the spirit possession ritual, rather than expressing their desire to exercise masculine prerogatives, women were in fact expressing their fulfilment of the feminine role, just as the men expressed fulfilment of their masculine roles in their own rituals. Her conclusion was, much as mine has been here, that in spite of certain elements of cross-sexual hostility contained in the ritual, participation did not constitute either an attack on male identity or a desire to assume male roles. What it did express was maintenance of the existing social order, in which the husband publicly provided for the health and well-being of his wife.

Notes

1 The pre-Independence Census of 1955–6 was still the most recent full census at the time this paper was written.
2 These are both quite complex and painful operations. The most commonly practised form of female circumcision in the Sudan involves the complete excision of the external sexual organs – clitoris, labia minora, and labia majora – and the sealing together of the wound leaving only a small orifice for the passage of menses and urine. The resulting tough scar tissue sometimes has to be incised to allow sexual intercourse to take place at marriage. This again is performed by the midwife, usually for a considerable fee and in secrecy, since it is considered shameful for a man not to be able to penetrate his bride, no matter how severe the circumcision. The scar tissue has to be incised to allow the passage of a baby, and is re-rendered after each birth.
3 For more on the correspondence between *zaar* ritual and female life-cycle ritual see Constantinides 1977.
4 For a more detailed account of ritual similarities see Constantinides 1972.
5 Northern Sudanese believe that the only true homosexuals are passive homosexuals who act as female substitutes in the sexual act and are therefore also equated with females in a more general sense. The attitudes of Sudanese men and women towards such homosexuals is very similar to that described by Unni Wikan of Omanis towards Omani male transsexuals (Wikan 1977).
6 For comparative data on women's networks in an urban Muslim society see Vanessa Maher's study of women in Morocco (Maher 1974; 1976).
7 In recent years there have come into existence several women's voluntary associations, mostly allied to previously existing political parties (women were enfranchised in 1965) or among 'educated' women – that is the tiny percentage of women with secondary and university education. The latter, possibly because they have benefited from other means of cross-ethnic association through their schooling, are not much represented in *zaar* followings.

References

BARCLAY, H. B. (1964) *Buurri al Lamaab: A Surburban Village in the Sudan.* Ithaca, New York: Cornell University Press.
CONSTANTINIDES, P. M. (1972) *Sickness and the Spirits: A Study of the Zaar Spirit Possession Cult in the Northern Sudan.* Unpublished Ph.D. dissertation, London University.
—— (1977) Ill at ease and sick at heart: Symbolic Behaviour in

a Sudanese Healing Cult. In I. Lewis (ed.), *Symbols and Sentiments: Cross Cultural Studies in Symbolism*. London: Academic Press.

DEWEY, A. (1970) Ritual as a Mechanism for Urban Adaptation. *Man* 5(3):438–48.

HARRIS, G. (1957) Possession 'Hysteria' in a Kenyan Tribe. *American Anthropologist* 59:1046–66.

LEWIS, I. M. (1966) Spirit Possession and Deprivation Cults. *Man* (N.S.) 1:307–29

—— (1971) *Ecstatic Religion: An Anthropological Study of Spirit Possession and Shamanism*. Harmondsworth: Penguin.

MAHER, V. (1974) *Women and Property in Morocco*. Cambridge: Cambridge University Press.

—— (1976) Kin, Clients and Accomplices: relations among women in Morocco. In D. Barker and S. Allen (eds.), *Sexual Divisions and Society: Process and Change*. London: Tavistock.

SAIFULLAH-KHAN, V. (1976) Pakistani Women in Britain. *New Community* V(1–2):99–108.

WIKAN, U. (1977) Man becomes woman: transsexualism in Oman as a key to gender roles. *Man* 12(2):304–19.

EIGHT

Two contexts of solidarity among pastoral Maasai women[1]

MELISSA LLEWELYN-DAVIES

'Let's raise our voices so our song will be heard, loud
and annoying, through the cracks in the house-plaster.
We'll be quiet the day our husbands give up drinking beer.
Look! I've dared to announce in my song that we love
the young men [moran] of our district.'
(Maasai women's song in praise of young men)

'Solidarity', as I take it, is a commitment to some kind of
mutual aid or support, based upon the perception, by those
who are solidary, that they share certain significant characteristics, or that they are equal with respect to some social principle. This formulation is derived from Pizzorno, who points
out that, for an inferior status group, solidarity can be a double-
edged sword (Pizzorno 1970).[2] In some cases, it constitutes a
challenge to the existing social order, but in others it is supportive of the *status quo* and of the group's own inferior position
within it. In this paper, I shall describe two contexts in which

pastoral Maasai women manifest solidarity, and I shall look at their differing implications for the social order.

The Maasai have no social movements, consciously aimed at changing institutions, of the kind that Pizzorno is concerned with industrial societies. Nevertheless, I believe that his discussion of the concept of solidarity is illuminating in the Maasai context. He suggests that when the disadvantaged unite around an issue that has universal applicability (such as 'equal rights', 'universal suffrage', and so on) their solidarity is potentially subversive, because it challenges the social boundaries that circumscribe the group in its inferior position. When it is focused on non-universalistic issues, and does honour to the supposed differences of the inferior group from the dominant culture, then it may have the opposite effect.

Following this view, I shall argue that when Maasai women unite in solidarity to protect those women who commit adultery with men who are prohibited to them, they are implicitly asserting their equality. They are claiming a privilege already enjoyed by men, namely, the right to dispose of their own bodies, as they choose, in sexual relationships.

Such adultery threatens to undermine the hierarchial basis of one of the most important features of Maasai social structure – the age-set system – which organizes men and women into separate but interrelated hierarchies of sex- and age-groups. The boundaries between these groups are marked by codes of conduct relating to food and sexuality. These embody two principles: first, all legitimate sexuality takes place between structural unequals; second, rights of sexual access to women are vested in the men's age-sets. Both these principles are denied when women engage in adultery with men of their own choice.

Adulterers also flout one of the most reiterated moral values of Masaai life, *enkanyit*, which I shall translate as 'respect'. 'Respect' can be summed up as meaning courteous behaviour towards others, appropriate to their relative social positions. It has two more particular meanings, consistent with the importance of hierarchy and sexual prohibitions in the structure of social relations. It means deference and obedience towards one's superiors, and also the sexual avoidance of those who are forbidden to each other by 'incest' regulations. These include specific kin, and also the sex- and age-groups defined, by the age-set system, as related as 'parent' and 'child'. These people should 'respect' each other.

Overall, 'respect' can be seen as the moral justification of the social order, as it is represented in ideology, and in particular, the structural relations of the age- and sex-groups, and the fundamental inequality between them. Adultery calls into question the inevitability of these relations and it also constitutes gross disrespect to the woman's husband and his age-set, on the part of both lovers. It is, therefore, seen by men and women, as threatening social stability.

Maasai women also exhibit solidarity with each other on the basis of their common potentiality as child bearers. Fellow-villagers, and especially co-wives, are expected to support each other in practical matters and in rituals connected with childbirth. Their solidarity in this context may be highly conspicuous: they may, for example, gang together to humiliate or beat up individual men whose behaviour is believed to have endangered women's fertility. However, this behaviour does not threaten the institutionalized inequality between the sexes. On the contrary, it reflects women's acquiescence in the conventional Maasai wisdom that men care about cattle while women care about children.

This maxim, harped upon in myth as well as conversation, implies a certain complementarity between men and women. In fact, it devalues women's labour on the family herds and justifies men's control of all domestic animals, the basic means of production. This control, in turn, permits their domination over women and their progeny. Thus, when women unite in solidarity in the interests of human fertility, they confirm this representation of the relations of production and reproduction and concur in an ideology that assigns them an inferior social position.

Moreover, there is evidence, as I shall show, that women's social and political inferiority is explicitly linked, in Maasai thought, to childbearing. Indeed several writers have suggested that such an association may be culturally universal. They hold that women's biology (specifically their 'life-giving' powers) places them, conceptually, closer to nature than to culture (de Beauvoir 1953; Ortner 1974). Rosaldo and Atkinson find that cultures in which 'the sexes are seen as different and unequal by right' are also those that are likely to glorify

208

motherhood and feminine sexuality (Rosaldo and Atkinson 1975).[3]

Appropriately, women's procreative powers are believed to flourish, among the Maasai, when everyone in the community behaves with 'respect' and, implicitly, acknowledges their 'proper' position in the social order. Women are 'blessed' every four years or so, at a major ceremony (*inkamulak oonkituaak*), which promotes their fertility and, consequently, that of the human population in general. This ceremony is preceded by delegations of women (*olamal*) touring the country and levying fines upon those men who have persistently violated the more trivial food or 'respect' prohibitions, in relation to their real or age-set 'children'. In addition, they may mount punitive expeditions against more serious offenders against 'respect'. Moreover, it is thought that women may cause their children to be stillborn or deformed if they ignore certain food and sexual prohibitions during pregnancy. I suggest that these prohibitions are also concerned with the maintenance of 'correct' relations within the age-set system.

Women's solidarity in the interests of motherhood, then, invokes the principles of 'respect' and demands its acknowledgment by both sexes. By contrast, in the context of adultery, women unite to protect those who have disrupted the orderly hierarchical relations between men's groups and between men and women, by choosing to have sexual relations with members of an age-set that has no legitimate rights of sexual access to the women concerned.

To return to Pizzorno's comparison between the universalistic and non-universalistic aims of solidary action, it is clear that women's solidarity in relation to childbirth is based upon the perception of irreducible differences between men and women, and it dwells upon women's unique role in social reproduction. The ideal it celebrates – healthy motherhood – is not (obviously) applicable beyond the boundaries of the female sex, so it poses no threat to any of the biologically arbitrary rules and conventions that delineate women's inferior status. It is, in fact, supportive of male hegemony and the *status quo*, although it may have an important psychological effect. Pizzorno suggests that non-universalistic solidarity which celebrates the differences between the 'subculture' and the dominant culture, is significant in this respect. I do not wish to maintain that Maasai women's activities on behalf of their own fertility constitute a subculture, but I believe that Pizzorno's remarks are apposite nonetheless.

> '[The subculture] comes into existence because man does not want to accept a definition of his conduct according to which he has no choice: he needs to justify it, to present it as a choice or preference, or somehow be proud of it ... [Subcultural products] have the potentiality of transforming failures into preferences, and inferiority into pride.'
>
> (Pizzorno 1970:55)

Family and property

This paper draws upon material that I obtained during a period of research between 1970 and 1972, followed by short return visits in 1974 and 1977, in the Loita section of the pastoral Maasai, Loita Hills, south-west Kenya.[4] My material is mainly drawn from an area within Loita which is dominated by members of a particular sub-clan, *oloonkidong'i*. This sub-clan provides the Maasai people with its prophets and diviners (*oloiboni*). The social organization of the 'laibons', as they are known to English speakers in East Africa, differs in some ways from that of other Maasai. But exogamy rules forbid inter-marriage within the sub-clan, so laibons' wives are all drawn from non-laibon Maasai. In any case, the disparity of the laibons is not relevant to the material discussed in this article which is broadly characteristic of all Loita, laibons and non-laibons alike.

The Loita Maasai are herders of cattle, sheep, and goats. Up until 1976, the cultivation of cereals or vegetables was insignificant in the area where I carried out the most concentrated work. The staple food is milk, supplemented by meat and (bought) grain. Villages (*enkang*) are semi-permanent, moving every three or four years, when the site is considered to have become too muddy and insect-ridden. They are surrounded by a circular thorn fence.

Every adult woman builds her own house, from heavy posts, sticks, and cow-dung, for herself, her husband, and her children to live in. Villages vary greatly in size: a large one may contain twenty or more houses and about 100 people, while the smallest may consist of only two houses and half a dozen residents. A herd-owner is free to choose whether to live alone with his women and children in his own village, or whether to move in with other herd-owners who may be kinsmen, affines, or friends. In this case he is likely to pasture his animals in co-operation with his fellow villagers.

The livestock normally leaves the village in the morning and returns from grazing in the evening, but the herds are sometimes divided to take advantage of distant grasslands or salt-licks. When this happens, some of the men and women drive the bulk of the animals to temporary cattle-camps, constructed by the women from sticks and cow-hides, leaving behind just sufficient milch-cows to feed the population that remains in the village.

Land, among the Maasai, is administered in common by the herd-owners who use it, but livestock is owned by individual men. Roles in production are, ideally, determined by sex, and age (as defined by the formal age organization), but labour is actually appropriated by individual herd-owners on the basis of kinship. To maintain a self-sufficient household, a man needs not only animals, but also women and herders to work for him. It is believed that circumcised men become sick, or even die, if they perform certain 'women's' chores for themselves, such as drawing water.

It is also considered inappropriate for an elder to go herding every day. Ideally, a man's herds and flocks are grazed by his uncircumcised sons, while his wives see to the milking and the welfare of the youngest animals, aided by their uncircumcised daughters. Women decide how much milk to leave the calf, and how much to take for the human population. Women and girls also build and maintain the houses, fetch water and firewood, and, of course, take care of the smallest children.

The herd-owner himself has overall responsibility for the herds and for the members of his household. He makes all the important decisions involving the disposal of resources, the sale, slaughter, or gift of livestock, and the marriage of daughters. He also decides alone, or in association with other men of the village, where the animals will pasture, and where and when they will be watered, or taken to the salt-licks. The village elders are also jointly responsible for the construction of the village fence, which is expected to protect the inhabitants from the dangers and disruptions of the untamed world outside (notably animal predators and cattle diseases).

Maasai men are usually ambitious to become 'rich'. The concept of 'riches' (*karsisisho*) embraces rights over women and children as well as rights over livestock, and it has spiritual as well as material consequences. A man who lives to old age, surrounded by wives, children, and grandchildren who are supported by his flourishing herds, is believed to be immortal. Such a man will never die, but merely go to sleep; his name will not be forgotten quickly, unlike those who die young or poor, whose names must never be spoken in the presence of their descendants. This ideal is achieved only in old age, and only by a few. In practice, men often find themselves without enough animals or personnel to form a self-sufficient household, especially while they are comparatively young. Indeed the process by which uterine brothers take possession of their 'own' animals from their father's herd is a very gradual one. (It is not formally completed until their father's death.) Men remain dependent on the services of their mothers or their brothers' wives until they themselves have found a wife. Moreover, herd-owners often decide to pasture their animals as one unit, pooling their sons' or younger brothers' labour; elders may even go herding themselves or keep an adult unmarried daughter at home, to tend the sheep and goats. However, through all the variations in the composition of the household, and the allocation of tasks within it, one element remains unchanged: women never have full rights of ownership over livestock, so they must always be attached to the household of a male herd-owner.

When she marries, a woman is allocated limited rights over a number of her husband's animals. She has milking-rights, and the right to the sale or use of hides of all stock which die or are slaughtered. These animals constitute the nucleus of the herds and flocks her sons will eventually come to possess. She alone is responsible for the allocation of specific animals to them, and she can decide to give nothing at all to a particular son. At her death, any unallocated animals pass directly to her youngest son.

Nevertheless, she herself is never in charge (*aitore*) of the stock, with rights of alienation over it: these rights pass directly from father to son. Even a widow, caretaking her late husband's animals until her sons come of age, must find a male guardian to protect her against the cupidity of unscrupulous affinal kin. She must consult this man before taking any important decisions, and he may administer her herds without seeking her advice. A husband may give away or slaughter any of his wife's allocated animals, including those that she has been given by her own kin. However, a wife has the right to complain to her father or brother if her husband tries to reallocate any of her stock to another wife. Unless there is a very compelling reason for doing so, such as the death of most of the co-wife's herd, this action will be taken as grounds for divorce.

A woman's aim is to bear sons to take over her allocated herd and when this occurs, she continues to 'milk her own cows' in the household of one of her own children. As mother-in-law to her sons' wives, she is much respected and also relieved from some of the more arduous chores by the younger women. Sometimes a woman who has borne daughters but no sons, persuades her husband to let her keep a daughter at home, unmarried, to produce sons who will inherit the herd. The herds of barren women who have not been given a child to adopt, are divided up among the sons of her co-wives or other male relatives of her husband. Such widows must depend upon their own or their husband's kin for support.

Women, then, are excluded from almost all important decisions relating to the welfare of the herds. They have no right to sell or slaughter animals, or to give them away to anyone outside the household of which they are a member. They have no right to dispose of themselves in marriage, and mothers have no right to a say in the marriage of their daughters; women are 'bought and sold with stock' as they put it. Women diagnose their lack of autonomy as a consequence of their lack of rights over livestock. In an interview, a married woman said:

'There's nothing a woman is in charge of. Because the cow that is in the village – she just looks after it. She can't say "I shall sell it today because I have a purpose in mind". Because she can't dispose of it ... You have nothing. If your husband sells a cow [from your herd] you don't have rights over the money. None of it belongs to you, unless your husband gives you a little to buy flour, or something to buy tea – that's what you get. If your father comes [to visit], if your mother comes, it's only your husband who can sell a cow [to buy liquor for them]. There is no woman in Maasai who can decide to do what she wants.'

Moreover, women's poverty also inhibits their ability to consolidate social relationships because, in Maasai, all important dyadic relations, including kin relations, are marked by the gift of stock from one party to the other.

However, women do not unite to protect those of their fellows who suffer particularly badly from their separation from the means of production. For example, in 1970, a man died leaving a widow with two immature sons. Shortly after her husband's death, one of her sons fell sick. She and many other women believed that he had been bewitched by her husband's brothers who were supposed to be looking after her herds until the boys grew up. The widow fled with her sons and the brothers divided up her herd among themselves. The general view among the men was that she must have been at fault in arousing her guardians' dislike in the first place; they denied that the men had actually used witchcraft. Women disagreed, and said that the men had only been interested in the livestock. But they did little to help her, and laughed at her sad fate. She took refuge in her mother's house and her eldest son was adopted by one of her mother's brothers. Eventually, after the death of her youngest son, and having no father or brothers, she married a wealthy elder. She was by this time past the menopause and it was generally believed by the women that her husband would throw her out once she was too old to work. She was sometimes addressed, by women, as 'the unfavourite wife' (entinki), and her plain appearance was joked about. Those involved hope that when her eldest son grows up, he will look after his mother.

Women do not unite around the issue of their economic dependence on men, rather, they stress the importance of bearing children who will mitigate the effects of not owning animals. Mothers assume that they will be able to exercise an important influence over their adult sons, who, after all, obtained many of their animals from them. Women may refer to their sons' initiation into adulthood as the time when they 'become strong' (*tenagolu*). An informant, whose son was shortly to be circumcised, boasted to me that she would soon be able to slaughter a goat for her friends to eat, because her son would not refuse his mother such a favour.

Women, then, are very much aware of the economic basis of their inequality with men, but in this case their awareness of their common lot does not lead to solidary action. They are divided by their immediate economic interests because their individual well-being depends upon their raising to maturity sons, who are successful herd-owners, and who fulfil their obligations to their mothers. A myth, often told by women, reflects the relation between their propertylessness, their lack of solidarity on economic matters, and their emotional focus on their children. However, it reflects this 'true' relation in an 'illusory' way, laying the blame for their dependence on the atomism which in fact flows from that dependence.

'Elephants used to move the houses of women; buffaloes were their cattle; Thomson's gazelles were their goats; wart-hogs were their sheep; zebras were their donkeys. Those were women's herds before. And then one morning, they got up early to slaughter an ox. And there were many women in the village. And there was not one who did not say, "My child is not going herding because he will stay to eat some kidney". One said, "My child is not going". And another said "Neither is mine" ... So the cattle went off on their own. They went into the forest. The zebra became wild; the gazelle became wild; the buffalo became wild. But they were our cattle before. We let them go on account of a kidney ... So we no longer have cattle. These cows all belong to men. We have become the servants of men because we let our cows go off into the forest and become wild beasts ... We no longer have cattle that we can dispose of ... It was us who put the herds in danger through putting our own individual interest first, so off they went. So we are not in charge of anything any more. All we have is calabashes to milk into.'
(As told by a married woman in 1974)

In the myth, women become the servants of men because they attach more importance to their children than to their livestock. The polarity underlying the myth, that men care for

215

livestock and women care for children is, as I have said, fundamental to Maasai conceptions of male superiority. It follows
that any solidary action which acknowledges this polarity can
only underline their own inferiority.

The age organization and 'respect'

The age organization ranks all men and women in separate but
interlocking hierarchies. Circumcision, in early adolescence,
denotes the end of childhood for both sexes. The male hierarchy
consists of three age-categories: uncircumcised boys (*olayioni*),
circumcised young men (*olmurrani*), and elders (*olpayian*); the
female hierarchy consists of only two: uncircumcised girls
(*entito*) and circumcised women (*enkitok*).

The older girls of a village (from about nine years old and
upwards) form a kind of labour pool for the women, similar
to that of the boys for the men. They run errands, fetch water,
and help to look after the toddlers. They are often given responsibility for a younger sibling, or for another child. In the
latter case, the girl will usually be 'given to' the mother of the
baby she is looking after, as a foster-child. In general, the older
girls sleep together in one of the houses where there is no elder
in residence. An uncircumcised girl must have sexual relations
with young circumcised men, but she is not expected to conceive. Pregnancy before circumcision brings shame upon herself
and her family, but it is not uncommon since a girl's circumcision may be delayed until a year or so after the onset of the
menses.

The operation involves the excision of the clitoris, but Maasai
women do not see the operation as significant in terms of sexual
fulfilment. They deny that uncircumcised girls (*entito*) or circumcised women (*enkitok*) ever reach sexual climaxes in the
way that men do. The main significance of the rite to the initiate
is that it confers upon her the status of a fertile adult, entitled
to become pregnant and to marry. Adult women have no formal
age-sets, but there is an informal division between fertile
women (*esiankiki*) and those past the menopause (*entasat*),
which is only really apparent at the time of the women's 'blessing'.

Men automatically belong to the age-set that is 'open' at
the time of their circumcision. Age-sets (*olporror*) are organized

on a Maasai-wide basis, and each age-set recruits for about 14 years. A man remains a member of the same age-set into which he was initiated, for the rest of his life. The age-set as a whole moves through various *rites de passage*, and its members change status together as the age-set grows older, and as the more senior age-sets die out.

The youngest age-set belongs to the age-category (or 'age-grade') of *olmurrani*, which is usually anglicized as 'moran'. It is often translated as 'warrior' because the young men were primarily responsible for raiding and warfare in the days before such activities were largely stopped by the government. Even now, the main activities of the moran are independent of the family herds, and they are formally segregated from the elders' villages and thrown into each other's company by two rules. They may not drink milk (the staple food) alone, but only in the presence of other 'moran', and they may never eat meat which has been seen by a circumcised (and therefore formally fertile) woman.

These rules are two of a number, concerning eating and other kinds of behaviour, which mark the boundaries between the various sex- and age-groups. Non-observance of any of them results in *enturuj*. There is no English equivalent to this term, but it shares some similarities with the notion of 'embarrass-ment', although its application is limited to the context of the relations between different age- and sex-groups. *Enturuj* and 'respect' both maintain formal distance between these groups. Unlike 'respect', *enturuj* has no moral content, but a person who deliberately or carelessly 'embarrasses' another, is guilty of 'disrespect' (*meenyit*). Both ideas are often expressed in terms of the 'fear' (*aure*) aroused by another age- or sex-group, in specific contexts. Thus, an elder is said to 'fear' his age-set daughter, while a moran is said to 'fear' the skirt (*olokesena*) of a circumcised woman. A woman's skirt is said to be 'dirty' because it may have been in contact with *kereek*, the lard with which newborn babies are smeared. While they are eating meat, the eyes of moran dare not look upon it.

After her circumcision, a woman's social maturity is un-equivocal. She is considered quite ready for childbirth and most women are married within a year or so after the operation. However, a man's circumcision may be seen as only the begin-ning of a *rite de passage* of which moranhood is the 'rite of seclusion'. During this period, men build up their moral strength apart from women, and gain experience denied to them. It ends in their gradual reincorporation into domestic life, as elders, worthy of women's 'respect', and entitled to be their masters.

The moran of one district have their own special encampment (*emanyata*), where many of them live with their mothers and uncircumcised brothers and sisters, and this provides a headquarters for the activities of the age-set. Also, all moran spend a lot of time (perhaps a month or more at a time) living in small groups of ten or so, in the forests which surround Loita, and other areas of Maasai. They take with them an ox, or a succession of oxen, which are killed and eaten by the members of the camp. No milk or grain is consumed at these forest camps (*olpul*), where the young men are thought to build up their physical strength, by gorging themselves on animal flesh, and their courage, by learning to face the dangers of the wild together. The friendships they form at this time are supposed to last a lifetime.

The legitimate sexual partners of these young men, when they are visiting the elders' villages or staying in the *emanyata*, are uncircumcised girls, although (as we shall see) they also have love affairs with circumcised wives of elders. Girls sometimes accompany moran to the forest camps for a few days to share their meat. However, sexual relations are considered inappropriate in the forest, and, moreover, the girls must never become 'dirty' (like circumcised women) through contact with animal fat; their food is prepared on skewers so that they never touch it with their hands.

Age-sets in most territorial sections are divided into an older 'right-hand' and a younger 'left-hand' group. After about seven years or so as moran, the reincorporation of the group begins, in a series of rituals that relax the rules setting them apart, and draw attention to their new roles as herd-owners, husbands and fathers. These rituals take about fifteen years to complete, by which time almost all the men in the age-set should have married. However, they are in some contexts referred to as 'elders', as soon as the first 'promotional' ceremony (*eunoto*) is completed. Nowadays, approximately two years after this ceremony, most have ritually 'drunk milk at home' (*aok kule ti ang*) with no age-mate to drink with them. This enables them to return to their fathers' villages and begin to take responsibility for their share of their fathers' herds. A year or two later it is appropriate for a man to marry, although a very few may have been lucky enough to find a wife before *eunoto*, and others may be unable to find a wife for another five years or even more. As a result, when a man takes his first wife, he is likely to be at least ten years older than her.

As Spencer has shown, one of the important effects of the age-set system of the Maasai-speaking Samburu (which is substantially similar to that of the Maasai) is that it permits the older men a fairly high level of polygyny. This is because the young men are sent off into moranhood, which delays their entry into the competition for wives (Spencer 1965). In the population I censused, the relationship between age and polygyny was very marked (ilKiseiyai were still 'recruiting' at this time).

Table 1   *Age-sets and their wives in Kisokon, Loita Section* (1972)

age- category	age-set name	number of members	number of wives	average number of wives per elder
moran	ilKiseiyai	15	0	0
elders	ilTerekeyani	17	52	0·67
	ilNyankusi	34	23	1·50
	ilTerito	22	33	3·05

The hierarchy of age- and sex-groups can be schematically drawn as follows:

superordination ↑	elders	
	moran	circumcised women
subordination ↓	uncircumcised boys	uncircumcised girls

All legitimate sexuality takes place between structural unequals. Elders may have sexual relations only with circumcised women; moran should take their girlfriends from among the uncircumcised girls; uncircumcised boys, being superior to no one, are required to be chaste. The right of a particular category of men to have sexual relations with a particular category of females is often expressed as their right to physically punish them. Thus, elders beat their circumcised wives and moran beat the girls.

In 1971, a young elder in Loita refused to take his full brother's widow as his wife in defiance of his father; he was happy to take responsibility for her, but only as a dependent widow. Eventually, his father threatened to 'embarrass' him by beating him if he himself failed to beat the woman in full view of the village, as a public statement that he was taking her as a wife with full rights of sexual access. Corresponding with the sexual rules, elders should not eat in front of girls; moran should not eat in front of circumcised women; boys, who are not supposed to be engaged in sexual activity of any kind, may eat with anyone.

The age-sets with the status of elders are also differentiated from each other in terms of their relations with, and rights over, women. In the first place, there is some sense in which the members of an age-set hold in common the rights of sexual access to their wives. A man may have sexual relations with the wife of an age-mate without fear of reprisals; indeed if the husband should voice his objections to such behaviour, his age-set has the right to fine him nine head of cattle. A hospitable friend should offer his house (and by implication his wife) to a visiting age-mate, although women say that they do not feel obliged to respond to the sexual advances of men other than their husbands.

On the other hand, the age-set must give away its daughters, as wives, to men of other age-sets. With respect to its daughters, the age-set is 'exogamous'. This 'exogamous' principle is expressed in terms of the rule that no man may have sexual relations with his own daughter or with one of an age-mate. This is forbidden by a rule of 'respect' which is taken very seriously and fairly frequently referred to. Rumours of 'lack of respect', in this sense (meenyit), on the part of fathers towards their daughters are particularly common at the time of the women's 'blessing', as we shall see. A man may not even sleep under the same roof as his own or his age-set daughter; nor may he beat her if she misbehaves.

Women, in their turn, are prohibited from having sexual relations with their sons, and with the age-mates of their sons, for reasons of 'respect'. However, this rule, in its transgression, does not become a matter of concern for the whole community, unlike the transgression of that which enjoins 'fathers' to 'respect' their 'daughters'. There is, however, public concern about the violation of the rule that forbids pregnant women from having sexual relations with men. In Maasai thought, this is the equivalent for women, of the rule that forbids men to have sexual relations with their 'daughters'. It is equivalent, I believe, because both offences bring a man into sexual contact with his offspring, in this case, because the man's seminal fluid is believed to enter the foetus.

An age-set should 'respect' all the age-sets senior to it, but the relationship between alternate age-sets differs from that between adjacent age-sets. Alternate age-sets are perceived as following the same traditions, and the senior one acts as the moral guardians of the junior, officiating at all its *rites de passage*. Adjacent age-sets, on the other hand, follow slightly different ceremonial traditions, and there is a certain rivalry between them. The relationship may also be conceptualized as one between affines, because Maasai say that an age-set gives its daughters to their immediate juniors. They, in return, should accord the senior age-set 'respect', as their potential fathers-in-law.

The importance of the concept of 'respect' and the related idea of *enturuj*, in the age organization and family structure of the Maasai is by now, I hope, clear. The virtues of respectful behaviour are constantly dwelt upon by men and women, in speeches, debates, and general conversation. The following quotation is part of a harangue delivered by a member of the ilNyankusi age-set, to the 'right-hand' of the junior alternate age-set, ilKiseiyai, at *eunoto*, their first collective ceremony of reincorporation. (IlTerekeyani are the age-set in between.)

'Go, and "respect" the people, wherever you go. "Respect" is the best thing on earth ... [Singling out a counsellor] You were disrespectful as an uncircumcised boy. You behaved like a moran when you were a boy. Later you thought, because you'd become so involved with women you were no longer a moran. You thought you were an elder like me ...

You think you've become an elder and we are equal simply because you "eat" tobacco and women, and because I can no longer call my women my own ["to eat" can also mean to have sexual relations] ... I shan't have to tell you again to stop stealing animals to take to the forest camps. I shan't have to remind you again to stop going to the wives of ilTerekeyani. Put that age-set in "respect" because it's their daughters you marry [literally=it's they who you marry from].'   (Recorded in 1974)

The transgression or the upholding of 'respect' is, indeed, a constant theme in Maasai rituals. The rules may be played upon in jokes, insults, and mock battles, or they may be invoked by honouring those who have not offended against them, and by forcing those who have done so to reveal their guilt.

At *olkiteng' loolbaa*, the last *rite de passage* undertaken by an individual man, the women from surrounding villages make themselves sticks and engage in a mock battle with the men which is regarded as very hilarious. Women describe the ceremony as the time that 'they beat up the elders'. *Eunoto* honours those moran who have not had sexual relations with circumcised women; women themselves must confess to such offences before the ceremony that permits their husbands to eat meat in the village where it may be seen by women. The women's 'blessing' is preceded by the invocation of rules forbidding sexuality and commensality between 'fathers' and their 'children'.

Nevertheless, the idea of 'respect' rests upon the assumption of inequality in social relations, and for women, the latent meaning of the sexuality and commensality rules, as a whole, is their own inescapable inferiority to men.

Solidarity and fertility

When a man brings home a new bride to his village, her arrival is marked by a ceremony, which begins by dramatizing the very reverse of female solidarity. The bride is met outside the entrance to the village by her fellow-villagers, women who are likely to be strangers to her. The women descend upon her, screaming threats and insults. Her appearance and character are abused: she is ugly, she is known to be a thief, and so on.

In addition, the women threaten her with branding irons and man-eating lions, and other terrifying or comical dangers. She is not allowed through the gates of the village until she has broken down and wept; at this point, she is invited to enter the village. Traditions vary from family to family, but the bride usually responds by refusing to enter until she has been promised gifts of livestock (and therefore friendship) by some of the women.

Those, in particular, who should give gifts to the bride are her co-wives, but other women, whose husbands are related to the groom, may also promise stock. No woman can alienate an animal from her husband's herd without his approval, but women who belong to the household of the same man (and are, therefore, supported by the same herd) are expected to give to each other. Full brothers, for example, consider it appropriate for their women to give gifts to each other, especially if their herds have not yet been completely separated. Relationships that have been initiated or consolidated by the gift of animals are taken very seriously by Maasai. Indeed, the participants in such relationships of friendship are expected to help and support each other in trouble, throughout their lifetimes. Men have many stock-friends, but women have only a few. These almost invariably include their co-wives, and women consider it very important that a man's wives should help each other as male stock-friends do.

Women's work varies from season to season but, broadly speaking, they devote the middle of the day, while the animals are away at pasture, to domestic work. This includes fetching water and firewood, maintaining their houses and the village walkways, and cleaning the milk calabashes. Women, like men, express a dislike of being alone, and they perform many of their chores together, in informal groups of women from within the village or from neighbouring villages. They also spend some of the day sewing and chatting together, collected in the shadow of a wall, and playing with the smallest children. Older girls often join these groups, but they run the risk of being sent on errands.

Women are expected to help each other in many small ways, and they constantly request and receive small gifts of tobacco, tea, and sugar from one another. However, it is around events connected with childbirth and fertility that collective and co-operative activity is most evident. Women supervise all births and organize the ceremonies that follow. Every circumcised woman in the village must attend the tea-parties which celebrate the birth itself and the first shaving of the child at about three months old. It is very unpropitious (and also very rude) if anyone fails to share the tea, which is brewed in one huge aluminium bowl on the new mother's hearth. Less formally, all the women are expected to go to her house to sing and keep her company after dark, for several evenings running. If her mother-in-law is alive and living close, she will usually take primary responsibility for the mother and baby, but the child will also be cared for by various women visitors to the house, in the days following the confinement.

Women's autonomy and support for each other, in this important context, does, I assume, have a positive effect on their view of themselves as a sex. However as I have suggested, solidarity in the interests of childbirth and fertility is based on a concern that is 'non-universalistic', in Pizzorno's sense of the term. It does not challenge the existing distribution of roles in social reproduction and, therefore, it does not challenge male hegemony. This can be seen most clearly by considering the four-yearly 'blessing' of the women (*inkamulak oonkituaak*), which protects the community against barrenness and infant mortality.

Women are responsible for initiating the ceremony and for making all the early arrangements. In the months leading up to it, the informal hierarchy between the women's 'age-sets' (*olporror*) becomes visible. This is based on the distinction between fertile women and those past the menopause, and it is copied from the men's age-set system. Many of the same terms are used. For example, women who distinguish themselves in debate become known as 'counsellors' like their more formal male counterparts. However, the 'age-sets' are differentiated by indigenously female characteristics unlike other women's groupings which are derived from women's relationships with men (for example, the wives/daughters of age-set X; the women of Loita, and so forth).

I participated in a blessing ceremony in June 1972, the preparations for which began in the autumn of 1971. These were carried on in an atmosphere of excitement and euphoria. For about three months, the women held almost daily meetings in different villages to discuss among other things, the problems of finance and choosing a man to lead the ritual. Sometimes women would have to travel for a couple of hours on foot to reach them. Fines were threatened for persistent non-attendance. In late 1971, the junior (fertile) women accused their seniors of procrastination, because their interest in the birth of children was less urgent than their own. In one very heated meeting, both sides tore off their leather belts and a fight began, but this was quickly suppressed. Eventually, everyone was organized into delegations (*olamal*), which roamed the country in search of contributions of money from men, to finance the event.

The women's delegations have a powerful curse; when they arrive in a village, they approach the house of an elder, singing and dancing. As soon as they reach the doorway women plant a stick, upright and sing until the owner of the house emerges with a contribution, or with a convincing promise of such a gift; the women then remove the stick. If the owner should refuse to give, the women will leave the stick in place and this can bring dire misfortune (death or disease) upon himself or, more likely, his children. The women can single out any elder for these unwelcome attentions, though they should never approach more than one or two men in a single village. In practice, they tend to choose men who are known to be rich in cattle, and who therefore have cash to spare; or they choose men who have offended against one of the less seriously held rules of 'respect'. Men sung to in this way include, for example, those who have been often discovered drinking milk at home in the presence of uncircumcised girls, or men who, perhaps tired or drunk, have inadvertently allowed their clothes to fall open to reveal their genitals in front of their children.

These 'delegations' are usually regarded by women as occasions to be enjoyed. They possess an uncharacteristic degree of autonomy: if an elder should beat his wife, for no good reason, while a delegation is visiting his village, they have the right to exact a fine from him. But the 'blessing' is sometimes preceded by more hostile proceedings because suspicions of the most serious kind of 'disrespect' are in the air. In 1972, the ceremony was temporarily suspended because a man complained to his age-set council that his mother-in-law had insulted him by shouting at him, when they were both drunk, 'You fuck your daughter'. This, with appropriate variations, is the standard Maasai insult (women are accused of 'fucking' their fathers). However, in the heady atmosphere before the 'blessing', it did not pass unheeded, even though no one thought that the woman had meant to actually accuse her son-in-law of the offence. The elders involved refused to allow the ceremony to take place until the women had sent several deputations to plead with them. Eventually, they agreed to let it go ahead on the payment of a fine, imposed collectively on the women.

Women have the right to punish only one serious offence in Maasai, the offence of 'eating one's children' (*ainosa inkera*) and *olkishoroto* is the penalty they exact against the offender. A man 'eats his child' if he has sexual relations with his real or age-set daughter; a woman 'eats her child' if she has sexual relations with a man while she is pregnant. In this latter case, the seminal fluid is believed to enter into the foetus through its orifices, and to cause it to be stillborn or deformed at birth. Women are also said to commit this offence if they drink milk from a cow infected by foot-and-mouth disease while they are pregnant, the milk being thought to affect the foetus in the same way. However, the women do not talk of *olki-shoroto* being organized in this case and they do not seem to have a technique for diagnosing this latter offence as they do for the former.

When a woman is delivered of a stillborn or deformed baby, the midwife, or a woman skilled in the technique, massages her stomach to find evidence of seminal fluid distending in it. If she claims to have found such evidence, the culprit is abused by everyone present. At some point thereafter, *olkishoroto* is organized (opinions vary among the women about how long it takes to get ready). I have never witnessed it, either against a man or woman, but I have received descriptions, from memory, of the events that take place when a woman is punished in this way. The outline that follows is based on several accounts. I have no first-hand account of *olkishoroto* when it is levied against a man, but all my informants assured me that is is substantially similar.

The women who participate put on ceremonial garments and descend upon the guilty person's house singing obscene and abusive songs. They beat her with sticks and raze her house to the ground. Then they seize one of her animals for slaughter; the animal is known as *olkishoroto*, 'the levy' and it is this which gives the event its name. Her husband will raise no objection to this slaughter; indeed, he is likely to have fled the scene. After the animal has been butchered the offender is humiliated. The contents of the animal's stomach are emptied over her head, and the large intestine is draped around her neck. The women dance in circles round her, singing insulting songs and pricking her chest and shoulders with pointed sticks. The flesh of the *olkishoroto* animal is then consumed, but it must be eaten exclusively by circumcised women, because any girl or man who swallowed a mouthful would fall ill. When a woman who has been publicly censured in this way goes, later on, to the 'blessing', she is said to be forced once again to wear the large intestine around her neck, in acknowledgement of her past offence.

Olkishoroto actually happens, I believe, quite rarely. Only one of my informants had seen one within the last five or ten years, and that was outside Loita. But rumours about supposed offenders, both male and female, are rife. Women seem to be accused of the offence only when they give birth, although mothers may remain uneasy about the interpretation that might be put on any small defects on their young children. For example, a six-month-old baby developed a fold of skin on one of his thighs because, his very young mother said, she was too tired to turn him over in his sleep at night. She was afraid, she told me, that people thought she had 'gone to men' while pregnant and caused the blemish herself. The fold of skin in fact quickly disappeared as the baby grew older.

Suspicions against men, on the other hand, tend to build up over a period of time. Men who choose to live alone with their wives and children are particularly vulnerable to imputations of father-daughter incest, as are, to a lesser extent, the fathers of women who have remained at home, unmarried, after circumcision. When the women's 'blessing' is mooted, the preceding series of women's meetings provide them with an opportunity to voice these rumours and decide whether they should take action.

In general, then, childbirth and human fertility flourish when men and women 'respect' their children. Women, who are acknowledged to have special responsibilities towards children, are assigned the task of policing the important as well as the minor rules which protect children from the sexuality of the parental generation. Events surrounding the 'blessing' force everyone in the community to recognize the validity of the rules as well as the women's right to enforce them. Nevertheless, it is a right which, in practice, women can rarely exercise without the consent of the elders.

In 1976 the women decided before the blessing to organize *olkishoroto* against a particular man. I was not present, but I have gathered accounts from informants. An elder was accused of having sexual relations with his real daughter by a number of speakers at a women's meeting. It was decided that he was indeed guilty of the offence, and that *olkishoroto* would would be organized. The man in question heard what had happened and went at once to complain to members of his own age-set. They responded by cursing the beer that the women had brewed for the age-set of the man who was to lead the ritual (the age-set immediately senior to that of the offended man). Any elder who drank the cursed beer was expected to die and, since liquor is an essential ingredient in any ceremony, their action effectively put a stop to the arrangements. The senior age-set announced that the 'blessing' would be cancelled unless the women withdrew the charge. For their part, the women remained convinced that the accusation was true, but decided, after much discussion, that the 'blessing' was more important than the punishment of the offence. They sent two representatives to apologize publicly to an age-set council called by the supporters of the accused man. The women were then fined two blankets and a large quantity of home-brewed beer, and the curse was withdrawn.

Moreover, it is an elder who actually blesses the women, and his age-mates who help to decide the details of the ritual. When the women have collected enough money for the ceremony through the *olamal,* and through individual contributions begged from husbands, brothers, and sons, or supplied from their own resources (the sale of hides), they consult a 'laibon' (diviner). This man consults his oracle and suggests a suitable candidate who must be an elder of proven fertility. In 1972, the women asserted that if the oracle were to choose a man who was likely to become too drunk to carry out the proceedings properly, they would consult another laibon. In fact, they were happy with the choice of the oracle, so I do not know if they would have succeeded in doing so. However, as soon as the blesser is appointed, the women lose control of the whole affair. Elders decide how much beer the women should brew for them. The elders also decide the locations of the ceremony and administer the various stages of it. It is they who 'bless' the women, and conifer fertility upon them, by spitting beer over their heads. They can even, as I have described, call the ceremony off, if they hear reports of 'disrespect' on the part of the women who are hoping to attend.

In 1976, the ritual was held in common by the whole of Loita, laibons and non-laibons alike. In 1972, the non-laibon elders of Loita decided to refuse their women the blessing because, they said, they had 'thrown away all respect'. The main reason for this judgement appeared to be that one of the women of the non-laibons was suspected of trying to kill her husband, by putting poison in his tea. The man chosen to lead the 'blessing' was himself a laibon and he rigidly enforced the prohibition on the participation of any women who were not 'women of the laibons' (that is, their wives and their circumcised, but not yet married, daughters). Many 'women of the non-laibons' pleaded with him to let them enter the 'blessing', and many 'women of the laibons' also entreated him on their behalf. He refused them all; even women who had been born laibons, but who were now married to non-laibon men, were not allowed to participate.

Men, obviously, cannot themselves give birth, but they must have legitimate children if they are to achieve 'riches'. In asserting that women were eligible to be blessed, according to their relationships with individual men, the blesser was re-affirming the principle of men's ultimate rights over women's fertility. This principle was also expressed in the fact that the ceremony was eventually taken completely out of the women's hands. It is worth noting, in this context, two other ways in which men (and culture) assert their control over women's powers of reproduction. It is believed that girls do not develop breasts until moran have 'opened up the way' by having sexual relations with them. Moreover, girls are not considered fully fertile until they have been further opened up in a rite of circumcision.[5]

Women's solidary action, in the interests of children, does

nothing to challenge men's control over women and their progeny. Indeed, it celebrates the existing relations of production and reproduction, which are rooted in the inequality of the sexes, and it reaffirms the principles of 'respect'. Moreover, Rosaldo and Atkinson's suggestion that there may be a direct association in many systems of thought, between women's inferiority and their role in biological reproduction, is borne out, for the Maasai, in a 'secret' myth, supposedly known only to women. The myth describes a time when there was no fertility (*enkishon*), no human reproduction, and no inequality. It is usually told with great guffaws and innuendos; what follows is summarized from several versions.

Once, men and women were equal, there were no elders in the land, but only women, known as *ilpongolo* (women-warriors), and moran. The women were braver than the men. At that time, they had no vaginas, but only tiny holes for urine to pass through. One day they accompanied the moran to war because they needed assistance. That night, as they were sitting round their separate fires, the moran crept up behind the women carrying bows, weapons the women knew nothing about. The moran pushed the sharp ends of their bows into the women's bodies and created vaginas, and the women and the moran lay down together. In the morning, the moran got up and said 'Ahah! These are only women, after all!', so they took them and married them. Women lost their bravery, and fertility began.

Solidarity and sexuality

The hierarchical organization of men's age-sets is partly defined, as I have said, in terms of their rights over women. When women decide to dispose of their own sexuality, as they choose, and to engage in sexual relations with the 'wrong' men, they not only manifest a lack of 'respect' for their husbands, but they also disrupt the orderly relations between age-sets. 'Adultery' with a man of the same age-set as a woman's husband is not regarded as a breach of her husband's privilege, so 'adultery' in what follows, should be understood to mean a relationship between a woman and a man from a different age-set than the one she 'married'.

'Adultery', then, expresses and creates tensions between the

230

men's age-sets. For example, in 1971, the elders of a Loita village occupied exclusively by ilNyankusi age-set members, called upon their age-mates to curse the current age-set of moran, their juniors by two age-sets. This was due to their 'disrespect' for the elders as evidenced by their persistent seduction of their wives. The age-set council decided not to accede to this request; some of the men had sons in the younger age-set and it was said that they did not want them to come to harm. The elders of the village originally concerned with the problem decided to issue a total ban on visits from any moran to any person in the village.

The antagonism between adjacent age-sets concerning this issue is perhaps even more marked than that between alternate age-sets. In 1974, relations between the two youngest age-sets, ilTerekeyani and ilKiseiyai, became particularly tense, I was told, because a member of ilTerekeyani had found a moran in his wife's bed. There was a fight between the two men, which threatened to escalate into general fighting between the age-sets, and the junior elders decided to announce that they would deny the moran their daughters as wives, when they were ready to marry.

'Adultery', as I have said, may take place between a woman and any man who is from an age-set junior to that of her husband. However, 'adultery' with a man who is still formally in moranhood is regarded as a more serious offence than 'adultery' with an elder. All age-sets are partly differentiated from each other by the sharing of legitimate rights of sexual access to its women, and the denial of these rights to other age-sets. Moran are further differentiated from elders by the principle that elders are supposed to monopolize the sexual services of the adult women while moran have rights of sexual access to uncircumcised girls.

It is precisely as a relationship between a woman and a moran, however, that 'adultery' is conceptualized. Moran are regarded, by everybody, as more handsome than elders. Moreover their ability to seduce the wives of their seniors depends entirely upon their personal characteristics, including their reputation for bravery, their physical attractiveness, and their skill in pleasing women. They cultivate their beauty and anoint themselves with ochre and sweet-smelling herbs. They are supposed to stay awake for most of the night, telling their mistresses how much they are loved, and engaging in 'talk for the bed' (*olderrie lerruat*). Women sometimes characterize the difference between moran and elders in a rhetorical question, which refers to their different clothing; 'Would you rather have a fresh clean sheet', they ask, 'or a smelly old blanket?'

Moreover, the myth of the women-warriors, *ilpongolo*, relates that when men and women were equal, all men were moran. In this respect, the myth expresses the structural equality between women and moran in the age organization. It also casts more light upon the disapproval with which 'adultery' between such persons is viewed by men, as well as the tendency of women to regard all their lovers as moran, even when they are no longer formally in moranhood. 'Adultery' is a relationship freely entered into by a woman, and it is characterized by none of the 'respect' and obedience required of her by her husband and his age-set. Thus, when I asked one of my informants which age-set she was married into, she replied, laughing, that she was married to ilNyankusi age-set, but that her 'moran' whom she loved were ilTerekeyani (the immediate juniors of ilNyankusi), in spite of the fact that both age-sets were already elders.

When a woman calls her elder lover a moran she is implicitly calling attention to the egalitarian and voluntary nature of the 'adulterous' relationship. I believe it is these very qualities that contribute to the self-assertive pride women take in their 'adultery'.

A woman caught *in flagrante delicto*, by her husband, faces severe punishment: she may be beaten and fined nine head of cattle by him.[6] The beating, women say, consists of forty strokes with a long stick. Men believe that women are cowards and although, in most contexts, women ruefully agree, in the context of 'adultery' they flaunt their physical bravery. One woman told me: 'We Maasai women are very brave. We buy our lovers with forty strokes. After a beating we get straight up and go and find them again.' It is my impression that most husbands beat their wives badly, once in their lifetimes. The justification for it is, frequently, that they are suspected of 'adultery' with moran. Thus it is around this issue of women's sexuality that antagonism between men and women erupts into violence. It is also around this issue that women unite in opposition to men's control.

No woman would ever give information, about the 'adultery' of another woman, to any man: women's solidarity on this issue is absolute. It pits all women against all elders, even cutting across the ties between a mother and her son because a mother would never betray her daughter-in-law to her husband. Women are adamant that this is so, and that they would 'cut the throat' of a tale-bearer. I have never, in fact, heard of a case in which this happened (although Spencer describes an occasion, among the Samburu, when a young woman was frightened into giving information by some elders (Spencer 1965)).

Men can only learn about their wives' love affairs if they catch them with their lovers, except in the case of the youngest age-set of elders who learn of their wives' relationships with the age-set immediately junior, the moran, before two particular *rites de passage*. These rites require confessions from the wives of all the participants and it is believed that any guilty wife who failed to confess, would sicken and die. (Women married to age-sets that have already passed through these ceremonies need only worry about being caught out.)

However, a woman who is faced with the necessity to declare her state of guilt can usually avoid a beating. She runs away from her husband to try and beg the nine animals, for which she is liable, from her own family and clan. If she fails to obtain promises of sufficient stock, her husband may take the remaining head of cattle from her allocated herd. In practice, the fine may be reduced according to individual circumstances. In one case that I managed to follow up, occurring in 1972, the guilty wife managed to obtain only one animal from her family, which had suffered very severely in a recent drought. Her agnates, nevertheless, pleaded for her, and she was let off with this single payment. (She had, in any case, only one cow in her allocated herd, since her husband had also suffered badly in the drought.) It is my impression, though, that the fine is usually paid in full. Indeed, two elderly co-wives of a laibon explained to me that their husband had decided to call in their fines when his herds were depleted by natural disasters. They had both obtained the full nine head of cattle and had 'made him a rich man'. This is, I suspect, normal; debts in Maasai can remain outstanding for many years but this does not mean that they have been forgotten.

The guilty wife referred to above was forced to declare herself at fault when the ilTerekeyani laibons held the *rite de passage* that relaxes the prohibition upon their eating meat seen by women, in the villages. The ceremony took place in 1972, and two out of approximately thirty wives confessed to taking lovers from among the moran. Five years later, at *engang' oolorikan*, another *rite de passage* held by the same age-set but not attended by laibons, about one-third of the women confessed, according to an estimate made (I believe reliably) by an informant. The explanation of this discrepancy may be partly because laibons' wives are less 'adulterous' than non-laibons' wives. I believe it is also because women's 'adultery' tends to increase as their husbands grow older, and they acquire more than one wife. Men continue marrying until they are very old, and as a particular age-set becomes more senior, the desire and the ability of its members to control their wives decreases.

I believe, in fact, that most women engage in 'adulterous' love affairs, although much of my data on this subject is inevitably anecdotal. Nearly all older women (now beyond reproach from their husbands) openly claim to have had lovers in the past; those who did not seem to be the exception. Among those I knew fairly well, there was one woman of about sixty who was believed never to have 'gone to moran'. I have overheard her contemporaries laughing about her and saying that she had gained nothing by her abstinence.

Women who discover that they share a lover are expected to become close friends, and small groups of young women are sometimes seen at inter-village gatherings, exchanging the names of their lovers and joking about their new-found friendships. Unlike the Samburu, Maasai girls do not form exclusive sexual relationships with moran, and nor do adult women with their lovers (Spencer 1965). If asked, women and girls usually claim to have four lovers (I assume because four is a propitious number). Men for their part claim that women are divided by jealousy of each others' beauty and attractiveness to men. This, in fact, is the common male interpretation of the marriage ceremony described above. However, women deny that they are divided by their sexuality, and I believe that this denial, and the suppression of feelings of sexual jealousy, if they do occur, are most important matters to women.

234

They are also important factors in the relationship of co-wives. Women believe that jealousy can drive a woman 'mad' (*aata oloirirua*: to have a little spirit) because she cannot express her anger, as can her husband, by beating her spouse. Women tell stories which provoke much hilarity about jealous wives, but the stories nearly always concern non-Maasai women. One favourite story concerns a European woman who, discovering that her husband had a mistress, went out and shot him with a gun. Another example concerns a barren Kikuyu wife of a Maasai elder who went 'mad' in 1971. She began to rave and hit out at people, more or less at random. Eventually her husband threw her out of the house and she slept in the open for a few days, before returning to her family. Her 'madness' was caused, in the opinion of the Maasai women, by her discovery that her husband had made another Kikuyu woman pregnant. They had little sympathy for her because, they said, it is silly to be jealous. She should have tried to persuade her husband to marry the other woman and then she could have adopted a child from her.

Maasai women, then, not only support each other in 'adultery', but they refuse to allow themselves to be set against each other by their sexuality. In this respect, they are acting like male age-mates, who also forbid expressions of such jealousy within the age-set. 'Adultery' certainly expresses and exploits tensions between age-sets, but from the women's point of view I believe there is much more to it than that. When a woman flaunts her husband's authority by disposing of her sexuality in a relationship of her own choice, she is implicitly attacking the principle of male superiority, and asserting the possibility of a more egalitarian social order. Women's solidarity, in the context of their procreative powers, punishes those who 'lack respect'; their solidarity in the context of their sexuality arises to protect them.

Maasai men tend to ignore the implications of widespread 'adultery' and to separate the ideas of sexuality and pro-creation, in their pursuit of prolific fatherhood and the acquisition of 'riches'. A man has full social and spiritual rights of fatherhood over all the children of his wives, so long as they were born into his household. Thus, 'adultery' does nothing to challenge the unequal relations of production and repro-duction. It does not affect the contingency of women's rights

235

in the fruits of their productive labours, nor the right of their husbands to dispose of their daughters in marriage and to appropriate the labour of their sons. Indeed, women's love of the moran is itself an ambiguous weapon. Moran may be the equals of women, but moranhood is the period in which men are thought to prove themselves, in formal isolation from women, to be worthy of women's 'respect', and entitled to assert their control over their sexuality and fertility.

Notes

1 In the preparation of this paper I have been indebted to valuable discussions with the other contributors to this book, and with Peter Loizos, James Faris, and Chris Curling.

2 It is closer to Durkheim's concept of 'mechanical solidarity' than to his opposed idea of 'organic solidarity', which is based upon the principle of the mutual interdependence of unlike social actors (Durkheim 1964).

3 Shulamith Firestone takes this view further in her assertion that women will never achieve equality with men until biological motherhood is replaced by ectogenesis (Firestone 1970).

4 The bulk of the fieldwork on which this paper is based was funded by the Child Development Research Unit (now the Bureau of Education), University of Nairobi, and by Harvard University. I should like to thank them, and also John and Beatrice Whiting for their advice and encouragement while I was carrying out the research.

5 This view of female circumcision is derived from Jean La Fontaine's analysis of Bugisu women's rituals (La Fontaine 1972).

6 The injured husband is entitled to try to beat or even kill the young man concerned on the spot, but the latter is expected to run away as fast as possible. The husband's age-mates will then demand that the age-set of the lover send a delegation to the husband's village to apologize and pay him compensation of one or heads of stock as well as smaller gifts. The husband should then slaughter an animal to feed them.

References

DE BEAUVOIR, S. (1953) The Second Sex. London: Jonathan Cape.

DURKHEIM, E. (1964) The Division of Labour. New York: The Free Press.

FIRESTONE, S. (1970) *The Dialectic of Sex.* New York: William Morrow & Co. Inc.

LA FONTAINE, J. S. (1972) Ritualization of Women's Life-Crises in Bugisu. In La Fontaine (ed.), *The Interpretation of Ritual.* London: Tavistock.

ORTNER, S. B. (1974) Is Female to Male as Nature is to Culture? In M. Rosaldo and L. Lamphere (eds.), *Women Culture & Society.* Stanford, California: Stanford University Press.

PEHRSON, R. H. (1966) *The Social Organization of the Marri Baluch.* Compiled and analysed from his notes by Frederik Barth, Chicago: Aldine. (Viking Fund Publications in Anthropology 43).

PIZZORNO, A. (1970) An Introduction to the Theory of Political Participation. *Social Science Information* 9(5):29–61.

ROSALDO, M. and ATKINSON, J. (1975) Man the Hunter and Woman: Metaphors for the Sexes in Ilongot Magical Spells. In R. Willis (ed.), *The Interpretation of Symbolism.* London: Malaby.

SPENCER, P. (1965) *The Samburu.* Berkeley and Los Angeles: University of California Press.

NINE

Désirade: a negative case

JULIA NAISH

In the situation to be described, we find a case where solidarity among women is very restricted. On the island of Désirade, in the French Caribbean, women express only limited support towards each other, and on the basis of kinship rather than friendship. There are few opportunities for women to get together; when they do they may be accused of gossip. Differences of rank and colour between them are perceived as instrumentally more important than that which unites them. There is a vast difference between men and women in relation to initiative, autonomy, and decision-making powers. Women have to find their social identity in terms of dependency on *men*, not on each other. In this case, the structures of production and of reproduction as expressed in family structure, fail to allow women to support each other *as women*, and there is a corresponding lack of solidarity as an ideology. Both the physical segregation of women from each other at work and at home, and the imputation of gossip largely to women are modes of social control used to keep them apart from each other and from the world of men.

Désirade and its economy

Désirade, a dependency of Guadeloupe, has a population of 1,600 living on an island measuring roughly seven miles long and one mile wide. The political status of Martinique and Guadeloupe was changed in 1946 from that of colony to overseas department of France, and the islands were assimilated into the administrative system of metropolitan France (Mathews 1971). With this transition Martinique and Guadeloupe lost their fiscal autonomy but gained access to many of the social security benefits of France (Bradley 1975). These Caribbean islands are poor, relative to the mother-country, per capita income being one-third to one-quarter that of France, and the poverty is largely accounted for by the high level of underemployment and seasonal work. Half of the actively employed population work on small farms, and France is the main customer, receiving 90 per cent of all exports from Guadeloupe (Andic and Andic 1965). Links between the French islands and France are much stronger than with neighbouring British islands – shops, town architecture, cooking, clothes, and a host of other things show a strong French influence. The weather forecast on the radio gives temperatures for French towns but does not mention neighbouring British islands; there is extremely limited coverage of West Indian news.

Guadeloupe has five small island dependencies under its administration, including Désirade, which lies off its east coast. The economy of Désirade is considerably different from that of the island of Guadeloupe. It is mountainous, with infertile soil and unpredictable rain. There are three villages joined by one road on the island, and various households dispersed from the main settlements. Villages tend to be endogamous, but kin do not necessarily live near to each other as there is a housing shortage and people have to take what they can find. The main source of income is fishing, followed by *Aide Sociale*, a form of social security. The fish is sold to traders on Guadeloupe; some is then frozen and flown to France. Land is owned individually by men and women, but it is not highly productive, does not fetch high prices, and can easily be borrowed, share-

239

cropped, or bought. Most people own some land, although most plots are very small and dispersed. Land ownership does not define a class of people here, as in some other Caribbean areas. It is mostly used by women to graze animals, though many families have a small garden where they grow vegetables.

Each boat-owner, or *patron*, owns his own equipment and markets his own fish; there is no joint ownership of materials. A *patron* works with one or two *matelots*, who may earn enough to set up as *patrons* themselves. In any case, the composition of fishing crews constantly changes. A successful fisherman can earn large sums of money and is thus able to save enough to get married, buy a house, and support a wife while still a young man. This is significantly different from mainland Guadeloupe where the man may be a financial drain on the household because of lack of employment. He may, therefore, remain marginal to the family, giving rise to the matrifocal family. *Patrons* tend not to accumulate capital but to spend earnings on consumer goods and re-investing in equipment. A successful fisherman is one who works long hours – in certain seasons going out at three in the morning and not returning until seven the next evening. He needs a wife or a mother to look after his material needs, so the patrifocal family suits his kind of work.

Most Désiradien households have more than one source of income, though generally speaking the division of labour is sexual; men fish, women either do not do waged work or do a little gardening and raise some sheep and goats. There are very few jobs for women, though there is some cleaning work available from the *commune* (the local politico-administrative division), some dressmaking, and there are several women shopkeepers. Shops are mostly small and sell the same range of goods, so there is competition, and little scope for capital accumulation. Of adult islanders, 26.13 per cent of men are fishermen, 12.35 per cent of men and women farm and raise animals, 16.9 per cent trade, have shops, or work in the Town Hall, and other clerical posts. The remainder of the population are dependent, retired, unemployed, or disabled.

Apart from activities connected with the church, ideally women stay at home and look after their children, sending the latter to do the shopping and run errands, so that they do not need to go out except, perhaps, to water the animals. There is no market where women can get together as they do on other islands. The typical house and courtyard symbolize their isolation: the houses have no windows on the front wall, only narrow louvre doors, the courtyards are enclosed by a high wall or fence so that women cannot chat to neighbours, or be observed in the privatized domestic domain. The sexual division of labour leads not only to sex segregation but also to the isolation of women from each other. The division of labour is geared to the nuclear family structure, whereby the household needs are supplied from the sea and the plots of land, and co-operation in larger groups is not necessary. If land needs to be cleared for cultivation, it can be done by a woman and her husband or mate. Men tend to discourage women from having friendships with each other by suggesting that other women are not good enough to be a friend because they gossip, are promiscuous, or lazy.

Women earn little money for themselves, usually their only source of earned income is to sell an animal to a trader or kill and sell a pig to neighbours. Small children take orders, deliver the meat, and collect the money, so that women do not need to go out of their own domestic sphere. Although women have access to social security, if living with a man it is usually the latter who will go to the Town Hall to pick up the monthly payment.

The French welfare system is tripartite: it consists of family allowances, social security, and social aid. Since the First World War, and increasingly since the Second, French social policy has been dominated by *la politique familiale*. The population of France was not considered to be rising fast enough, and so a vigorous family policy was pursued, including financial aid to persuade women to stay at home. By contrast in the French West Indies, the population growth is the reverse; in Martinique the annual rate of increase is 2.7 per cent – which would double the population in one generation. Social benefits in the French West Indies are more restricted than in metropolitan France, with certain benefits tied to marital status, and non-salaried, part-time workers, and handicapped persons not being eligible. Also certain family allowance benefits are restricted to metropolitan France.

However, the majority of the population in the overseas departments are only eligible for social aid, since they do not pay insurance contributions, and many are not married. If able to demonstrate insufficient means both men and women can claim a cash allowance for themselves and their dependants, obtain free medical treatment, and grants for children's school books. They can obtain these benefits regardless of marital or birth status, so, unmarried women living without resident males but with children are eligible. However, the amount that social aid provides is much less than social security or family allowances, so a woman on her own may enter a liaison with a man who will support her. The poorest people on Désirade are single or separated women with children too old to qualify for social aid payments. There is also an organization called 'La Marine' to which active and retired fishermen belong, and which provides pensions, widows' pensions, and allowances for children, the money being paid to the male household head or his widow.

Colour

About 250 of Désirade's population are genotypically white (that is, white by reference to descent, not merely appearance). They refer to themselves as white, and there is fairly widespread agreement by others concerning their colour, though for non-whites, colour categorization is shifting and inconsistent. Désirade differs significantly from larger Caribbean islands where status hierarchies are perceived and expressed in terms of skin colour and white skin denotes a high position in the economic sphere, if no longer necessarily in the political. On Désirade, whites and non-whites are all in a broadly similar socio-economic position.

Under slavery the slave-owning whites controlled all political and economic resources and denied non-whites access to them. The solidarity of the whites was based on their property-owning role and their colour as an expression of political status. There was a marked division of labour between whites and non-whites, though perhaps not as strong here as on the islands where sugar cane was grown and great wealth amassed. The main crop on Désirade at this time was cotton, but its importance has subsequently diminished as fishing has become more profitable. Miscegenation was common, but did not imply equality: marriage with slaves was not legally possible, and sexual relations were between white men and non-white women, never vice versa. Another manifestation of white solidarity at this period was in the maintenance of the purity of the group. White women, therefore, could not have children by any but white men, and until very recently one could predict the colour of an individual islander according to his or her surname. Preconditions for white solidarity were present, but this was not the case with the non-whites, who were denied any autonomy to organize themselves.

Racial awareness and preference for pale skin and 'good' hair and features is still much in evidence. White skin is generally thought to be indefinably better than other skin colours. However, colour is usually of secondary importance in most interactions, because people know each other not as strangers – where labels would be significant – but as fellow-islanders. Although islanders do not operate in response to stereotypes, they do exist as the background to interaction, and are partly taken for granted.

Since the emancipation of slaves in 1848, racial relations have no longer reflected the differential distribution of *collective* power. There have been few economic differences between whites and non-whites – at least, few that are commonly perceived – and there are no legal differences of status, nor a clear-cut social boundary between whites and non-whites. No longer can skin colour automatically confer high status, nor does it refer to collective identity. Moreover, the ethos of the French Caribbean is to minimize colour differences. The lack of residential segregation based on race, the degree of inter-marriage and mating, and the confusions in the colour classification all show that race is not an organizing principle or a dominant ideological theme.

However, there is a difference between what is experienced and expressed by the islanders, and what can be observed. Désiradien whites still express a feeling of moral superiority. They were never slaves (though in fact they are descended from indentured labourers taken from prisons and hospitals of France), they claim to be able to trace their ancestry to France, and their ethno-history gives them a vague but golden heritage. Among themselves they may express contempt for non-whites, perhaps particularly since the number of pure white households is diminishing as mixed unions increase. Non-white women are perceived as being at the bottom of any hierarchy on double grounds of sex and colour. Of the 340 households, twenty-eight contain whites, twenty-seven mixed unions, and the rest are black.

The minority of whites are prominent in public life; there is a relatively high proportion of white men in positions of legitimized office. More white men than non-white are commune councillors, workers for the Post Office, employees in the Town Hall, and employees in water and electricity services. There is a high proportion of whites in commerce and as *patrons* in fishing: 18.3 per cent of adult white men are *patrons* as opposed to 4.9 per cent of non-whites. Although the whites express a feeling of *moral* superiority, they fail to recognize their political and economic dominance, and they do not think of themselves as a group. Part of the reason for the latter is that they do not have valuable land to protect and prevent from splitting up, as is the case with other poor white communities in the French Caribbean (Chartrand 1965).

Since World War Two, whites have been marrying or having relationships with non-whites on Désirade almost as frequently as they marry people of their own colour and even the feelings of white moral superiority seem to be dying out among the young. The diminishing importance of race is indicated by the lack of racial segregation, the degree of inter-marriage, and the confusions in colour classification. However, the whites' unacknowledged politico-economic prominence seems no weaker.

Ranking

When asked about differences in wealth and power, the islanders emphasize the equality of all. There is some occupational differentiation, but no enormous differences in life-style, and no evaluation of others in terms of a single scale of ranking. Although Désiradiens subscribe to the idea that they are all equal, the men, in particular, are intensely individualistic and competitive. They gossip about each other and use jealousy and accusations of sorcery in order to prevent others rising in prestige. One of the cohesive elements in this society is the competition to remain equal – to prevent others gaining more prestige, and becoming more powerful. Indeed it can be perceived that not all are treated in the same way, and one of the key criteria in the ranking system is respect.

Those meriting respect have certain characteristics: good financial standing, respectability, family background, age, wisdom, ability to speak French (rather than the local Creole), verbal skill, and wide contacts. These apply largely to men, since women do not earn, or spend time in groups practising verbal skills, and, indeed, may be accused of gossiping if they chat in the streets.

What verbal skills women do possess are, in fact, very divisive, usually being directed against other women as a sanction. For example, they engage in street shouting matches – swearing and being obscene – behaviour that contravenes what is expected of a woman, and is much to the entertainment of onlookers. Such behaviour may occur if a woman's husband is having an affair with another woman. The wife hurls abuse at the mistress, who loses face by the liaison being made public, as this indicates her promiscuity. However, there is no gain in prestige for the wife either, since she is going against the ideal of womanhood. In any case, the sexual double standard requires women not to make a fuss if their men are unfaithful, so long as they themselves are not being deprived of any material comfort.

Gossip

Friendship is regarded ambivalently on Désirade: although you may love your friend, you may have a treacherous friend who is spreading gossip about you and telling people your secrets. Notions of jealousy and treachery militate against friendship. Women say that they had friends at school, but not subsequently and that on Désirade one has more enemies than friends. Many mention treachery and hypocrisy in the context of friendship.

There is no word for gossip, merely one for those who engage in it: *macro/macrelle* (Creole). Someone who is *macrelle* eavesdrops with the intention of passing on the gossip, exaggerates, and wants to know other people's business at all costs. Of course, all do gossip, but the rules of the game constrain the islanders in different ways, and the person who is gossiping would not describe it in those terms. Gossip is an important means of social control – not only is it used to

245

combat men's claims to prestige, but it is also used against women as a means of keeping them in their place. It is considered normal and acceptable for men to sit in loafing-groups and chat. If women go out and chat, they are labelled *macrelle* and in this way made to see that the street and other areas where they may encounter people are not their domain. Married women who stay at home are least likely to be accused of gossip.

The ideology of keeping oneself to oneself means that much information has to go through neutral channels, the grapevine. This includes shops, the post office, and dances as well as loafing-groups. Women do not loaf, or visit neighbours, and they send children to run errands. They may accompany children to dances where they will sit separately from the men and nurse younger children. However, many married women will not go even to dances, considering them frivolous or unsuitable. As stated earlier, gossip is imputed to women much more than to men, and both sexes support the idea that women should stay at home to avoid being accused of it.

As in Alpine communities in Europe, on Désirade one can observe assertions of equality on the one hand, and willingness of islanders to rank each other, especially on moral grounds, on the other (Hutson 1971). The situation is complicated by the fact that the objectively observable political and economic prominence of the whites is not expressed; and always, the individual is a much more significant unit in social life than a group or category.

Family structure

I shall first discuss the general Caribbean pattern before going on to show how Désirade differs from this pattern. Slaves in the Caribbean were not allowed to marry but were free to cohabit consensually or mate extra-residentially. They could contract or dissolve unions at will, and men often had two or more mates, living with one and visiting others (Smith 1962). The family system is still based on extra-residential mating and consensual domestic unions, partly due to the heritage of slavery, and partly to economic factors of casual and seasonal labour, physical mobility, and low income (Smith 1971).

Usually in the Caribbean, monogamous marriage is the ideal

type of union for all classes. However, the young in rural areas find it difficult to achieve because they are not sufficiently self-supporting to be able to pay for a wedding celebration, a house, and preferably a non-earning wife. Two-thirds of West Indian children are born illegitimate, but most parents eventually wed (Lowenthal 1972). Some children are born to couples living in non-legalized unions, others to women who are not in co-residential unions and who enjoy varying degrees of stability in their relations with the father of their children. This latter group characterizes the matrifocal family, and is neatly summed up in the title of a book on West Indian family structure: *My Mother who Fathered Me* (Clarke 1957).

Other characteristics of Caribbean family organization are a large family circle, but a weak man-woman link, with the sexes spending little leisure time together. The tie between parents and children is stronger than between partners. A sequential pattern of sexual relationships for women is usual: a girl will have a clandestine relationship which results in pregnancy, her family rear the child while she goes out to work. After one or more much relationship, she may enter a common-law union with a man, and in this case it is frequently the woman who owns or rents the house, and the household is likely to include her children by former partners. Formal marriage may follow in late middle age – often with the birth of a first grandchild.

Temporary migrant labour leaves the woman in charge of domestic affairs most of the time, and even when present men frequently lack authority. Women are independent agents, they make important decisions about children, jobs, and so on, aided by their relatives. Common-law unions are more egalitarian than 'formal' marriages, and the latter 'may have definite drawbacks for both partners. For women it entails a loss of equality, less freedom to move about, fewer contacts, more loneliness. For men it means an economic burden, a less carefree or venturesome style of life, a more demanding and perhaps less satisfying relationship' (Lowenthal 1972:111). The advantages for women are higher status, for men a greater claim to their children's support. The non-participating father finds it difficult to get a foothold in a family group as time goes on. Legitimacy confers higher status on the children, though there is little moral stigma attached to illegitimacy.

Under French law, illegitimate children who are not legally recognized by their father and do not bear his name inherit only from their mother; if recognized they inherit half as much as a legitimate child from their father as well as their mother's share. If there is little to inherit, this has little effect on attitudes to illegitimacy.

Kinship and family structure in Désirade

In an island with such a small population as Désirade, one might expect everyone to be related. This is not the case, largely because the number of Désiradiens is much greater than 1,600, but many of them are in France. Moreover, there have always been some white families who have not mixed with non-whites. Kinship is a powerful commitment and source of help, but it can also be extremely negative – some of the most bitter and long-lasting disputes I witnessed were between siblings, or parents and children. The kinship link is perhaps most useful away from the island, as it provides an islander with someone to stay with when migrating to France, supplying a network of people she or he knows, or knows of, and cushioning the newness of metropolitan life.

It is striking to observe the extent to which loyalties to one's family of procreation minimize those to one's family of origin. Quarrels with one's children are not infrequent, but happen when the child has set up its own household and not usually while it is still living in the family of origin. The ideology of kinship is not strong enough to prevent the split of families into factions, for example, over politics. Quarrels between siblings are usually perpetuated by their children.

Désirade family structure differs from that of mainland Guadeloupe. It is closer to the French pattern than the Caribbean, having a lower illegitimacy rate than the latter generally, with more people getting married than living together or in single-parent households.

During the year I was there, (1971–2), a third of all households were headed by women. This high figure is deceptive, however: when we break it down and look at colour composition we see that there is a much lower figure of white women household heads than non-white. When we look at their past history, it can be seen that all the white women household heads are widows, as are half of the non-white. Only a quarter of the total figure, then, are women who have not married, or are divorced, or separated.

Women household heads

Women household heads under forty years old tend to be non-white, single, divorced, or separated, and most of them have children. The fact that they are independent of their own families of origin suggests that they have some other form of economic support – either from social security or from a man. Although there is a large number of men living alone, it is generally not these men who are supporting women, but economically successful married men. Forty-two per cent of all households contain a legally married couple with or without children and/or grandchildren. Again, if we break down the figures and look at colour composition, we can see that 64 per cent of white households fit this pattern, as opposed to 40 per cent of non-white households. Only 6 per cent of all households contain a couple living together *en ménage;* these are nearly all non-whites. Divorce rates are low – only 2.7 per cent of marriages have ended in divorce since 1920.

Although a third of the households are headed by women, on Désirade, the norm – ideal and statistical – is marriage and the nuclear family, and the number of white nuclear families is higher than elsewhere. There is a significant difference between whites and non-whites; white women, with relationships concerning white men, marry them. Non-white women, and women in mixed unions are more likely to have a wider range of choice about relationships – extra-residential unions, common-law unions, or the matrifocal family.

Developmental cycle of women

All girls may have secret sexual relationships from puberty onwards, meeting boys at dances, getting out of the house by running errands, or going to water animals. White families seem to have a more inward-looking family life and to exert greater sanctions against young girls being left alone with men. If a girl of any colour gets pregnant, she may be turned out of the house by her parents for a day or two, but usually returns. Although her parents support her, she is now a much freer agent having lost her virginity. They cannot oblige her to stay at home and this usually causes such friction that she will try to persuade her lover to support her, and move out to live on her own. As long as the man supports her she fares quite well, but if he is married or will not marry her and they split up, she has to live on social aid – rather a small income. So she will try to find another man to support her, and probably have another child (men are keen on having children not only for themselves but to prove their virility), and so it goes on.

Such women usually keep themselves to themselves *vis-à-vis* others in the same situation – especially since they may not be living near similar women. Many girls do, in fact, get married after the birth of one child; though thought to have been tricked, they are not necessarily thought to have been ruined. However, they consider themselves, and are considered, lower in the respectability stakes than a girl who has avoided pregnancy.

If a woman's husband dies, she may well set up with another man whom she does not marry, or have an extra-residential affair. She is not censured for this as a young woman would be, the fact that she *has been* married is important.

Sexuality

Although everyone holds that the climate gives them 'hot' blood and that sexuality is an expression of this, men are believed to be more highly-sexed than women, and this is used as a justification for a dual standard of sexual morality. One of the worst things that can happen to a man is to be cuckolded, as this reflects upon his virility and makes him an object of ridicule. However, if a man is unfaithful, it is thought that a woman should not make too much fuss, particularly about a casual affair. If a legal or common-law wife has all she needs materially and the man does not deprive her of financial help, she is perceived as having little cause to complain.

Children start to experiment sexually at an early age, and contraception is fairly easily available and known about, although little used by young people. Secrecy about pre-marital affairs is maintained as far as possible, and since sexual activity is particularly frowned upon for unmarried girls, their affairs are the most secret. In spite of the ideology stressing marriage, most girls do have clandestine sexual relationships. This does not conflict with their desire to get married: they may hope either not to get pregnant or that the boy will marry them if they do.

Why do women in Désirade, particularly white women, exchange the free expression of their sexuality for a restricted role in the nuclear family? From what the women themselves say, the prime reason is financial. Although they can get social aid as single mothers, they are better off with a man to support them. This is a society where people want to buy consumer durables – refrigerators, radios, and televisions. One must also take account of the sexual double standard which entails great moral pressure being exerted on the women.

Ideology

Despite differences in terms of composition between white and non-white households, ideas underlying domestic relations are shared by everyone. The most significant difference is that the whites emphasize marriage as the only form of union, while the non-whites see marriage as one alternative and will quote various sayings likening it to slavery. Generally speaking though, women are keener to get married than men. They talk in terms of marriage being more respectable, better for the children, and showing that the man is ready to accept responsibility and recognize the woman as his partner. The church also emphasizes it, and most islanders are aware that in French society it is important to be legally married.

Women who have children as single mothers are often regarded as having been tricked or fooled. From their own point of view they may see it as something they wanted to do, but there is no prestige for women becoming pregnant outside marriage. However, a formal proposal of marriage does give limited right of sexual access to the prospective wife: the man is allowed to visit the girl and stay the night with her in her parents' house. Indeed the wedding date may not be set until she is pregnant.

Some single women household heads argue that they are better off without a husband or resident mate, but others express the fact that they had failed to achieve the norm, and feel it particularly for their children. The Roman Catholic Church is important here; for church is one of the places women may go to freely, and it is also one of the strongest platforms of formal marriage. If a woman is not married, it is often said that this is because the man did not think enough of her to marry her, not because *she* did not want to marry.

Apart from ideological pressures, there are financial incentives for a woman to marry. There is more financial security if the marriage ends, a widow can get a pension where a common-law widow cannot. As well as these pressures, since there are virtually no voluntary associations or group organizations, women need to be with men in order to have access to the public world of formal and informal politics.

However, the strongest reason why more white women achieve the ideal type of union is linked with the structures of production. White men earn more because of being 'patrons', and are thus able to afford to build a house, pay for the wedding, and support a wife. So for women the prevalence of marriage and the nuclear family is closely linked with economic incentives which enable the family to acquire goods and thus merit prestige. It also enables a formal wedding to be held and thus gives the couple a higher position on the scale of respectability. Men want to get married for prestige reasons also – as an indicator of their financial standing – and the free expression of their sexuality need not necessarily be restricted, although very few white men have outside women.

Leisure

Men and women on Désirade, as generally in the Caribbean, spend leisure time apart from each other. However, on Désirade, there is a marked lack of formal associations which would provide an opportunity for people of the same sex to come together. The islanders cannot co-operate for any length of time, individual differences always outweigh the perception of common interests, and only those groups organized by outsiders have any chance of survival. As stated previously, this is connected with the ethos of egalitarianism. No islander will take it upon himself to initiate group activity because his claims to be organizer will fast be challenged by others in order to restore equality. Behind his back he will be accused of financial dishonesty, using sorcery to better his position, and so on.

In spite of this lack of formal associations, men do sit and chat in loafing-groups on street corners. One of the marks of being respected is being able to hold the attention of the other men by being witty and verbally skilled. In the loafing-groups a man's reputation can be made – this is the arena of informal politics, the small politics of daily life which is about having a good name, about gossip and insult, about one-upmanship, and being socially bankrupt (Bailey 1971). The loafing-group is the arena where Désiradien men compete to remain equal.

For women, there is no equivalent to the loafiing-group, no informal area which they can wander into and chat, and they stay at home so as not to be accused of gossip. Their reputation, then, is either linked with that of their husband, or is low because they are not married. In order to know what is going on, and who or what is being discussed, it is easiest for them if there is a resident male from whom information may be gained, and to whom they may pass their own opinions and influence situations.

Women may co-operate with kin, for example, making the twice daily trip to water animals together, but it is unlikely that this will last long. A more permanent bond will arise over the informal adoption of children – a woman may bring up one of her daughter's children. This, however, does not mobilize more than two women, and their supportive role towards the infant is emphasized more than their relationship to each other.

Women get together regularly in groups only in activities connected with the church, in relationships fraught with rivalry and jealousy. There are two small Roman Catholic churches on the island, served by a metropolitan priest. Most women go to church on Sunday, and some attend a prayer group called the Légion de Marie, the members of which attend meetings twice a week, elect a President, and are most devout in terms of church attendance. Members have certain tasks to perform, like visiting the sick, or visiting people living together and persuading them to regularize their union. Not surprisingly given Désiradien ideas about visiting, these women are not very successful, and may be thought to be prying. They give a little money each week, which may be used to buy a new statue for the church, or given to a sick member, or to someone in the event of a disaster, for example, a home burning down.

The women who attend must be married, or single without children. The group is organized by the priest, who usually attends meetings, but it consists of only a very small proportion of the female population, and would express very little solidarity if not held together by an outsider. The women seem to be as competitive as the men; in one case a prayer-group formed in which a statue of the virgin went round the houses of the members, and each member went to that house for prayers on that day. However, the group fell apart because of hostility and competitiveness arising from the fact that some meetings were bigger than others. The women were unwilling to devalue the differences between them.

Because of the lack of opportunity for women to get together informally, they can enter neither into the game of making a reputation and competing for equality, nor into situations where they could express solidarity as women. In terms of reputation they can participate only as appendages of men; since they do not work together and the general ethos is one of individualism, solidarity has little chance of emerging.

Politics

Apart from informal politics, men participate more than women in the formal political field. The administration in the French Caribbean is divided into three levels: the *Préfecture*, the General Council, and the Municipalities. The municipality, or *commune*; is the smallest politico-administrative division; there are thirty-four of them in Guadeloupe, of which Désirade is one. The municipal council governing it is elected, and headed by a mayor, and its duties are the administration of municipal interest, including preparing the *commune* budget, regulating local commerce, and so on.

In the present (at the time of my research) and previous administrations, there have been a higher proportion of whites than generally on the island. Only one of the twelve councillors is a woman. Interaction of the islanders in various disputes centred around the political field shows, as in other situations, that the scene is acted on by individuals and not by groups, whether based on race or party affiliation. Political unification does not occur along colour lines. More important, political processes succeed at the local political level because relationships established in one context are utilized in another. Because men can work at their reputations in the loafing-groups, they are known when the time comes for them to be voted for the positions of municipal councillors. Since women are barred from men's groups and have no equivalent themselves, it is much more difficult for them to enter the formal political system.

The woman who is a councillor (non-white but fair-skinned), owns a shop and is in her sixties. Her youthful indiscretions – having two illegitimate children and not marrying until late middle age – have been cancelled by her age, her financial standing, her range of contacts (due to her occupation : shopkeeper), being a regular church-goer, and having a forceful personality. However, she still conforms to the ideal of womanhood by not going outside her shop except to church or to the Town Hall, and by being moralistic about the behaviour of her family.

Women, men and solidarity

In this community, everyone sees themselves operating in a potentially hostile social environment, divided by colour, rank, and negative evaluations of others. Although the islanders maintain a spoken commitment to egalitarianism, people are constantly ranking others relative to themselves, and all prefer to remain isolated individuals rather than entering into group activity.

Apart from those factors that militate against group activity among either sex, there are more specific ideological and structural factors which prevent women perceiving their oppression and expressing solidarity with each other. In terms of ideology, there is an underlying feeling that because women do not participate in work for wages and other key areas of social life they are 'naturally' unfit to do so. This provides ammunition for the men's argument that women should be docile and dependent as long as they are provided for. Sexuality is also used as part of the ideology militating against women being able to devalue their differences – they view each other as competitors for men's favours, since men, but not women, can have more than one sexual relationship at a time. Men use sexuality, largely unconsciously, as a divide and rule policy. The other ideological factor keeping women apart is the use of gossip, which plays a significant role in defining the areas in which women may operate. Often ideas about gossip are expressed more forcibly by the women themselves than by the men.

The main structural factor preventing women from expressing solidarity is tied up with production. Women are virtually excluded from productive activity, and although they can get social aid as single women, few wish to do that on a long term basis as it does not provide them with enough cash to acquire the goods all aspire to own. Few of them are in a classic matrifocal situation, where they would find themselves in a supportive female group with males being peripheral, and where they would not be excluded from production. On Désirade, there is constant work for men and virtually no employment for women. The situation is, therefore, the reverse of that of American black women, where men's unemployment or seasonal labour leads to a drain on family resources supplied by women's welfare payments (Stack 1974).

Moreover, on Désirade women's non-participation in production is a status symbol for men in an ideology to which all subscribe. Because there is a clear-cut sexual division of labour in this society, it does not automatically follow that women will form solidarity groups. The isolated character of women's domestic role militates against co-operative activity.

Nor does the fact that women are clearly oppressed in this situation necessarily make for female solidarity – ideological factors work against this. Women are socialized into not wanting women friends on the assumption that those friends will be hypocritical and that they themselves will be accused of gossip. They rationalize this by concurring with the view that women are less adequate than men and denying themselves any possibility of solidary action, that is, power. Instead they direct their energies towards having personal influence over particular men. Although such influence may better the position of individual women, it merely reinforces their general status in that society by being expressed as the 'women's way' of operating (like 'feminine wiles' or 'intuition' in our own society).

If the economic system were to change, for example, as a result of the development of tourism and the need for women workers in hotels and so forth, and even if men's work continued to be profitable, we might find Désiradien women beginning to perceive their *common* situation as being significantly lower than that of men. At an individual level they would have the financial power to achieve an alternative family organization whereby they were not dependent on men but could be relatively autonomous. However, it is hard to see any existing factor that will force the evaluation of their present position on their consciousness. Although one woman expressed the plight of women's dependence on men by saying 'Pou cheché di pain, ou ka prend on ti-moun' (to get food, you get pregnant), as yet, Désiradien women have evolved no critical analysis of their status, and consequently they are not in a position to develop a strategy for change.

References

ANDIC, F. M. and ANDIC, S. (1965) *Fiscal Survey of the French Caribbean*. Special study no. 2. Puerto Rico: Institute of Caribbean Studies.

BAILEY, F. (ed.) (1971) *Gifts and Poison*. Oxford: Basil Blackwell.

BRADLEY, S. C. (1975) *Colonialism and Welfare: a comparative study of the development of welfare services in the British and French West Indies*. Unpublished M.Sc. dissertation, London School of Economics and Political Science.

CHARTRAND, F. (1965) Le Choix du conjoint chez les Blancs-Matignons de la Guadeloupe. *Anthropologica* 7(1):81-102.

CLARKE, E. (1957) *My Mother who Fathered me*. London: Allen & Unwin.

HUTSON, S. (1971) Social Ranking in a French Alpine Community. In F. Bailey (ed.), *Gifts and Poison*. Oxford: Basil Blackwell.

LOWENTHAL, D. (1972) *West Indian Societies*. London: Oxford University Press.

MATHEWS, T. G. (ed.) (1971) *Politics and Economics in the Caribbean*. Special study No. 3. Puerto Rico: Institute of Caribbean Studies.

SMITH, M. G. (1962) *West Indian Family Structure*. Washington: University of Washington Press.

SMITH, R. T. (1971) Culture and Social Structure in the Caribbean: some recent work on family and kinship studies. In M. Horowitz (ed.), *Peoples and Cultures of the Caribbean*. New York: National History Press.

STACK, C. B. (1974) Sex Roles and Survival Strategies in an Urban Black Community. In M. Z. Rosaldo and L. Lamphere (eds.), *Woman, Culture and Society*. Stanford, California: Stanford University Press.

TEN

Segregation and its consequences in India: rural women in Himachal Pradesh

URSULA SHARMA

In the field of racial politics, segregation is transparently connected with inequality of access to various sources of advantage and power. The apologists of apartheid may claim that to be separate is not necessarily to be unequal but such protests are hardly convincing. The social segregation of castes in India does not even pretend to be in the interest of 'separate but equal' development. It is understandable, therefore, that feminists have usually assumed that where women are segregated from men they will occupy an inferior status, and be denied access to sources of power and influence.

On the other hand, there is some anthropological evidence that the actual or symbolic separation of the sexes in social life does not necessarily indicate a hierarchical relationship. Mary Douglas points out that the rules concerning pollution which segregate menstruating women among the Lele may be manipulated by men to control women, but they may also be manipulated by women to control either sex (Douglas 1975). Even where segregation clearly places power in the hands of men, there may not be a predictable relationship between the stringency with which segregation is enforced and the actual loss of power by women. For instance, data on Muslim women suggest that even where segregation is very strictly enforced and where women are virtually invisible in public life, they are nevertheless not forced into total economic and political passivity (Maher 1976). Their segregation may even create a sense of solidarity among women in so far as the enforced realization of their common situation provides the basis for co-operation and mutual support.

In this paper, I shall consider how segregation may be related to other aspects of gender roles in general, and to solidarity in particular, in the context of Indian society. I shall make special reference to data from Ghanyari, the north Indian village where I carried out fieldwork.

Segregation and gender roles

I would distinguish three main aspects of gender roles found in any given society. They are, of course, analytical distinctions, useful for the purpose of discussion; empirically they may be very difficult to disentangle.

First, there is the extent to which either sex is denied access to positions of control, whatever these may comprise in the society in question. This is the element that is generally accorded the most explanatory power by sociologists. It has, therefore, frequently been observed that in western capitalist societies women generally have a marginal role in production because of the primacy given to their domestic and socializing roles. So while they are, for the most part, no longer formally debarred from positions of economic and political power, it is in practice difficult for them to gain access to such power except through their relationships with men. In rural India, land is not usually held in the name of women; they are excluded from the direct control of the main productive resources and also from public participation in political processes. As in Britain, this exclusion is nowadays enforced by convention and not by statutory law. However, it has the effect of ensuring that if women enjoy access to sources of power and prestige they do so through their relationships of dependency on men.

Second, in most societies there is some kind of division of labour between the sexes in terms of what kinds of work are thought appropriate to, or efficiently done, by either sex. According to its nature and degree of rigidity, this division of labour may have various consequences for women. It may strengthen the extent of mutual dependence of men and women; for example, among many hunting and gathering societies the men hunt and kill animals while the women spend most of their time collecting fruits or plants; in such societies the activities of men and women are complementary.

Alternatively, the division of labour may mitigate the effects of women's dependence on men when they are debarred from the direct control of property. For example, in the well-known case of the Nuer the prohibition on initiated men milking cows places them in a position of practical dependence on their women-folk. This occurs even though the herds are (nominally, at least) in the control of the men.

Or it may reinforce such relations of dependence, as when women are debarred by the conventional division of labour from playing any productive role outside the home and are restricted to domestic work and child-care. This is the case in many sections of both British and Indian society. The division of labour will frequently be supported by notions about the different capacities of men and women, ideals about what it means to be truly masculine or truly feminine, or by ideas about skills that only men or only women are supposed to possess.

Third, there are in most societies structural arrangements that segregate men from women in some degree, irrespective of whether their tasks are the same or different. Men and women may sleep or bath in separate places or at separate times; they may perform productive work in separate groups or in separate places. Such segregation is characteristically supported by notions of shame or modesty, and sometimes by the belief that the mixing of the sexes will lead to special kinds of ritual danger or pollution.

The sexual division of labour is bound to give rise to a degree of segregation in so far as specific tasks need to be done at distinct times or in special places. In Britain, today, there is little, if any, opposition to men and women working together in the same room or office on the grounds of decency. However, the fact that in most bureaucratic organizations women are generally employed to do the secretarial, clerical, and cleaning tasks while men are employed to carry out executive and administrative functions means that men and women will, in practice, be segregated from each other during much of the working day. I would make a distinction between this kind of situation and that in which men and women perform similar tasks but at separate times or places. I am aware that it is a conceptual distinction only, and one which may be difficult to make in practice in some societies where the two kinds of separation reinforce each other.

The relationship of this last component of gender role to the relations of dependence established by the other two is not at all clear from the comparative literature. For instance, what are we to make of the Bushmen, a hunting and gathering people, where men and women may not even sit on the same side of the hearth? For a man to sit on the woman's side (or vice versa) is to court all kinds of danger (Marshall 1959). Yet the relations of dependence between the sexes in this society probably do not place women in so disadvantageous a position *vis-à-vis* men as in our own society, where such symbolic separation is almost absent. The problem is harder to solve because ethnographic accounts often neglect to mention those forms of segregation that are 'merely' conventional and not supported by special ritual or magical sanctions. On the whole, the segregation of the sexes has been seen in terms of the obstacles it presents to field investigation rather than as a theoretical problem in its own right (Singh 1975).

A number of problems attend the study of sexual segregation in India. Segregation is a very general feature of Indian society, but there are wide variations in the degree of rigidity with which it is observed. In some communities, and not only Muslim, women are actually secluded (Hitchcock and Minturn 1963; Wiser and Wiser 1963). In other communities segregation is maintained through a well developed etiquette of avoidance, or through informal or implicit understandings about the way in which distance between the sexes is managed. Among educated urban Indians the chief concern is to protect women from unnecessary contacts with men outside the home; inside the household the physical segregation of the sexes is less obvious.

Another problem is that anthropologists have not as yet worked out a satisfactory terminology to deal with these various forms of segregation. The same indigenous term *purdah* (literally, a screen or curtain) is used to refer to different aspects of the separation of the sexes. Thus Saifullah-Khan uses it to refer to all aspects of segregation, from actual seclusion to the kind of situation where men and women merely sit on opposite sides of the room (Saifullah-Khan 1976). Jacobson uses the term 'purdah' to refer also to the types of veiling behaviour and avoidance etiquette practised by women towards specific men, especially affinally related men (Jacobson 1970).

Anthropologists are perhaps not to be blamed too severely for this lack of precision since Indians themselves use the word 'purdah' to refer to all these kinds of avoidance and segregation. However, it has meant that anthropologists have not distinguished satisfactorily between the kinds of respectful avoidance which are *specific* to certain roles, and the avoidance of men *in general* by women *in general*. The two kinds of avoidance are mutually reinforcing at the local level, but they need to be distinguished since in India, although all communities practice sexual segregation to some degree, the patterning of relations between affines is not everywhere the same.

In view of the comparative project of this volume I shall restrict my discussion to the consideration of the general aspects of segregation: the arrangements which divide men *as men* from women *as women*. My material from Ghanyari will illustrate the ways in which segregation is related to other aspects of gender roles in a particular community. It would be rash to claim any kind of typicality for this village in view of the wide variations that exist in India.

Segregation of the sexes in Ghanyari

Ghanyari is a Himalayan village, situated in Himachal Pradesh in north-western India. I conducted fieldwork there in 1966 and 1967 and have visited the village several times since then. My remarks here are based mainly on my observation of Brahman households, Brahmans being the dominant landowning caste in Ghanyari. The non-Brahman population of the village were

263

formerly tenants and artisan dependants of Brahman households, although recent economic changes have enabled them to
acquire small landholdings.

Nowadays, though, the more important variation in wealth
between households stems less from the amount of land held
than from the amount of cash earned by male members of the
household employed outside the village, this being an area of
heavy outward migration and a 'money order economy'. In
this respect the Brahmans are still pre-eminent as they were the
first to avail themselves of the educational opportunities that
are the passport to lucrative employment. However, the variations in wealth and life-style between the richest and the
poorest villagers in Ghanyari are not wide, and most of what I
shall say here is applicable to women in all groups in Ghanyari.
I recognize that in other areas of India this is not the case, and
indeed I shall refer to some of these differences subsequently.

In this area of subsistence farming, women have traditionally
played an important part in agricultural production and do not
observe the stricter forms of seclusion. They are not confined
to their houses or courtyards (although they travel outside the
village less often than men) and without exception they work
in the fields as well as in the home. In fact a young married
woman is likely to spend a greater proportion of her time on
agricultural tasks than on purely domestic work. Unmarried
girls are taught agricultural as well as domestic skills by their
parents. In this area a strict system of village exogamy is
practised and a girl's parents will, ideally, find her a husband
in a village at some distance from her own. Her prospective
in-laws will expect her to have already learnt basic agricultural
skills and will not favour her if she proves slow or inefficient
in tending crops and animals.

In Ghanyari the main economic resources are land and cash
wages. Land is almost invariably held in the name of the eldest
male member of the household, although it may occasionally
be registered in the name of a woman. Traditionally land was
divided equally among the sons only, but recent legislation
allows daughters to also inherit equal shares of the family
property. Cash is chiefly earned outside the village through
urban employment or military service carried out by migrant
workers who divide their time between the village and the
cities. As yet, no women from Ghanyari has ever sought

264

employment outside the village and very few work for wages within it, apart from a few low caste women who hire their labour out at harvest time.

Women perform agricultural work as members of their husbands' or fathers' households, working on land that is registered or rented in the name of the senior male of the household. Family labour is not renumerated individually, so women receive no personal 'wages' for this work. They have only a general right to be maintained from the produce of the land which they help to cultivate. Women are, therefore, excluded from direct control over the two most important sources of economic power, and their dependence on men is unequivocal. They do, of course, exercise a great deal of control (of an indirect and informal nature) over the way in which land is used or cash saved or spent. However, formally, even senior women are subordinated to their husbands or their husbands' male kin. The etiquette that controls personal relations between villagers of opposite sex symbolizes the formal subordination of wives to their husbands, who control the chief economic and political resources.

Women are also subordinate to other women, for the household is internally structured according to seniority as well as to sex. A wife is expected to submit to the authority of her mother-in-law and to the wives of her husband's elder brothers. So long as a wife lives under the same roof as her mother-in-law, her agricultural and domestic tasks will be directed by the latter. In Ghanyari the stringency of this supervision is often mitigated by the fact that an older woman is only too glad to hand over the responsibility for heavy agricultural work to a capable daughter-in-law, as soon as she can decently retire from strenuous outdoor work to concentrate on lighter domestic tasks. However, the daughter-in-law is still formally under her control and must be seen to obey her, showing deference and respect.

Given the rule of village exogamy, the women of the household will generally be strangers to each other initially. It is unusual for brothers to take wives from the same village, although it does sometimes happen. These relations of authority among the women of the household pre-exist whatever bonds of affection and common interest may develop among them. Indeed, it is generally expected that there will be tensions between mother-in-law and daughter-in-law, and between sisters-in-law.

The daughter, as has been noted in the literature on Indian family structures, has a privileged position in her natal household (Mandelbaum 1972). She is allowed a much more informal relationship with the senior men and women of her own kin group than with those of her husband. In Ghanyari, as elsewhere, a woman may expect much more affectionate treatment from her mother than she will ever receive from her mother-in-law. Nonetheless, while unmarried, she too is subordinate to the control of the older women and must obey her mother and aunts. In Ghanyari, she will not have much more leisure or freedom from responsibility in her parents' home than in her husband's household. Her labour is needed and she will be expected to work hard under the supervision of her mother. It is true that her behaviour towards the men of her parents' village may be much more relaxed and informal, but the general segregation of women's activities from those of men will ensure that she has relatively little social contact with men outside her immediate household.

How do women in Ghanyari view their dependent position? I do not think that their subordination has led them to experience themselves as powerless or feeble. So long as a woman identifies herself with her husband's household she sees herself as strong or weak largely to the extent that her household occupies a strong or weak position in the village. Also, women in Ghanyari recognize that any grown up woman has a battery of moral weapons at her disposal – verbal abuse, persuasion, and manipulation. If she learns to use them well there is no need for her to feel weak or put upon. As many observers have noted, village woman may stick rigidly to the conventions of outward submissiveness and subordination without sacrificing self-confidence and self respect.

My own impression was that it was only in the rather unusual situation in which a woman's relationship with her husband and his kin had deteriorated to the point where she no longer identified herself with the interests of his household, that she would realize subjectively the true extent of her economic dependence. In two such instances which I observed, the women did not behave in a cowed defeated manner so long as they had the active support of their own parents or brothers.

In Ghanyari the most stringent segregation practices relate to bodily functions and the care of the body. There are no separate rooms for bathing and excreting in the village houses; these functions are performed in the open air in the fields at the back of the houses. There are, though, certain locations that are recognized to be the preserve of women, and others which are only frequented by men. In a small household consisting of one nuclear family, all the members will sleep in one room or in one courtyard. In bigger or more complex households it is the practice for the men to sleep in one room or on one side of the house, and for the women to sleep in another room or in another courtyard. Privacy for the married couple is difficult to achieve in such households. It is accepted that a married man and his wife will take advantage of the opportunities provided by grass cutting expeditions to lonely parts of the jungle to enjoy sex together. Such expeditions sometimes also provide opportunities to enjoy sex relations with other men's wives.

There are no special 'women's quarters' as there are in some parts of India (the houses are not large enough to allow this kind of division) but generally the sleeping arrangements distinguish and separate the sexes. Men and women also eat separately, though at separate times rather than at separate places. Generally the women eat after the men have been served, at any rate the junior women eat after everyone else. It is a gross violation of ideas about propriety for a junior married woman to eat in front of her father-in-law or any other senior kinsman of her husband. At feasts, men and women will be seated in separate lines, as are also members of different castes. A spatial separation of men and women occurs at virtually all social and ritual gatherings. Where kinsfolk are gathered to celebrate a wedding, the male and female guests will tend to congregate in separate parts of the house. While watching a domestic ritual, the women will sit on one side of the room and the men on the other, and this is also the practice at public temples or shrines. In even the most informal gathering there is a tendency for the women to sit together, apart from the men. This is strongly reinforced by the fact that married women are forbidden by concepts of sexual propriety and courtesy from showing their faces to their husbands' elder male kin.

Outside the home, girls sit separately from boys at the village school. Men and women travelling together on foot will not walk side by side, but the women will follow at a little distance. When villagers travel long distances, the women may occupy special 'ladies only' compartments in trains, and if women are present at a bus station or railway ticket office, a special ladies' queue may be formed so that they may obtain their tickets separately.

It is interesting that this universal stress on separating the sexes does not inhibit the formation of mixed sex work parties concerning agricultural tasks. It is not unusual to see married women going to the fields in the company of their husbands or the younger men of their households. Some tasks, such as sowing or threshing, are usually performed by parties including both men and women. On the other hand, young married women rarely go to the fields in the company of the older men of the household.

On the whole a high degree of segregation is achieved with very little special allocation of space to either sex. It operates through the exercise of informal discretion and avoidance. At a public gathering no one will explicitly mark out certain areas for the occupation of women and others for men. However, women entering the scene will automatically sit with other women and the men will move towards the other men. Within the household there is a tendency for men to congregate in the more public parts of the house, the verandah and the court-yard, and for the women to gather indoors. Yet if a group of women have staked a claim to part of the courtyard to carry out some task which cannot conveniently be done indoors, for example, washing clothes, cleaning grain, and so forth, then any older male of the household wishing to sit outdoors will automatically place himself at a distance from them. As I shall argue later, there is a disproportionate responsibility on the part of women to avoid men in areas defined as public space. Within the household this assymetry is less pronounced and men and women maintain a distance from each other by means of tact and silent discretion.

Segregation and the division of labour

In Ghanyari the degree of segregation between the sexes is clearly only very crudely related to the sexual division of labour, which is not particularly rigid. There are certain tasks that are usually done only by women (cleaning and feeding small children, sweeping the house) and some that may only be done by men (notably ploughing), but these 'restricted' tasks are relatively few. There is quite a large category of tasks that will usually be done by women, but may if necessary be done by men. Usually women cook, but there is no particular shame if a man cooks when no women of the household are available. The majority of agricultural tasks may be done by members of either sex indifferently.

With this relatively weakly developed division of labour between men and women we find a strong sense that the sexes ought properly to be segregated in all activities where this can be arranged. In those Indian communities where women are actually secluded, seclusion itself necessitates a strict division of labour, since women are excluded from all kinds of outdoor work. However these communities constitute an extreme case. Elsewhere we find an extraordinary degree of inventiveness and ingenuity applied to the problem of ensuring that men and women can engage in economic co-operation and even perform identical tasks, while maintaining as marked a social distance from each other as possible. So at the level of gross generalization, the relationship between the sexual division of labour and the degree of segregation in India is only a clear cut one when the latter is so extreme as to automatically necessitate a strict division of labour, even the exclusion of women from any kind of productive work. Otherwise it is not a straightforward relationship. Segregation is clearly a component of gender roles in a particular community, but we cannot infer the structural relations between the sexes from this factor alone. Perhaps it is more useful to look at segregation in terms of its consequences and the work to which it is put, rather than in terms of what it indicates.

Segregation in India and elsewhere: its uses and consequences

Segregation in India is clearly asymmetrically organized: that is, men and women have different kinds of responsibility for maintaining this separation. A man who tries to enter a ladies' compartment in a train will be laughed at, even abused, but there is no male equivalent to the concept of female modesty which every girl has to learn from an early age (Jacobson 1970). This involves not only the proper concealment of her body but also her whole demeanour in the presence of men. Thus, in any neutral public space in which men and women are likely to interact – such as the area round a bus stop, the verandahs of village grocery stores, the open space near wells or the village streets – it is the business of the women to protect themselves from unnecessary contacts with men.

Women themselves are highly critical of other women who break this norm. A certain amount of extra-marital sexual activity is tolerated so long as it remains clandestine. However, a woman who does not maintain a discreet distance from men in public will be severely censured by her own sex. Only to a much lesser extent is it the business of men to withdraw from interaction with women. This responsibility has the obvious effect of debarring women from many activities that are not in themselves regarded as unfeminine. For instance, in Ghanyari neither men nor women were particularly opposed in principle to the idea of women holding political office. Indeed most of them have voted for a woman candidate, or the candidate of a party that had a woman at its head. However, relatively few Indian women enter politics unless their menfolk are also in politics, and women in Ghanyari are politically invisible. The very nature of the formal political processes would involve overt and public interaction with men. So while it would be quite untrue to suggest that women in Ghanyari play no political role whatsoever, they are in fact constrained by the norm of separation to play only backstage roles. The concepts of modesty and separation are not explicitly appealed to in order to bar women from political office – they do their work without this being necessary.

This assymetrical responsibility is not exclusive to India and may even be seen in industrial countries. One case of alleged discrimination in Britain involved a situation where workers would be required to pass along a catwalk (*Women's Report* 1976). It was argued by the employer that this would cause embarrassment to women workers as presumably the men would be able to peer up their skirts. The fact that they might wear trousers was not considered, nor the possibility that if their presence caused embarrassment to women workers it might as well be the men who were excluded from employment. As in India, the demands of modesty require, very conveniently for the employer, that women withdraw from the situation, not men. Therefore the ideas of separation that follow from such concepts of modesty can very easily be manipulated to ensure the exclusion of women (but not men) from particular places or activities.

We have a similar instance when Indian men argue that they do not wish to send their daughters to school unless separate classes are provided. If no single sex education is provided then it is the girls who must go without. For them to have contact with boys once they are over a certain age would be damaging to their honour, but not to the boys'. Again, the assymetrical nature of the concept of modesty ensures that it is the girls who are excluded.

In spite of these similarities, the ideology of separateness in India is capable of much more complex manipulation on the part of both sexes than in Britain. I am not suggesting that the concept of modesty in the latter relates solely to the disposition of the body, but it certainly applies to a far narrower range of situations than in India. Therefore, it offers much more limited scope for manipulation when it comes to the exclusion of women from positions of control, and recourse is made to other notions (for example, the primacy of women's roles as wives and mothers).

Another salient difference is that in South Asia the separation of the sexes is closely connected with status distinctions. (It bears little relation to status differentiation in Britain today, although it may have done once.) This is most conspicuously true of Muslim groups in India and Pakistan (and indeed of Muslim societies in general), but it is also true of many non-Muslim groups, notably the Rajputs of northern and central India. The ability to preserve one's womenfolk from unnecessary contacts with men becomes a diacritical mark of prestige and economic security. Upward mobility is often accompanied by a tendency for the women of the group to withdraw from outdoor work and to lead increasingly segregated if not actually secluded lives. This is especially true of agricultural castes, and I have no doubt that many families in Ghanyari would prefer to approximate to the ideal of maximum segregation were it practically possible.[1]

It is because of the association of segregation with high status

271

that Indian women can find seclusion tolerable, and even desirable, difficult though this may be for western women to understand. Those women who are so poor that they have to work at menial tasks outside the home have lost dignity as well as economic status and no woman of status will envy them their freedom wholeheartedly. Indeed, many economically depressed groups go to considerable lengths to avoid the necessity for their women to work outside the home (Darling 1928; Vreede de Steuers 1968).

For those who have some dignity to maintain, certain types of work outside the home can be approved, depending very much on the extent to which some kind of segregation can be maintained in the workplace. For middle-class educated women most teaching positions are acceptable; even if the teacher has a class of boys they are likely to be much younger than herself and hence socially 'harmless' as males. Similarly, in nursing and medicine a woman must come into contact with men, often quite close physical contact. Here again the male is 'harmless'; he is socially ineffectual by virtue of his disease or injury, and so these professions have long been practiced by women. (If nursing actually has low prestige this is probably due more to ideas about pollution than to those concerning modesty and segregation). Work as a stenographer or receptionist is regarded as injurious to social honour by many. This is because in a busy office it is hardly possible to order interaction between men and women to ensure any kind of acceptable distance is maintained between them.

In agricultural work, as we have seen, the idea that men and women should not come into close contact with each other does not in itself necessitate the exclusion of women from such work. A group of young men and women working together at tasks like weeding or harvesting can remain spaced out in the field and quite easily maintain a proper distance for most of the time. Thus in agriculture the 'workplace' is large enough to permit this and no-one need lose face.

However, when women move into industrial and clerical employment, conventions about segregation and distance become more restrictive. Urban space is, after all, at a premium. In Britain, the chanelling of women into certain types of urban employment had little to do with segregation as such and much more to do with: a) the lack of access to many forms of specialized training; b) conceptions about what kinds of work were 'women's work'; and c) the fear that they would compete with men and reduce the opportunities for male employment. On the other hand, one aspect of factory work which was found most disturbing in the early days of the industrial revolution (though admittedly by those who contemplated it rather than by those who actually did it) was the fact that men and women were obliged to work in close proximity in mills and mines. This caused much fear concerning their morals, especially for those of the young, who began working in such environments at an early age (Alexander 1976).

One way of looking at the sexual banter which one hears between men and women in factories, shops, and similar workplaces is to regard it as a means of maintaining a kind of sexual social distance through what anthropologists call 'joking relationships' (Sykes 1966; Whitehead 1976).

Another consequence stemming from the conception of proper female modesty is that the segregation it demands may cause women to be 'lumped together' as an undifferentiated social category, irrespective of the various distinctions of age, education, and experience. Joyce Pettigrew notes that the separation of men from women among landowning families in Punjab means that educated and illiterate women are like members of the same category within the household, and the educated must obey the illiterate if, as is usually the case, they are the juniors (Pettigrew 1975). If separation involves actual seclusion, then relations of dependence and authority among the women themselves are likely to be more pronounced. The senior women of the household will have some access to the affairs of men, and therefore the junior women will depend upon them for the channelling of information and requests. The senior women come to occupy a key position in the women's segregated world.

Mrs. Ranade, in her autobiography, has described how her husband's stepmother and aunts would try to discourage her from studying and educating herself. They felt that her efforts reflected upon themselves (who were for the most part uneducated) and that it implied defiance of their authority (Ranade 1938). The young wife was in a difficult position, for in conforming to one aspect of her role (obedience to her husband, who wanted her to study) she was effectively flouting another

273

set of demands (obedience to the senior women of the household). Her husband could offer her little useful support since he could not intervene on her behalf without flouting the conventional separation of the sexes in the household and (worse still) without seeming to act disrespectfully to his own stepmother. The segregation of the sexes here gives the older women increased control over the young women and it is difficult even for senior men to intervene. There is no better means of social control than the devolution of internal control onto the group that is to be subordinate.

We may add that where the segregation of women is very rigid, the positions of control within the women's sphere may not even be held by high status women. Rama Mehta, in her description of the secluded women of the Oswal caste of Rajasthan, points out that so strict used to be their seclusion from the outside world that the maidservants employed to serve the women often came to occupy a crucial role within the household. They were brought in at an early age and trained, almost becoming members of the family, but because of their lowly position they could interact with the outside world unlike the purdah women. To a large extent these maidservants acted as very powerful go-betweens, mediating between the Oswal women and the community at large (Mehta 1976). Leaving women to control each other, as inevitably happens when they are very rigidly segregated from men, leads to the creation of positions of control and authority among the women, but not the kinds of control that they can use to challenge their position as women.

From these examples we can see that segregation in itself does not imply inferiority or powerlessness on the part of women. Segregation may confer positions of control upon some women, while denying it to others. Its assymetrical organization, though, ensures that all but a few women are denied access to important sources of influence in the household and in the community. It is interesting that in India the rule of segregation which limits women's social effectiveness in public is not supported by notions of feminine incompetence as found in western societies. There is hardly any feeling that women are inherently incapable of performing the work of, say, a trader or politician. Much more influential is the idea that for a woman to attempt

274

to perform such work, which involves extensive and public contact with men, would be immodest and – a term frequently used – 'unnecessary'.

Segregation and solidarity

To what extent does the segregation of the sexes lead to greater solidarity and mutual support among women in India? In Ghanyari, a considerable amount of informal co-operation takes place among women of different households. There is much mutual assistance of a material kind even if the goods lent or given are not great in value. For example, women frequently lend petty sums of cash or grain to a well-liked neighbour.

On the other hand, there is relatively little exchange of services. We do not find, as in some British communities (see, for example, Chapter 5), bonds between women based on mutual aid in domestic tasks: taking in another's washing, minding another's children after school, and so on. In their domestic and agricultural work women in Ghanyari co-operate with other members of their household rather than with friends or neighbours. Women who enjoy each other's company may, however, arrange to do some task together, for example, fetching water, or washing clothes at the well, or cleaning grain in the courtyard.

Nevertheless, there is little mutual reliance for practical help between women of different households. In domestic crises, for example, the birth of a baby, or severe family illness, a woman will be obliged to call on the services of other women to cook and share the household tasks. However, in such situations it is generally a relative or another female member of the household who will help. That is, it will be someone with whom the woman already has a determinate relationship in terms of rules of seniority and juniority which structure relationships within the household. Co-operation between women, therefore, is very important, but it is 'given' by the structure of household relations rather than developing spontaneously as a result of their common predicaments as women. Consequently this co-operation takes place in terms of the control and authority over younger women with which the older women are vested.

Friendships of a particularly intimate kind are formed between young married women in the village, and these involve a good deal of time together, exchanges of confidences, petty gifts, and loans. Every young bride is encouraged to make a bond of ritual kinship with some other young wife in the village when she first arrives in her affinal home. Such a ritual 'sister' will often be a girl who comes from her own natal village or is already related to her in some way. Frequently these relationships are an important source of moral support and help to a young wife during the period when she is getting used to her new household and 'learning the ropes' of village society.

On the other hand, I have the impression that such friendships among women of different households are not particularly stable. A woman who is reputed to be enjoying an intimate friendship with a certain neighbour one day will cool towards her the next and favour another neighbour. Alliances among the younger women seem to shift relatively quickly, although this does not mean that a particular friendship may have little significance at the time it flourishes.

I can only speculate about the causes of this pattern of friendships, but I would suggest two main reasons. First, a young wife cannot offer any kind of substantial support, apart from moral support, to another young wife who is in difficulties. For example, if a woman quarrels with her husband or is ill-treated by her mother-in-law other young wives are least likely to be in a good position to help her. They cannot enforce any important sanctions upon the behaviour of the offender because they do not have much say in their own households, let alone in the community at large. In one instance a young wife was repeatedly beaten by her husband. She was unable to put her complaint to the caste council in the village until it had been drawn to the attention of the elder males of the village. The younger women had known about the behaviour of the husband for a long time, but they were not in a position to offer her more than moral support.

Second, I have the impression that it is only the younger married women who seek friendships with members of their own sex outside the household. An older woman seeks her allies among her children, especially her sons, and as they grow to adulthood she will tend to seek moral and material support from them rather than from other women of her own age-group. She may also look to her sons' wives if she can secure their loyalty and goodwill when they are first married. Also, as she grows older and withdraws from active outdoor work, she has less occasion to meet other women of her own age in the course of her daily work. Her activities become more household centred and as her identification with the interests of her husband's household and kin group increases, so her inclination to seek independent friendships beyond this circle of kin decreases.

It is a commonplace in the literature on India that solidarity between the older generation of women within the household is particularly difficult to achieve. Influence in the household is achieved by women only with age and child-bearing, especially sons. A woman who has progressed from the lowly status of a nobody as a bride to the position of a respected matriarch is at last compensated for her lack of public prestige by her status within the home. She might be expected to sympathize with her own daughter-in-laws for their weak position in the household, but she is much more likely to attempt to keep the younger women in their places by asserting her own authority. The internal politics of the household constitute a zero-sum game so far as the women are concerned: the younger women's gain is the older woman's loss. The fact that neither of them has much power to assert outside the household means that much is invested in such adjustments within the domestic group.

Not all young wives are at loggerheads with their mothers-in-law, indeed many have very harmonious relationships. There are, though, differences in interest between women of different generations which make it unlikely that they will combine as women to form a solidarity group. To a large extent, the relations between older and younger women within the village community are modelled on those that exist between them in the household. Therefore an equal or solidarity relationship among the village wives would be difficult to achieve, even without the divisive effects of caste hierarchy, differences of economic status, and education which I have not discussed here.

I think that the women are well aware of these limitations which affect the potential of their relationships with each other. They would frequently express the idea that there are some problems that one could not discuss with a man. Only a woman would understand a husband's infidelity, medical difficulties in pregnancy and child-birth, and conflicts with an overbearing mother-in-law. On the other hand, many practical problems needed the understanding and co-operation of male members of the family. For example, the husband of a neighbour of mine was continually unfaithful to her and wasted a good deal of money on presents for his girl friends and mistresses. This woman obtained a good deal of relief for her feelings from pouring out her troubles to several sympathetic women friends, including myself. However, she would also bewail the fact that she had no brothers, for a brother could be asked to try and bring the husband to his senses. Nor, she pointed out, did her husband have any brothers, which was unfortunate since a younger brother-in-law might also provide some help and support within the household.

These limitations to the kinds of positive help that women can give each other also curtail their coming together as an effective group, a body with its own collective influence and interests.

Almost everything that I have said about the relationships among women also applies to relationships between men. Among the young men also, there are unstable factional alliances which quickly form and dissolve. This is, in part, due to the lack of a stable economic hierarchy within the landowning groups which might allow the rise of long term factional formations such as found in many other parts of North West India. A high degree of segregation in work and household activities does not mean that either the women or the men of the village form solidarity groups. Men seldom show solidarity *as men* in spite of the fact that they have grown up in the village and know each other well, unlike the married women who have all been recruited from outside the village. If women are controlled and disciplined in Ghanyari, it is through the assertion of authority on the part of their seniors (both male and female) rather than through the authority of men as a sex. The pronounced economic dependence of women on the household as a landholding or productive unit ensures the effectiveness of the system of internal authority in controlling their behaviour. The relative freedom of movement and activity that women in Ghanyari enjoy only accentuates the fact that women are expected to exercise responsibility for each other. Freedom from male interference in female activity does not mitigate the effects of the relations of authority and control among women.

Much of what I have said of Ghanyari would also be applicable to the position of women in other parts of India. However, in certain cases I am sure that important qualifications would have to be made. For example, in southern India where village exogamy is not practised, the women of a particular community are not necessarily 'strangers' to each other or to the households into which they marry. Unfortunately very little ethnographic work has been done on rural women in southern India. For similar reasons, the Muslim women of India must also constitute an exception, since among Muslims village exogamy is not a cultural ideal. The Muslim ideal is to marry within a circle of respected families of equal social status. In contrast, North Indian Hindus aim to spread the network of marriage alliances as widely as possible and to establish new relationships with each marriage that takes place in the family.

The community of women with whom a Muslim wife associates after her marriage is, therefore, less likely to be a group of strangers, and she will probably have prior ties of kinship with the men and women of her husband's family. This might be expected to mitigate the effects of the household hierarchy based on the position of the husband. On the other hand, as one anthropologist has pointed out, the fact that Muslim women generally practice stricter forms of seclusion than Hindu women of the same region and comparable social status means that they will have less occasion to meet each other. Consequently, they will be unable to build the kinds of relationship among themselves that might form the basis for female solidarity (P. Jeffery, personal communication). Although there is more ethnographic evidence on the consequences of segregation for Muslim women than there is on South Indian women there is still a need for more detailed data on Muslim women of different social strata.

Conclusion

From this discussion it can be seen that there are really two

279

levels at which we can describe segregation of the sexes in India, and thus there are two levels at which we can observe its consequences.

First, at the level of general public culture, there are widespread patterns of belief and morality supporting the expectation that men and women will be segregated from each other, even though, in practice, particular groups or communities may translate this expectation differently. All over India there is a general aversion to physical contact between the sexes in public except where it cannot be avoided, and indeed to any public expression of intimacy between the sexes. There is a widespread ideology of feminine modesty which governs both the disposition of women's bodies and their general social demeanour. There is a general expectation that women will not draw attention to themselves in public, or that it is worse for them to do so than for men. This is because the honour of a family or status group is especially vulnerable to the misdemeanours of its women.

There is also a widespread belief that female sexuality is more difficult to control than that of men. It is thought that women will be tempted to indulge in sexual misbehaviour unless restricted by rules which reduce their opportunities for contact with men. All these ideas can be manipulated, usually in favour of preventing women from doing certain things or excluding them from certain positions or activities. As we have seen, they may even be manipulated by women themselves to obtain a degree of freedom from male interference. In general, however, these ideas sustain a general expectation, which is not specific to any one social group, that the sexes will not mix too much in public and that arrangements (formal or informal) to keep them apart are necessary and desirable.

Second, at the level of specific local communities we can observe how these general cultural ideas and expectations are realized through specific segregation practices compatible with other aspects of the local community structure (for example, marriage practices, division of labour, and so on). In this paper I have described in detail only those that obtain in the village of Ghanyari, but this example does illustrate how the different aspects of gender roles mesh in the context of a particular community. We have observed, for instance, the consequences that segregation has for the kinds of relationships which women can establish among themselves and hence for the kinds of solidarity possible for them to achieve.

Among Hindus in North Indian villages like Ghanyari where village exogamy is practised the adult women are thrown together (by their common status as affines and 'strangers' and by the segregation that separates them from men). However, they are also set apart from each other by their membership of different household groups and by the structured relations of juniority and seniority that exist among them. Only at this level of description is it really possible to talk about the consequences of segregation in terms of solidarity.

It is likely that the relationship among the different components of gender roles varies widely between different Indian communities, in spite of the general adherence to the principle that a high degree of segregation is natural and desirable. More comparative work on the ways in which relations between men and women are ordered in different localities in South Asia would probably reveal a variety of community types among women which are the product of segregation.

Note

1 To the women, it was the constant physical toil that they had to perform which they saw as the most deplorable aspect of their lives, and any style of life that liberated them (and their menfolk) from such labours was seen as desirable. Several women referred to the urban housewife married to an office worker as living the ideal life for a woman. Her work is limited to domestic tasks, yet she has the amenities (electricity, tap water, shops, and so on) which make these tasks easy.

References

ALEXANDER, S. (1976) Women's work in Nineteenth Century London. In J. Mitchell and A. Oakley (eds.), *The Rights and Wrongs of Women*. Harmondsworth : Penguin.

DARLING, M. L. (1928) *The Punjab Peasant in Prosperity and Debt*. London : Oxford University Press.

DOUGLAS, M. (1975) *Implicit Meanings*. London : Routledge & Kegan Paul.

HITCHCOCK, J. and MINTURN, L. (1963) The Rajputs of Khalapur. In B. Whiting (ed.), *Six Cultures*. New York : John Wiley and Sons.

JACOBSON, D. (1970) *Hidden Faces; Hindu and Muslim Purdah in a Central Indian Village.* Unpublished Ph.D. dissertation, Columbia University.

MAHER, V. (1976) Kin, Clients and Accomplices: Relations among women in Morocco. In D. Barker and S. Allen (eds.), *Sexual Divisions and Society: Process and Change.* London: Tavistock.

MANDELBAUM, D. (1972) *Society in India.* Berkeley and Los Angeles: University of California Press.

MARSHALL, T. E. (1959) *The Harmless People.* Harmondsworth: Penguin.

MEHTA, R. (1976) From Purdah to Modernity. In B. R. Nanda (ed.), *Indian Women from Purdah to Modernity.* New Delhi: Vikas.

PETTIGREW, J. (1975) *Robber Noblemen.* London: Routledge & Kegan Paul.

RANADE, R. (1938) *Himself: the Autobiography of a Hindu Lady.* Translated by K. Gates: Longman, Green and Co.

SAIFULLAH-KHAN, V. (1976) Purdah in the British Situation. In D. Barker and S. Allen (eds.), *Dependence and Exploitation in Work and Marriage.* London and New York: Longmans.

SINGH, A. M. (1975) The Study of women in India: some Problems of Methodology. In De Souza (ed.), *Women in Contemporary India.* Delhi: Manohar.

SYKES, A. T. (1966) Joking Relations in an Industrial Setting. *American Anthropologist 65.*

VREEDE DE STEUERS, C. (1968) *Parda. A Study of the Life of Muslim Women in Northern India.* Assen: Van Gorcum.

WOMEN'S REPORT (1976) May–June 4(4):15.

WHITEHEAD, A. (1976) Sexual Antagonism in Herefordshire. In D. Barker and S. Allen (eds.), *Dependence and Exploitation in Work and Marriage.* London and New York: Longmans.

WISER, C. and WISER, W. (1963) *Behind Mud Walls.* Berkeley and Los Angeles: University of California Press.

Name index

Numbers in italics refer to
entries in the References

Aaby, P., 23, 35, *43*
Acker, J., 107, *126*
Adams, B. N., 182, *183*
Adlam, D., 180, *183*
Alexander, S., 273, *281*
Althusser, L., 180, 182, *181*
Anderson, M., 182, *183*
Andic, F. M., 239, *257*
Andic, S., 239, *257*
Ardener, E., 17, *43*
Astell, M., 13, *27*
Atkinson, J., 208–9, *237*

Baig, T. A., 100, 114, *126*
Bailey, F., 253, *257*
Banks, O., 146, *154*
Banton, M., 143, *154*
Barclay, H. B., 186, 190, 195, *204*
Barnes, C., *97*
Barnes, J. A., 79, *97*
de Beauvoir, S., 208, *236*
Beechey, V., 22, *43*
Belden, J., 37, *43*, 59, 65, *74*
Bell, C. R., 159, 183, *183*
Benston, M., 21, *43*
Bernstein, B., 133, 134, *154*
Besant, A., 101
Bettelheim, C., 125, *126*
Bhasin, K., *126*
Boissevain, J., 80, *97*
Bose, A., 100, *126*
Boserup, E., 32, *43*
Boswell, D., 80, *97*
Bradley, S. C., 239, *257*
Bujra, J. M., 13–45
Burchinal, L., 183, *184*
Butler, N., 133, *155*

Caplan, P., 16, 28, 99–127, 116, *126*, 150
Chartrand, F., 244, *257*
Chipp, S. A., 125, *126*
Chithis, I., 124, *126*
Chowdhry, D. P., 122, *126*
Clarke, E., 247, *257*
Cohen, A., 122, *126*, 147, 148, 151, 152, *155*
Cohen, G., 16, 29, 128–156, 140, *155*
Conger, S. P., 48, *74*
Connell, R. W., 162, *184*
Constantinides, P. M., 15, 32, 116, 185–205, 204, *204*
Cousins, M., 101, 102
Croll, E., 17, 37, 38, *44*, 46–76, 68, *74*

Crooks, D., 55, 66, *74*
Crooks, I., 55, 66, *74*
Cusack, D., 53, *74*

Dalla Costa, M., 13, 21, 25, *43*
Darling, M. L., 272, *281*
Das, V., 110, *126*
Davies, B., 133, *154*
Davies, R., 133, *155*
Davin, D., 59, *74*
Delphy, C., 25, 30, *44*
Dewey, A., 187, *205*
Diamond, N., 63, *74*
Douglas, J. W. B., 133, *155*
Douglas, M., 259–60, *281*
Durkheim, E., 236, *236*

Edholm, F., 41–2, *44*
Encel, S., 162, *184*
Engels, F., 23, 26, 35, *44*
Epstein, A., 80, *97*
Epstein, I., 53, *74*
Etherton, D., 79, *97*

Firestone, S., 236, *236*
Firth, R., 178, 181, 182, *184*
Fletcher, R., 173, 182, *184*
Forge, A., 178, 181, 182, *184*
Frankenberg, R., 130, 135, *155*
Fürer-Haimendorf, C. von, 122, *127*
Fyfe, C., 145, *155*

Gandhi, M. K., 102, 103, *127*
Gardiner, J., 182, *184*
Guettel, C., 33, *44*

Hardgrave, R. L., 126, *127*
Harrell-Bond, B., 144, *155*
Harris, O., 41–2, *44*
Harris, C. C., 29, *45*, 178, 182, *184*
Harris, G., 203, *205*
Harrison, J., 159, 182, *184*
Hart, N., 133, *155*
Hate, C. A., 100, *127*
Henriques, J., 180, *183*
Hinton, W., 54–5, 59, 62, 65, *74*
Hirst, P. Q., 180, *184*
Hitchcock, J., 262, *281*
Hoffer, C. P., 99, *127*
Hubert, J., 178, 181, 182, *184*
Hutber, P., 133, *155*
Hutson, S., 246, *257*
Hutton, C., 107, *127*

Ifeka-Moller, C., 43, *44*
Irschik, E. F., 126, *127*

Jackson, B., 133, *155*
Jacobson, D., *97*, 263, 270, *282*

283

Subject index

kinship
  Creole education and, 146, 147–8
  and Creole female solidarity,
    151–2
  and family structure on
    Désirade, 248–9
  ideology of in Australia, 167–70
  and production, 31–3
  in rural Sudan, 191–3
  zaar groups as substitute for,
    201

labour, sexual division of, 13–45,
    261–2, 268–9
  on Désirade, 240
  female perpetuation of, 26
  and low status of women in old
    China, 52
  persistance of, in China, 63
  see also domestic labour
Labour Law in China, 56
learning, in women's organizations
  in India, 105, 114–15
legislation and women
  in China, 56–7
  in India, 103, 125
leisure activities, sexual
  separation of, 252–4
Lin Piao, criticism of, 72
livestock in Maasai society, 211–13
  gifts of, 223
  women's lack of, 213–16
'loafing groups', 253

Maasai, 24
  solidarity amongst women of, 16,
    17, 206–37
Madras, women's organizations in,
    28, 99–125
Mahdi, The
  rebellion of, 188
  and *zaar* cult, 203
marriage, 33
  Caribbean, 246–7, 251–2
  in China, 37, 54
    Laws, 56, 65
  in Creole society, 144–5, 151–2
  in India, 108, 109–10, 264, 265
    child, 101
  Maasai, 222–3
  in Mathare Valley, 90–1
  in northern Sudan, 191–3
Mathare Redevelopment Project,
    91
Mathare Valley villages, 95–6
  beer brewing in, 77, 79, 80–3
  criticism of people of, 93–4
  self-help action in, 91, 94
  squatters in, 78–9
  women's solidarity in, 88–95
menstruation, segregation during,
    259–60
middle-class solidarity, 128–56

and kin relations, 157–84
and women's organizations in
  India, 106–10
modesty, 273
  assymetric nature of, 270–1,
    274–5, 280
Mohamed 'Ali, conquest of Sudan
  by, 186, 188
Montagu Commission, women's
  deputation to, 101
mother-daughter link, 168
Mundarucú Indians, and
  reproduction, 39, 42
Muslim brotherhoods, in Sudan,
  192, 194–5
myths of Maasai, 215–16, 230

Nairobi, Kenya, beer brewers of,
  16, 77–97
National Children's Bureau, 133
National Committee on the Status
  of Women, Report of, 113
networks, in lives of Mathare
  women, 79–80, 83–88
non-violent campaigns, women's
  role in, 103

obscenity, as protest, 36, 43
'outcasts', women of Mathare as,
  88–9, 93

parental attitudes to education,
  132–4
Peasants' Union, in China, 57
Peking Women's Federation, 60
petty commodity production
  and female status, 34–7
  in urban Kenya, 78
  success in, 92
'place of women', Mathare as, 90
Plowden Committee, 132
police raids on *buzaa* brewers,
  83, 96
political activity of women, 34,
  46, 58–9, 68–70
  denial of, in old China, 48
  on Désirade, 254–5
  in India, 121–2, 126
    segregation and, 270
  in Mathare, 90–1, 94
  opposition to, by men, 54
  and 'women's war', 36
polygyny amongst Maasai, 219
pregnancy
  and circumcision in Maasai
    society, 216
  sexual relations forbidden
    during, 221
  in unmarried girls on Désirade,
    249–51
privitization of domestic labour,
  23, 25

287

288